Introduction to SBOM and VEX

Introduction to SBOM and VEX

Software Bill of Materials and Vulnerability Exploitability eXchange

Tom Alrich

Table of Contents

Author's Preface

This book has been a long time coming. It started in 2020 as notes on meetings of workgroups that were part of the Software Component Transparency Initiative of the NTIA (the National Technology and Information Administration, part of the US Department of Commerce); this Initiative was started and led by Dr. Alan Friedman of the NTIA. The meetings were focused on the relatively new concept of software bills of materials, or SBOMs. The notes were prepared for a client of mine, Fortress Information Security, Inc.

Since that time, those notes have coalesced into this book. However, the contents have regularly been revised as thinking on SBOMs (both mine and others') – and on the new concept of VEX or Vulnerability Exploitability eXchange, a concept that grew out of the NTIA meetings – has evolved.

Of course, the purpose of the Software Component Transparency Initiative (which ended at the end of 2021) was not just to produce some good meeting notes or white papers, but to make progress on getting SBOMs used in the real world. How did the Initiative do in this regard? Some available data, discussed in this book, shows that SBOM use has been growing almost exponentially since at least 2020, due in part to the efforts of the Initiative.

That is certainly good news, but the picture is mixed when you distinguish between the two main cybersecurity use cases[1] for SBOMs: a) use by software developers to identify and mitigate vulnerabilities that appear in their products during development, and b) use by organizations whose main purpose is not software development (i.e., every public and private organization in the world, except for developers). The latter group can use SBOMs to identify and mitigate

---

[1] The original use case for SBOMs was not cybersecurity but managing licenses in open source components. SBOMs are still being actively used for license management, but this is primarily a concern for suppliers, not for end users. This book is focused on the use case of managing cybersecurity risks for end users, and primarily risks due to vulnerabilities found in components included in a software product.

vulnerabilities found in the software they use to run their organizations, although very few of them are doing that now. This book broadly identifies these organizations as "end user organizations".

More details will come in the book, but in brief, the developer use case is growing by leaps and bounds, while the non-developer (end user) use case has not progressed much at all in the nearly four years since I joined the NTIA Initiative.

Why are end users hardly using SBOMs at all, even though almost everything that has been written about SBOMs (for example, Executive Order 14028 of May 2021) has focused on the great benefits that end users will realize from using them? Moreover, what can be done to change this situation? This book tries to answer both of these questions.

Who should read this book? How should they read it?

The author believes there are two general groups of people who will want to read this book, although there are others as well.

The first group is people who work in the software development or software security communities and want to learn more about SBOMs. If you are part of one or both of those communities, you will find this book to be different from almost anything you have read about SBOMs so far. This is because most articles today are aimed at developers and focus on issues with producing SBOMs.

However, as described earlier, my big concern is how *non-developers* can receive and utilize SBOMs. As a developer, you might think this is irrelevant to your concerns – and it is, if you think the only use for SBOMs is to help developers improve the security of software they're building.

But software developers wouldn't exist if there weren't software end users willing to buy the software they create (or at least download it, if it's open source); they are the other group addressed by this book. End users are concerned about their organization's security, which might suffer due to vulnerabilities (and other sources of risk) present in the software they use.

Currently, very few organizations that use software (but are not primarily in the development business) are able to learn about risks due to third-party components included in the software they use, since very few organizations are able to learn about those components in the first place. This is why SBOMs and VEX documents are needed by end users, along with the tools and third-party services required to make proper use of them: SBOM and VEX provide "transparency" into the software products used by an organization, so the organization can identify for themselves the risks they contain.

How to "shorten" this book

I admit this is a dense book. Many readers – especially those in the end user category – will not have the time or inclination to read every word between its covers. How can less technical readers save themselves some time, while still catching the meaning of the book? There are two ways to do this:

One way to save time is to bypass the chapters marked "Advanced". A reader who is just trying to get a general idea of what SBOM and VEX are can safely skip those chapters. Of course, if they decide they would like more details later, they can always return and read them.

The other way to save time, while not missing the full meaning of the book, is to skip the footnotes[2]. While reading this book, you should think of the body text as a continuous road you are traveling, while the footnotes are more like side trips. Like side trips, the footnotes are interesting in themselves, but it is not necessary to read them to reach your destination. Many readers will feel more comfortable if they start by just reading the body text and ignoring the footnotes. If you later find yourself wondering what's in the footnotes, you can always return and read some or all of them.

Of course, you could also combine these two suggestions: That is, you could only read the "non-advanced" chapters, and also skip the footnotes in the chapters you do read. If you do that, I promise you will still come away with a decent understanding of both SBOM and VEX. Again, you can always come back later to read some of what you skipped earlier.

Acknowledgements

I wish to thank the following people for their contributions to this book, both directly and indirectly: Cassie Crossley, Alan Friedman, Anthony Harrison, Ed Heierman, Olle Johansson, Jean-Baptiste Maillet, Jon Meadows, Philippe Ombredanne, Kevin Perry, Steve Springett, Tony Turner and Jeff Williams, as well as all the members of the OWASP SBOM Forum.

I also want to express my appreciation to Fortress Information Security, Inc., the organization that originaly requested that I follow and report on developments in the SBOM world. This book would never have been written without their support.

Please give me your comments!

I strongly encourage any reader who wishes to comment on this book to email me their comments, both positive and negative, at tom@tomalrich.com. Please also leave your comments on the Amazon web page!

---

[2] In the Kindle version, the footnotes are gathered at the end of the book (where they are called "endnotes").

Foreword

Perhaps the most important development in software during the last two or three decades has been the rapid growth in the availability and use of components, which the author defines as sections of code (they are sometimes entire programs in themselves) that can be used by multiple programs and can be replaced when needed. The day in which a single developer, or a single team of developers, wrote every line of code in a software product – or even most lines of code – is long past.

Nowadays, it is common for up to 90% of the code in a software product to be written by third parties, usually in the form of pre-written components that are available as open source or commercially. It is no exaggeration to say that the cost of developing an average software product today would be many times larger, and in many cases the cost would be prohibitive, if components were not available.

However, this revolution has not been entirely a "free lunch". Along with cost savings and increased functionality, components have brought a much higher level of cybersecurity risk to software users, due to vulnerabilities and other flaws found in those components. While it is not at all clear that the components found in a software product are inherently riskier than the "first-party" code contributed by the supplier itself, it is certainly true that just because the customer trusts a particular supplier enough to purchase their product, this doesn't mean they would find each of the product's component suppliers to be equally trustworthy, if they knew who they were. However, the customer doesn't have a say in choosing the product's component suppliers; when they choose the product supplier, they involuntarily "choose" all the component suppliers at the same time.

Of course, nobody is suggesting that software users demand that suppliers write all the code in their products themselves; this would be both unnecessary and extraordinarily expensive, and would force many suppliers to go out of business. Like almost everything else in life, cybersecurity is a risk management exercise. Risk can never be eliminated, but it can be managed. Managing any

4

security risk requires learning about and assessing threats posed by deliberate or inadvertently harmful actions taken by others.

While software is subject to many types of cybersecurity risk, the risks posed by third-party components far surpass risks posed by the code written by the supplier of the product, because a) components represent a much greater part of the code included in the product, and b) currently, most software users have no good way to learn about the risks present in components, since they have no way to learn about the components themselves. Software bills of materials (SBOMs) enable software users to learn about the components included in the products they use.

This book contains three Parts. The first Part introduces the reader to SBOMs, while the second Part introduces them to VEX. VEX can be thought of as an "enabling technology" for SBOM. As will be discussed at length in Parts 2 and 3 of this book, the author believes that SBOMs will not be distributed to end users in any meaningful way until the current confusion over VEX can be resolved.

The book is intended for use by both suppliers and end users of software, since both groups need to understand these two important concepts. However, currently there is a huge asymmetry between software suppliers and end users, when it comes to experience with SBOMs. On the one hand, a large percentage of software suppliers (although probably not the majority) have discovered the importance of having up to date SBOMs for their products while they are being developed, so they can continually track the vulnerabilities and other risks that may be present in components in the software.

On the other hand, those same suppliers are reluctant to distribute those SBOMs to their customers - and even if they want to do that, the customers are not generally requesting them. Why are we in this situation? We will discuss this topic in "Chapter 7: What's the current state of SBOM use?" later in this book.

Note that "software end users" in this book refers primarily to government and private organizations and not to individuals, although individuals may also draw lessons from this book. The word "users" is utilized in the same sense.

In addition, this book distinguishes between organizations whose main business is software development (e.g., Microsoft™ or Oracle™) and organizations whose main business is not software development, but which utilize software developed by third-party developers to run their business. Of course, the latter category includes well over 99% of organizations worldwide, both public and private.

This distinction is valid, even though in many cases the "non-developer" organizations may develop software that furthers the interests of their main business (e.g., a restaurant chain that develops an app for their customers or an auto manufacturer that develops software utilized by the engines they develop). However, that fact alone does not make them developers, any more than the fact that an insurance company offers exercise classes for its employees makes it a health club.

There are two main use cases for SBOMs: open source component license management (the original use case for SBOMs more than ten years ago) and security vulnerability management. The former use case relates almost entirely to software developers; they need to know what legal commitments they are making by using open source components in their products. In most cases, non-developers will not face any risks due to the licenses carried by open source components in the software they utilize. Therefore, this book will not discuss the license management use case.

Instead, this book addresses the use case of component vulnerability risk management. This is the use case most discussed – at least implicitly - in public discussions about SBOMs and in government documents like Executive Order 14028[3]. Ironically, it is also probably the use case least implemented in practice, as we will discuss further in this book.

---

[3] https://www.whitehouse.gov/briefing-room/presidential-actions/2021/05/12/executive-order-on-improving-the-nations-cybersecurity/

Part One: Introduction to SBOMs

1. Why are SBOMs important?

Just about every organization of any size today not only uses software but depends on it. This includes banks, insurance companies, electric utilities, churches, mosques and synagogues, federal, state and local government agencies, nonprofit social service organizations, etc. At the same time, anyone who follows the news knows that the threats posed by cyberattacks on software are all too real.

However, what many people do not know is that cyberattacks don't emerge from nowhere. Instead, they almost always target *vulnerabilities* – i.e., flaws in the code - that are present in software. These vulnerabilities can never be eliminated, but they can certainly be managed. SBOMs can play a key role in managing software vulnerabilities.

To understand why SBOMs are such a powerful tool, you need to consider that one of the most important innovations in software over the past two or three decades is the use of pre-written components. To illustrate this idea, suppose you are a software supplier, and you want to include in a program that you are writing the capability to display up-to-the-minute stock quotations. Twenty-five years ago, you might have had no choice but to write all the code required to retrieve and display the quotations yourself.

However, today a developer can choose from a variety of commercially developed and open source components that retrieve and display stock quotes. The developer does not need to write more code than the small amount it will take to integrate the component with the rest of their software product.

The use of components in new software has gone from being an exciting innovation thirty years ago to simply being how software is built today. Nowadays, it is no exaggeration to say that most software products consist of many components (an average of at least 135[4]) along with a small amount of first-party code that "glues" the components together.

---

[4] This 2020 report from Sonatype states that the average software product includes 135 components, of which 90% are open source. The average number of components

The reason for this sea change is simple: Software developers save huge amounts of time and money by incorporating prewritten components into their products, instead of having to develop the code themselves. The time and money savings from using components are shared both by the developers and their customers, who benefit from having access to low cost software, which is developed much more quickly. A lot of today's software would never be feasible to develop, were it not for the availability of components.

But there is a downside to these benefits: Because components are developed by a wide variety of third-party software producers and open source communities with varying degrees of security knowledge and aptitude, it is no longer sufficient for the user organization to verify that the supplier of the software itself follows good security practices. Besides doing that, the organization needs to learn what the supplier is doing to mitigate the risks introduced by the third-party components included in their products. It is as if the job of managing risks in a single software product has suddenly ballooned to 135 times its original size.

The most important tool for identifying and mitigating third-party software component risks is SBOMs. An SBOM is a machine-readable inventory of components included in a software product or intelligent device. If a user has an up to date SBOM for a particular product and version that they utilize, they will in principle be able to identify vulnerabilities and other risks that apply to components included in that product. Very often, the user does this by looking up vulnerabilities that apply to those components in a vulnerability database like the National Vulnerability Database (NVD), the most widely used vulnerability database in the world.[5]

There are two broad types of vulnerabilities found in the average software product, both of which pose risk to the end user: vulnerabilities that are due to the supplier's own code and vulnerabilities that are due to third-party components included in the product. The end user normally has direct visibility into the former type of vulnerabilities; that is, by looking up the product and version number in the NVD, they may quickly find the vulnerabilities that apply to the product.

Moreover, since most product vulnerabilities are reported by the product's supplier, if an important new vulnerability is identified in the product and appears in the NVD, this means the supplier reported it, and has presumably already developed a patch for it. Given how visible the NVD is, any supplier that does not react promptly to a serious vulnerability will face pressure from their customers, since any delay between acknowledgement of the vulnerability and availability of the patch puts those customers at risk.

---

is undoubtedly higher today: https://www.sonatype.com/resources/white-paper-state-of-the-software-supply-chain-2020
    [5] https://nvd.nist.gov/

However, the same is not true for vulnerabilities that are due to third-party components in the supplier's product. Until very recently, there was no way for an end user to learn of these vulnerabilities, since they had no way to learn about the components that were included in the product. In theory, a supplier could harbor some highly vulnerable components in their product and the user would never know about them. In fact, even if a vulnerability in one of those components were exploited to attack the product and the end user were to experience a serious breach due to the attack, it is possible they would never learn that the breach was due to a risky component that the supplier allowed to remain in the product. Instead, they might well blame themselves for poor patching practices.

A 2017 study[6] by the software security company Veracode said, "A mere 52 percent of (software development) companies reported they provide security fixes to components when new security vulnerabilities are discovered. Despite an average *of 71 vulnerabilities per application* introduced through the use of third-party components, only *23 percent* reported testing for vulnerabilities in components at every release." (the author's emphasis) While it is hoped that more than 23 percent of software developers would say they test for component vulnerabilities today, this shows this was a serious problem only six or seven years ago.

Therefore, the main problem with third-party component risks is *transparency*: If there is no easy way for a user to learn about the components that are present in a software product they use, they are almost guaranteed not to know about those risks. What is the solution to this problem? Obviously, the solution is for there to be some means by which a software user can learn about the third-party components that are present in a software product they use. Knowing the identities of these components will in theory allow the user to identify vulnerabilities due to those components, and then to pressure the supplier to patch them as soon as possible.

Clearly, organizations of all types need to learn about vulnerabilities found in components inside software products they use. How can they do this? It will probably not be a huge surprise that the answer to that question is found in the title of this book. In fact, software bills of materials (SBOMs) can provide the transparency required for a user to be informed about the third-party components that are present in a software product they utilize, and to enable the user to learn about vulnerabilities that are applicable to those components.

Armed with knowledge about the components in the software they use, as well as the vulnerabilities that are applicable to those components, the user can have an informed conversation with the supplier, in which they ask them about individual component vulnerabilities and when they will be patched. The user can also ask the supplier more general questions such as, "What is your policy for replacing a component when a serious vulnerability is identified in the component, in a case where patching the vulnerability is not feasible?"

---

[6] https://www.veracode.com/sites/default/files/pdf/resources/ipapers/soss-2017/index.html

A brief history of SBOMs

The concept of a bill of materials – the list of physical components that make up a product like a motor - has been widely applied in manufacturing for decades. However, it was only in 2011 that the concept was applied to software, when the Linux Foundation led the development of the Software Package Data Exchange (SPDX[7]) format. SPDX 2.2 is now an ISO standard, although SPDX 2.3 is the current version. SPDX 3.0 is under development, but – as of early 2024 – does not have a release date.

In 2012, software security expert Steve Springett released what is now known as OWASP Dependency Track[8], the first open source tool for managing software vulnerabilities based on SBOM information. In 2017, Steve and Patrick Dwyer led the development of the CycloneDX SBOM format (sometimes abbreviated "CDX" in this book), originally intended for use with Dependency Track but now in widespread use as a general SBOM format. Thus, as of early 2024, there are two well-supported SBOM formats.

However, just having two SBOM formats will never in itself be sufficient for SBOMs to be widely used. There need to be guidelines and "infrastructure" for producing, distributing, and utilizing (or "consuming") SBOMs. To analogize this, there would be no electric car industry if there were not general agreement – guidelines - on how electric cars are developed, manufactured, marketed, and used. There also needs to be the infrastructure necessary for electric cars, such as charging stations, repair facilities, regulation of electric car producers, etc.

All of these did not need to be fully in place when the first electric car was produced, but at least there needed to be a clear path by which they would be put in place over time. If that path had not been visible, no electric cars would ever have been produced – and even if they had been, few end users would have bought them.

Similarly, just having two workable SBOM formats does not in itself provide the guidelines and the rest of the "infrastructure" necessary for SBOMs to be widely distributed and used. This infrastructure needs to be developed collectively by a variety of players, including software developers, end users, tool vendors, industry associations and of course government organizations.

---

[7] https://spdx.dev/.

[8] https://dependencytrack.org/. Dependency Track is now a mainstay of the software development community and is used by developers about 17 million times *every day* to look up vulnerabilities found in components (dependencies) of software products under development. Of course, these components are identified in SBOMs, whether created by Dependency Track itself or by other sources.

While free markets alone might eventually lead to development of the necessary guidelines and infrastructure for SBOMs to succeed, it is possible for government and private organizations to "help the markets along" by facilitating discussions among the players, aimed at developing guidelines for production, distribution and use of SBOMs. However, it is the author's opinion that, even though SBOMs (including their regular distribution as new versions of the software are issued) may be made mandatory in certain regions and industries, regulations will probably never play an important role in distribution and use of SBOMs. SBOMs will ultimately live or die due to actions taken by individuals in the private sector or by government agencies whose role is to encourage development - but not to mandate it.

The SBOM "industry" was very fortunate that, in 2018, the National Technology and Information Administration (NTIA) of the US Department of Commerce launched a "multi-stakeholder process", the goal of which was to facilitate discussions among industry players regarding guidelines for developing, distributing and utilizing SBOMs. That process was called the Software Component Transparency Initiative, hereinafter called the Initiative. The leader of the Initiative was Dr. Allan Friedman of NTIA, who is now part of the Cybersecurity and Infrastructure Security Agency (CISA) of the US Department of Homeland Security (DHS) and leads a similar effort to develop SBOM guidelines there.

The NTIA Initiative ended in late 2021, but by then it had produced a set of documents[9] that blazed the trail toward the goal of having an agreed-upon framework for production of SBOMs by software suppliers. Although that goal has still not been achieved, by 2021 a large percentage of software developers, including virtually all the larger developers, were regularly producing and utilizing SBOMs in order to improve security in the products they were developing. This was a significant achievement of the Initiative.

Fortunately, Dr. Friedman has continued his SBOM promotion efforts at CISA. In 2022, he convened five industry working groups under CISA's auspices. These working groups continue the work of the NTIA Initiative[10].

---

[9] Available at https://www.ntia.doc.gov/SBOM

[10] It is important to keep in mind that no document produced by either the NTIA Initiative or CISA's workgroups carries any special weight or authority, just because it was published by a government agency; neither the NTIA nor CISA has any regulatory authority over private industry, although CISA does have that authority over federal government agencies. All the NTIA and CISA documents on SBOM and VEX are based simply on the ideas and opinions of the members of the workgroups that developed them; there were and are no restrictions on who can participate in these workgroups, and they include participants from a wide variety of countries. Dr. Friedman and his team members help facilitate the workgroup meetings, but are not themselves responsible for the content of any documents produced by the groups.

This book draws from the NTIA and CISA SBOM and VEX workgroup discussions that have taken place since 2020, when the author started participating in them. This book also draws from documents developed by those workgroups. SBOM and VEX guidelines are now being developed by various other government agencies (e.g., ENISA, the European Union Agency for Cybersecurity: https://www.enisa.europa.eu/) and private organizations (e.g., the OWASP SBOM Forum: https://owasp.org/www-project-sbom-forum/ and the Open Source Security Foundation: https://openssf.org/).

2. What is in an SBOM?

An SBOM is at heart a list of the components (also known as dependencies) in a software product or an intelligent hardware device. Because the number of components usually reaches into the hundreds or even thousands, SBOMs must be machine readable to be useful. Both the SPDX and CycloneDX formats are machine readable, and both can be expressed in either the JSON[11] or XML[12] data exchange formats. Moreover, they can both be expressed in more human-readable formats like spreadsheets. Since JSON is the more modern and widely used of the two data exchange formats, all SBOM and VEX documents discussed in this book should be assumed to be in JSON.

As discussed earlier, there are two main use cases for SBOMs: open source license management and software component vulnerability risk management. Open source license management was the original use case for SPDX SBOMs; the SPDX format has always included excellent license management capabilities. However, while component license management is a big concern for developers, it is not a big concern for software user organizations (i.e., organizations whose main business is not software development).[13] This book focuses on the component vulnerability risk management use case, the use case most pursued and discussed today.

The two main SBOM formats, SPDX and CycloneDX, are both quite capable, but they are also quite different. While both software suppliers and end users should be aware of the differences between the two formats, the choice of SBOM format to use will normally rest with the supplier, not the end user. Moreover, the supplier's choice will often be dictated by the development tools they utilize.

---

[11] https://www.w3schools.com/whatis/whatis_json.asp

[12] https://aws.amazon.com/what-is/xml/#:~:text=Extensible%20Markup%20Language%20(XML)%20is,perform%20computing%20operations%20by%20itself.

[13] The only end users of software that might be affected by open source licensing concerns is entities that edit the code of open source software or components of proprietary software they have been authorized to edit, as is sometimes advocated by the "right to repair" movement.

However, even though end users will not usually have a choice of SBOM formats, that is not a serious problem. If the user utilizes a tool that only accepts one of the two formats (e.g., CycloneDX) and a supplier provides an SBOM in the other format (SPDX), the user should simply inform the supplier that they need to have a CycloneDX SBOM. There are many tools that convert SBOMs between the two formats (as well as between the two main data exchange formats, JSON and XML, which are supported by both major SBOM formats). However, depending on the fields used, the translation will not always be perfect.

What fields should an SBOM contain?

Both the SPDX and CycloneDX SBOM formats contain a wide variety of possible fields. What set of fields should a supplier include in their SBOMs, and how much say should their customers have in questions regarding the fields to be included in the supplier's SBOMs?

In discussing these questions, it is important to understand that currently, nothing regarding SBOMs is "required" of a software or intelligent device supplier, unless they sell to the US federal government or they have agreed to provide SBOMs according to a customer contract. Executive Order 14028 (hereafter, "the EO") of May 2021 required US federal agencies to start *requesting* "an SBOM" from each of their suppliers of "critical software", with an effective date of August 10, 2022.[14]

The EO left all the implementation details, including for SBOMs, to the federal Office of Management and Budget (OMB)[15]. However, the EO did

---

[14] While this was a nice gesture, and while receiving one SBOM is certainly better than receiving no SBOMs at all, every software supplier needs to provide, for all their customers, a new SBOM with every new version of their product. An SBOM for a previous version of a product should never be considered applicable to the current version (or any other version, for that matter).

[15] Memo 22-18, issued by the Office of Management and Budget (OMB) in the fall of 2022 (https://www.whitehouse.gov/wp-content/uploads/2022/09/M-22-18.pdf), stated that it is up to each federal agency to decide whether to request SBOMs from their suppliers, and if so under what terms. Since federal agencies must follow the contract terms in the Federal Acquisition Regulation (FAR), they have no authority to require SBOMs in a new contract, unless the FAR revisions which were ordered by EO 14028 include that requirement. As of early 2024, the FAR revisions are still being debated; it will likely be years before agencies might be able to "require" regularly updated SBOMs from their suppliers, if that even happens.

The OMB memo required attestations by suppliers regarding their software development practices - specifically, whether and how they follow the NIST Secure Software Development Framework (SSDF), available at https://csrc.nist.gov/projects/ssdf. CISA was supposed to have the attestation form mandate that the NTIA develop a document describing the "minimum elements" to be included in an SBOM. That document was published[16] in July 2021. It describes three types of minimum elements: "Data Fields", "Automation Support" and "Practices and Processes".

It is an excellent document, but unfortunately, close to 100% of what has been written about the document focuses solely on the first of those three types: data fields. This is probably because the other two types are not summarized in a table, while the data fields are. That table can be found on page 9 of the document. However, it is important to read the whole document and remember that nothing in the document (including the table on page 9) is in any way a "requirement", even for federal agencies.

The table specifies seven "minimum data fields" for an SBOM. They can be divided into two types of fields:

Metadata for the SBOM – i.e., fields that apply to the product described in the SBOM, but not to any of the components listed in it. Therefore, only one instance of each metadata field is needed in one SBOM. Note that both SPDX and CycloneDX require metadata fields that are specific to the format. For instance, a CDX SBOM needs to have fields for "BOM format" and "Spec version". These are in addition to the minimum fields in the NTIA document.

Data for each component listed in the SBOM ("Component-level data"). It is recommended that each of these fields be filled out for each component; on the other hand, there are many reasons why a supplier will not be able to fill them all out for one or more components listed in any SBOM.

Metadata fields required by the "Minimum Elements" document

1. Supplier Name. This field is used for two different purposes by the Minimum Elements document. One is to designate the supplier of the "product" described by the SBOM; the other designates the supplier of one of the components listed in the SBOM. The author would much prefer that the two SBOM formats, as well as the Minimum Elements document, distinguished between a "product" and the "components" included in a product; however, that is not the case. Therefore, "Supplier Name" and "Component Name" are listed in Minimum Elements as both metadata and component-level fields.

---

prepared by June 2023 and issued a preliminary version for comment, but so many objections were raised that OMB decided to postpone the due date for agencies to require attestations from their suppliers. As this https://tomalrichblog.blogspot.com/2023/06/what-are-new-due-dates-for-attestations.html blog post shows, that date is effectively postponed until at least the fall of 2024, and perhaps beyond that.

[16] https://www.ntia.gov/files/ntia/publications/sbom_minimum_elements_report.pdf

CycloneDX has both a "Manufacturer" and a "Supplier" field, in which "Manufacturer" refers to the entity that develops the product and "Supplier" refers to the entity that sells (or otherwise provides) the product. If the issuer of the SBOM wishes to make this distinction, they are welcome to use both fields.

However, in the author's opinion, there will not normally be a reason to make this distinction, since an entity that does nothing but resell a product developed by a software "manufacturer" does not need to be listed in an SBOM at all. Unless the reseller modifies the software product itself, it does not introduce any supply chain cybersecurity risk to the product. Therefore, there is no more need to name the reseller than there is to name the company that designs the label on the box.

This book always defines the supplier as the organization that developed the product described in the SBOM or VEX document, or the organization that developed a component of that product.[17] In CycloneDX, the product supplier name is entered in the "metadata/component/supplier/name" field, and the component supplier name in the "components/supplier/name" field. In SPDX, it is entered in the "package supplier" field.

2. Component Name. The same problem that was just described for "Supplier Name" applies to "Component Name". This term is used in two different senses, both as a metadata field (where it means "product name"), and a component-level field (where it is the name of a component included in the product). In CycloneDX, the product name is entered in the "metadata/component/name" field, and the component name is entered in the "components/name" field. In SPDX, both are entered in the "package name" field.

3. Version of the Component. This is the third minimum data field that is both a metadata field and a component-level field. The product version string is entered in the "metadata/component/version" field in CycloneDX. The component version is entered in the "components/version" field. They are both entered in the "PackageVersion" field in SPDX.

4. Author of SBOM Data. This will normally be the organization that created the SBOM, even though one individual may have played a primary role in that process. Only if the individual acted on their own in producing the SBOM (and probably the product itself) should their name be listed as the author.[18] In CDX, the author or authors of the SBOM are listed under "metadata/authors".

---

[17] See the discussion later in this Part of open source components, which have no "supplier" per se.

[18] CycloneDX (and probably SPDX as well) allows multiple authors to be entered, so one author might be the organization that developed the software and other authors might be the individuals at the organization who were heavily involved in that development effort. One reason for doing this might be to provide contact information for readers of the SBOM that have questions about it. The "metadata/authors" field in CDX has sub-fields for the name, email address and phone number of each author.

5. Timestamp. This is the record of the date and time at which the data in the SBOM was "assembled". In most cases, this will be the same as the date and time at which the SBOM was created. The timestamp is listed in "metadata/timestamp" in CycloneDX.

Component-level fields required by the "Minimum Elements" document

1. Component Name. The component name needs to be listed for each component in the SBOM. If the author of the SBOM does not know the name of a component or does not wish to reveal it[19], they should enter either NOASSERTION (in SPDX) or "omitted" (in CycloneDX). However, this *field* should always be present for each component listed in the SBOM, even if it is empty or contains NOASSERTION. In CycloneDX, the name of the component is entered in the "components/name" field. In SPDX, it is entered in the "package name" field.

2. Component Supplier Name. Every component listed in the SBOM should have a supplier name. However, if this is not known, the author of the SBOM should enter either NOASSERTION (in SPDX) or a "omitted" (in CycloneDX). In CycloneDX, the Component supplier name is listed in the "components/supplier/name" field. In SPDX, it is entered in the "package supplier" field.

3. Version of the Component. It is essential for vulnerability management purposes that the version string of every component installed in the product be included in the SBOM, unless it is truly unknown.[20] The component version is listed in the "components/version" field in CycloneDX and the "PackageVersion" field in SPDX.

---

[19] A supplier should not feel they are obligated to reveal the name of every component listed in their SBOM. It is legitimate to withhold the component name (or any other information about the component, such as supplier name) if they feel this might reveal proprietary information to competitors, or even if the supplier just finds it embarrassing to list the name of the component. It is important for both suppliers and software users to keep in mind that, since at the current time SBOMs are not being regularly distributed to, and used by, end users of software, receiving an SBOM with some missing information is still much better than receiving no SBOM at all. Yet, the latter will inevitably be the outcome if the supplier feels they must choose between revealing every piece of information about their components and not releasing any SBOM at all. Given that SBOM distribution to end users is still in its infancy, it is important not to let the perfect be the enemy of the good.

[20] If a supplier includes a component in their product whose version string they don't know, that raises the question whether they have even looked for vulnerabilities that apply to that component (since vulnerabilities are almost always listed by version number as well as product name). And if they have not done that, what does this say about their vulnerability management practices?

4. Other Unique Identifiers. To learn about risks due to components in a software product, it is essential to be able to look up the product in a vulnerability database like the National Vulnerability Database (NVD) or OSS Index. To do this, the user needs to know either the "CPE name"[21] or the "purl"[22] for the product. At the present time, CPE is the only identifier supported by the NVD, while purl (which currently is only applicable to open source products, and not all of them) is the primary identifier used by most of the other vulnerability databases worldwide. For a further discussion of CPE and purl, see the Chapter titled "The naming problem" later in this Part.

Other recommended SBOM fields

It is likely that most SBOMs exchanged in the US (and in many other countries) already include the seven NTIA minimum data fields. However, it must be noted that, even though the minimum data fields are necessary for a workable SBOM, any SBOM that just included those fields would be inadequate for most purposes. The important question is what additional fields need to be in an SBOM.

The answer to that question is that it is unlikely there will ever be a consensus regarding *all* the fields that should be included in a usable SBOM. Different use cases will always require different sets of fields.

However, this is not a problem. As long as any tools on the end user side can ingest most or all of the fields supported by at least one of the two main SBOM formats, it is up to each supplier to work out with their customers the fields to be included in the SBOMs provided by the supplier. This should not be done in contract negotiations because, at this very early stage of SBOM availability, there is no way to be certain that a set of fields enshrined in a contract today will still be considered adequate a year from now, or whether some required fields will prove to be excessively burdensome to the supplier and need to be removed.

At this point, it is much better for customers simply to have discussions with their suppliers about this subject and make their preferences regarding SBOM fields known. Since many suppliers and almost all end user organizations currently have little (if any) experience with SBOMs, it is far too early to be concerned about contract terms.

21

https://nvd.nist.gov/products/cpe#:~:text=CPE%20is%20a%20structured%20namin g,systems%2C%20software%2C%20and%20packages.

[22]https://github.com/package-url/purl-spec. For more context on purl and its importance, see this post: https://tomalrichblog.blogspot.com/2022/11/the-purl-in-your-future.html

It is also important to understand that production of SBOMs is a capability included in many modern software build tools; thus, in many cases it is easy for a supplier to produce an SBOM for a product they are currently building[23]. Moreover, the SBOM produced could potentially include every field in the format being used (there are around 80 fields in SPDX and a similar number in CycloneDX).

If the data required for other fields are readily available to the supplier, and including those fields would benefit their customers, it should not be difficult for a customer to convince their supplier to include those fields in their SBOMs. The point is that the supplier needs to engage in a dialogue with their customers (although the customers can certainly initiate it!) about how the customer will use the SBOMs provided by the supplier, and what fields the customer will need filled out, to enable that use case.

The following are fields that the author recommends for inclusion in an SBOM, which go beyond the data fields from the Minimum Elements document discussed earlier. Note that the four Metadata fields below are not currently included in either the SPDX or CycloneDX format, so they can't currently be used. The author hopes they will be added as soon as feasible.

Recommended metadata fields

Product name. As mentioned earlier, there are currently no fields in either format that refer to the "product". This makes it difficult for a user tool to learn about the software artifact that is described in an SBOM. It is problems like this one that are partly responsible for the lack of any "complete" user tools today (the author will describe what he means by a "complete user tool" in Part 3 of this book).

Product version string. Whenever the code in a software product or intelligent device changes, two things should happen. One is that the version number of the product should change. The second is that the supplier should produce a new SBOM, since the previous SBOM will no longer be valid. This means that, in an ideal world, there will always be a one-to-one correspondence between software versions and SBOMs. Of course, it will take a long time before this ideal is realized for a significant number of software products. But this shows that maintaining and using version numbers are essential for software security.

Product supplier. This is a third field that needs to be added to both SBOM formats.

SBOM Type. This refers to the stage of the SBOM generation process at which the SBOM was produced. The contents of the SBOM and the reliability of those contents can vary greatly due to the Type, which is why the end user should be

---

[23] Although the "naming problem" complicates this process. See the chapter with that title later in this Part.

informed of the type of every SBOM they receive. See the Section titled "SBOM Types" in Chapter 4.

CycloneDX v1.5 includes a field called "metadata/lifecycles", which is based on the same concept as Types, but with somewhat different names. While the Types are "Design, Source, Build, Analyzed, Deployed and Runtime", the lifecycle "phases" are "design, pre-build, build, post-build, operations, discovery and decommission".[24]

Recommended component-level fields.

These fields are all available in both major SBOM formats:

Component CPE name, if available. This is entered in the "components/cpe" field in CycloneDX and the "Other Unique Identifiers" field in SPDX.

Component purl, if available[25]. This is entered in the "components/purl" field in CycloneDX, and the "Other Unique Identifiers" field in SPDX.

Component version string. This is entered in the "components/version" field in CycloneDX and the "PackageVersion" field in SPDX.

Component download location. For open source components, it is important to include the download location in their SBOM so that, if desired, the user will be able to verify that the supplier downloaded the correct component (although the author has heard this is quite had to do in practice). In CycloneDX, this requires using the "externalReferences/" field. The mandatory sub-fields are "url" and "type". In the latter, the supplier has a good selection, but the most likely to be helpful will be "website", "distribution" and "distribution-intake". There are also optional "comment" and "hashes" sub-fields. The situation is more complicated in SPDX. See this section[26] of the SPDX documentation.

Components. The "Components" field in CycloneDX is quite powerful (there is no direct SPDX equivalent). The entries in this field will usually be the direct dependencies of the product, but they may also be "lower level" dependencies as

---

[24] https://cyclonedx.org/docs/1.5/json/#metadata_lifecycles

[25] The purl for an open source component should almost always be "available", since the purl can always be constructed, as long as the supplier (or user) knows some basic information about the component, and the component is available in a package manager (this excludes most C and C++ projects). This information includes, at a minimum, the repository (e.g. package manager) from which it was downloaded and its name and version number within that repository. For more information on constructing purls for open source components, see the chapter titled "The naming problem" later in this Part.

[26] https://spdx.github.io/spdx-spec/v2.3/package-information/#77-package-download-location-field

well. What's especially powerful is that "Components" is recursive. That is, each component listed in the field will have its own "Components" field, which can list any of its dependencies. Each of those dependencies will have its own "Components" field, etc. If the creator of an SBOM wants to copy or move, for example, Component A and all its dependencies to a different point in the implicit "dependency graph" (the inverted "tree diagram" often used to show the dependencies of a product and the "levels" they fall under), they can simply copy or move A. All the dependencies of A will follow with it.

3. Advanced: SBOM examples

The two major SBOM formats are SPDX and CycloneDX (the CycloneDX platform can be used for other types of documents[27] like VEX, while SPDX is only for SBOMs). Below is an example SBOM in each format, with a short discussion of what the example contains. Both examples are in the JSON data representation language. These examples (and the VEX examples in Part 2) are provided so the reader can have in mind what an SBOM or VEX document looks like when they discuss it or read about it, even though they may never have to develop or directly interpret an SBOM.

An SPDX SBOM

This table introduces the JSON code following it:

---

[27] https://cyclonedx.org/capabilities/

Field	Comment
	This SBOM is for an infusion pump, called "INFUSION". It was provided by the Healthcare SBOM Proof of Concept, which started in 2018 under the NTIA, and since 2021 has operated under the auspices of the Healthcare-ISAC.
Document Header	After the "Header" section, the rest of the SBOM consists of descriptions of each of the "Packages" in the infusion pump, as well as the pump itself, "INFUSION".
	The only function of INFUSION in the SBOM is to be the "container" for the five software components, which are listed below it.
"NOASSERTION"	A lot of the fields contain "NOASSERTION". These is the filler in mandatory fields (the filler is a blank line in CycloneDX, when it is needed).
"Relationship"	The "Relationship" fields define the hierarchy of components. Note that "INFUSION" has a "CONTAINS" relationship with each of the five components.
(components)	Each of the five components "CONTAINS" either "NOASSERTION" or "NONE". This doesn't mean there are no sub-components, but only that the author of the SBOM has no knowledge of those (or does have knowledge, but is not revealing it for some reason). In fact, all of the components very likely contain many components, which in turn contain other components, etc.

```
##Document Header
SPDXVersion: SPDX-2.2
DataLicense: CC0-1.0
SPDXID: SPDXRef-DOCUMENT
DocumentName:        ACME-INFUSION-1.0-SBOM-DRAFTv2021-
06-07T165013
DocumentNamespace:
http://www.hospitalproducts.acme
Creator: Organization:  ACME-Hospital-Division()
Created: 2021-07-31T16:50:13Z
CreatorComment:   <text>Draft SCME INFUSION PoC II
SBOM document in SPDX format. Unofficial content for
demonstration purposes only.</text>
```

```
##
## Packages
##
PackageName: INFUSION
SPDXID: SPDXRef-INFUSION-1.0
ExternalRef:          PACKAGE-MANAGER          purl
pkg:generic/ACME/INFUSION@1.0
PackageVersion: 1.0
PackageSupplier: Organization: ACME
Relationship: SPDXRef-DOCUMENT  DESCRIBES  SPDXRef-
INFUSION-1.0
Relationship:       SPDXRef-INFUSION-1.0       CONTAINS
NOASSERTION
PackageDownloadLocation: NOASSERTION
FilesAnalyzed: false
PackageLicenseConcluded: NOASSERTION
PackageLicenseDeclared: NOASSERTION
PackageCopyrightText: NOASSERTION


PackageName: Windows Embedded Standard 7
SPDXID:          SPDXRef-Windows-Embedded-Standard-7-
6.1.7601
ExternalRef:          PACKAGE-MANAGER          purl
pkg:generic/Microsoft/Windows-Embedded-Standard-
7@6.1.7601
PackageVersion: 6.1.7601
PackageSupplier: Organization: Microsoft
Relationship: SPDXRef-INFUSION-1.0 CONTAINS SPDXRef-
Windows-Embedded-Standard-7-6.1.7601
Relationship:  SPDXRef-Windows-Embedded-Standard-7-
6.1.7601 CONTAINS NOASSERTION
PackageDownloadLocation: NOASSERTION
FilesAnalyzed: false
PackageLicenseConcluded: NOASSERTION
PackageLicenseDeclared: NOASSERTION
PackageCopyrightText: NOASSERTION


PackageName: Windows Embedded Standard 7 with SP1
patches
```

SPDXID: SPDXRef-Windows-Embedded-Standard-7-with-SP1-patches-3.0
ExternalRef: PACKAGE-MANAGER   purl
pkg:generic/Microsoft/Windows-Embedded-Standard-7-with-SP1-patches@3.0
ExternalRef: SECURITY   cpe23Type
cpe:2.3:o:microsoft:windows_7:-:sp1:*:*:*:*:*:*
PackageVersion: 3.0
PackageSupplier: Organization: Microsoft
Relationship: SPDXRef-INFUSION-1.0 CONTAINS SPDXRef-Windows-Embedded-Standard-7-with-SP1-patches-3.0
Relationship: SPDXRef-Windows-Embedded-Standard-7-with-SP1-patches-3.0 CONTAINS NONE
PackageDownloadLocation: NOASSERTION
FilesAnalyzed: false
PackageLicenseConcluded: NOASSERTION
PackageLicenseDeclared: NOASSERTION
PackageCopyrightText: NOASSERTION

PackageName: SQL 2005 Express
SPDXID: SPDXRef-SQL-2005-Express-9.00.5000.00SP4
ExternalRef: PACKAGE-MANAGER   purl
pkg:generic/Microsoft/SQL-2005-Express@9.00.5000.00SP4
PackageVersion: 9.00.5000.00SP4
PackageSupplier: Organization: Microsoft
Relationship: SPDXRef-INFUSION-1.0 CONTAINS SPDXRef-SQL-2005-Express-9.00.5000.00SP4
Relationship: SPDXRef-SQL-2005-Express-9.00.5000.00SP4 CONTAINS NOASSERTION
PackageDownloadLocation: NOASSERTION
FilesAnalyzed: false
PackageLicenseConcluded: NOASSERTION
PackageLicenseDeclared: NOASSERTION
PackageCopyrightText: NOASSERTION

PackageName: .Net Frame Work
SPDXID: SPDXRef-.Net-Frame-Work-V2.1.21022.8SP2
ExternalRef: PACKAGE-MANAGER   purl
pkg:generic/Microsoft/.Net-Frame-Work@V2.1.21022.8SP2
PackageVersion: V2.1.21022.8SP2
PackageSupplier: Organization: Microsoft
Relationship: SPDXRef-INFUSION-1.0 CONTAINS SPDXRef-.Net-Frame-Work-V2.1.21022.8SP2

```
    Relationship:            SPDXRef-.Net-Frame-Work-
V2.1.21022.8SP2 CONTAINS NOASSERTION
    PackageDownloadLocation: NOASSERTION
    FilesAnalyzed: false
    PackageLicenseConcluded: NOASSERTION
    PackageLicenseDeclared: NOASSERTION
    PackageCopyrightText: NOASSERTION


    PackageName: Bobs Browser
    SPDXID: SPDXRef-Bobs-Browser-1
    ExternalRef:            PACKAGE-MANAGER            purl
pkg:generic/Bob/Bobs-Browser@1
    PackageVersion: 1
    PackageSupplier: Organization: Bob
    Relationship: SPDXRef-INFUSION-1.0 CONTAINS SPDXRef-
Bobs-Browser-1
    Relationship: SPDXRef-Bobs-Browser-1 CONTAINS NONE
    PackageDownloadLocation: NOASSERTION
    FilesAnalyzed: false
    PackageLicenseConcluded: NOASSERTION
    PackageLicenseDeclared: NOASSERTION
    PackageCopyrightText: NOASSERTION
```

A CycloneDX SBOM

Below is a basic SBOM example in CycloneDX format, showing dependency relationships among the product and three components; it is followed by the author's comments. This example is also in the JSON data representation language. It is taken from the "Use Cases" section of the CycloneDX website[28]. This table provides a "guide" to the JSON code below:

---

[28] https://cyclonedx.org/use-cases/#dependency-graph

Field	Comment
"serialNumber"	The "serialNumber" is a UUID[29] generated with a random number, meaning it is globally unique. Any globally unique character string is OK for this entry.
"metadata/component"	The "component" under "metadata" refers to the product that is the subject of the SBOM. A convention in SBOMs is that the subject of the SBOM is referred to as the "primary component", not the "product".
"bom-ref"	"bom-ref" provides a way to refer to a component (including to the primary component: the product itself). It can be any character string, as long as it is unique within the SBOM. The CycloneDX team recommends that it be the "purl" identifier, which is a unique identifier for open source software products. Because the product in this example, "Acme Application", is a proprietary product of Acme, it does not have a purl. Its "bom-ref" is a contraction of its commercial name.
"components"	The "components" section lists the components of the product. Note they are not listed by "levels". All the components of all "levels" are listed together. The "dependencies" section shows which components "depend on" which other components. If component A "depends on" another component B, this commonly means that B is a component of A.
	There are three components, all of which are open source and therefore have purl identifiers. Each of their bom-refs is the same as the purl.
"dependencies"	The "dependencies" section shows that: a. The application described in the SBOM, "acme-app", has two dependencies, "web-framework" and "persistence". These are the immediate components of the application. b. "web-framework" depends on "common-util", so the latter is a component of the former. c. "persistence" also depends on "common-util", so the latter is a component of both "web-framework" and "persistence". d. "common-util" has no dependencies shown. This should not be taken to mean that in fact it has no dependencies (very few software products nowadays have no dependencies at all). This just means that the author of the SBOM knows of no dependencies (probably because the author does not have an SBOM for "common-util").

```
    {
   "bomFormat": "CycloneDX",
```

[29]   https://www.techtarget.com/searchapparchitecture/definition/UUID-Universal-Unique-Identifier

```
"specVersion": "1.4",
"serialNumber": "urn:uuid:3e671687-395b-41f5-a30f-a58921a69b79",
"version": 1,
"metadata": {
 "component": {
   "bom-ref": "acme-app",
   "type": "application",
   "name": "Acme Application",
   "version": "9.1.1"
 }
},
"components": [
  {
   "bom-ref": "pkg:maven/org.acme/web-framework@1.0.0",
   "type": "library",
   "group": "org.acme",
   "name": "web-framework",
   "version": "1.0.0",
   "purl": "pkg:maven/org.acme/web-framework@1.0.0"
  },
  {
   "bom-ref": "pkg:maven/org.acme/persistence@3.1.0",
   "type": "library",
   "group": "org.acme",
   "name": "persistence",
   "version": "3.1.0",
   "purl": "pkg:maven/org.acme/persistence@3.1.0"
  },
  {
   "bom-ref": "pkg:maven/org.acme/common-util@3.0.0",
   "type": "library",
   "group": "org.acme",
   "name": "common-util",
   "version": "3.0.0",
   "purl": "pkg:maven/org.acme/common-util@3.0.0"
  }
],
"dependencies": [
  {
   "ref": "acme-app",
   "dependsOn": [
    "pkg:maven/org.acme/web-framework@1.0.0",
    "pkg:maven/org.acme/persistence@3.1.0"
```

```
      ]
    },
    {
      "ref": "pkg:maven/org.acme/web-framework@1.0.0",
      "dependsOn": [
        "pkg:maven/org.acme/common-util@3.0.0"
      ]
    },
    {
      "ref": "pkg:maven/org.acme/persistence@3.1.0",
      "dependsOn": [
        "pkg:maven/org.acme/common-util@3.0.0"
      ]
    },
    {
      "ref": "pkg:maven/org.acme/common-util@3.0.0",
      "dependsOn": []
    }
  ]
}
```

4. Advanced: SBOM best practices

The earlier discussion of fields has referred many times to the "supplier" of a product or component, which normally means a developer organization or an individual developer that produces and (usually) provides support for the product or component. Of course, the supplier usually charges for producing and supporting the software, but that may not always be the case. What is important is that there is some sort of agreement (usually written) between the supplier and the customer, that governs the obligations of each.

However, approximately 90% of software components are not provided by a "supplier" as defined earlier, but by an open source community that makes their software available free of charge. That community usually does not commit to providing support[30] for any developer (or anybody else) that downloads the software.

It is natural for a software supplier to wonder, when creating an SBOM for one of their products, how they should refer to the community that created an open source component. This is especially important when looking up vulnerabilities in the NVD, since the CPE name required to identify the component is based in part on the supplier name. Unfortunately, since open source communities are often referred to with many names and there is no database that lists a "canonical" name for every open source community (nor could there ever be one), the "supplier names" used to create CPEs for open

---

[30] Most open source communities provide some degree of support – at least, delivery of patches for serious security vulnerabilities – after a developer has downloaded a component and used it in one of their products. However, this is almost never guaranteed in a contract.

The exception to this statement is an organization like Red Hat™. Red Hat does not normally charge for their software (which is open source) but does charge for supporting it. The author considers Red Hat to be more of a proprietary supplier than an open source community, so this Section does not apply to RH.

31

source products vary widely. This often makes it difficult, and in some cases practically impossible, to locate a CPE name for a given component in the NVD. See the chapter titled "The naming problem" later in this Part.

However, most open source components have a purl, and there is no need for a central database to find a purl for an open source product. If the supplier does not know the purl for the component already, they can always create their own using their own knowledge of the location they downloaded the component from (often a package manager), the name of the component and its version number (version string).[31] Unless the supplier makes a mistake, the purl they enter for an open source component when they report a vulnerability to an open source vulnerability database like OSV or OSS Index should always match the purl listed for the component in an SBOM.

Since the purl for a component can be accurately identified without entering a "supplier name", the question about the proper name for an open source community becomes moot. Instead of the open source community, the product supplier just needs to know the repository from which they downloaded the component (e.g. Maven Central) – as well as the product name and version string - in order to construct a valid purl for the component.

Another important consideration regarding open source software is End of Life (EOL) date. For proprietary software, this means the date that the supplier will stop supporting the software, including issuing new patches. Usually, a proprietary software supplier will announce that a product (or a version of the product) is going into EOL status well in advance of the actual date. If the supplier of a product that includes a proprietary component learns that it will go EOL in the not-too-distant future, they need to decide whether to upgrade to a supported version of the component (if that is an option), to take on the open source maintainer responsibility, to branch or fork the code for purposes of internally maintaining it, or to replace the component with a different one.

However, open source project teams don't usually announce an end of life for their product, even if they might have some idea that it may be coming. Open source projects don't normally end with a bang but a whimper, as one-by-one the maintainers lose interest. Finally, there is nobody involved who can or will produce further patches.

If the supplier has the bandwidth and inclination, they might download the code and patch it themselves. At that point, the code is no longer a third-party component, but instead should be treated as the supplier's own code. Any vulnerabilities discovered in that code later should be reported as applicable to the supplier's first-party code, not to the previous component name.

How does the supplier avoid finding themselves in this situation? They need to monitor open source communities that maintain components that are important in their product and look for signs that the health of the community may be

---

[31] For further discussion of purl, see the chapter entitled "The Naming Problem" later in this Part.

declining. For example, if no patch or upgrade has been produced in the past year, or there have been no "commits" of new code to the project in the last six months, they might take these observations as warnings that they need either to look for a replacement for the component or commit their own resources to maintaining it.

"Forking" open source components

Software suppliers often edit open source components before they incorporate them into their product. This is called "forking" the component, since the supplier has now created a different component from the one they started with. They do this for multiple reasons, including fixing a vulnerability in a component and making a change to the functionality of a component. Of course, under most open source product licenses, this is a completely legitimate practice.

However, when they do this, the supplier needs to keep in mind that they should no longer list the original component in their SBOM. This is because the altered code means there can no longer be certainty that the forked component in the product is subject to the same vulnerabilities as the original component.

The supplier has the option of renaming the forked component and setting it up as a separate project on GitHub; they would then need to report vulnerabilities for it, make patches publicly available, etc. However, it will probably be much easier for the supplier just to treat the forked component as part of their own code, meaning that from now on they will report all vulnerabilities under the product's identifier and no longer list the original component name in their SBOM at all.

CycloneDX has a "pedigree"[32] field, which lets a supplier document "ancestors", "patches" and "commits" to an open source project. Also, the OWASP Software Component Verification Standard[33] (SCVS) project – a leading document in the software supply chain security field - includes a section[34] titled "Pedigree and Provenance Requirements".

How and when should SBOMs be supplied?

The NTIA Minimum Elements document states that a new SBOM should be supplied whenever there has been any change in the software. This includes every patch, every update, etc. However, this mandate will be quite difficult to follow in practice, and in fact a new SBOM is not necessary in the case of many of these changes. For example, a change in the supplier's first-party code, which does not

---

[32] https://cyclonedx.org/use-cases/#pedigree
[33] https://scvs.owasp.org/scvs/preface/
[34] https://scvs.owasp.org/scvs/v6-pedigree-and-provenance/

affect any of the third-party components in the product, should not require a new SBOM.

Based on conversations with software suppliers, the author believes that the best answer to the question of how often a supplier should produce a new SBOM and distribute it to their customers is that one should be produced with every new major or minor version of the software, or at least with every major version. Thus, when a supplier determines that a new version of their software is needed, they will understand that a new SBOM is needed as well. Thus, the decision on how often to distribute a new SBOM will always be related to the question of how often to declare a new version.

Of course, any change in the code of a product – whether in the first-party code or a third-party component – requires a change in the version number. If that does not happen, it becomes close to impossible to provide good support for the product.

However, requiring that a new SBOM be distributed whenever there is any change at all in the code of a product, as the Minimum Elements document implies, would be excessive, given that producing an SBOM for distribution outside the developer's organization will clearly take a lot of work today (including trying to find a CPE or purl for every component). In maybe ten years, it may be possible to produce a complete, accurate SBOM with the touch of a button, but that is far from being the case today.

The Transparency Exchange API

In both the NTIA and CISA SBOM initiatives, there has been much discussion of how SBOMs and VEX documents will be provided to end users. The option currently most used is making them available on an authenticated customer portal, although many other options have been discussed. Given that SBOMs are now being provided to customers very infrequently if at all (and VEX documents are being provided even less frequently), the customer portal is a workable solution.

However, the author does not believe that will be the case for very long. A customer portal is only a workable solution for distributing SBOMs if an SBOMs and VEX documents are not being distributed very frequently; once these documents need to be distributed frequently (and, as will be discussed in Part 2 of this book, a VEX document for a product may need to be distributed every day for many products), the portal will prove to be inadequate.

Fortunately, there is an excellent solution available for the problem of distributing both SBOMs and VEX documents in significant volume. It is the Transparency Exchange API[35], which is under development by the CycloneDX team. It is an API that can be embedded in an end user tool like Dependency Track or in the proposed "complete" component vulnerability management tool that is

---

[35] https://github.com/CycloneDX/transparency-exchange-api

described in Part 3 of this book. The API can retrieve an SBOM or VEX document, in any format, from a server maintained by a software supplier (or perhaps from a server maintained by a third-party that performs this service on behalf of many suppliers).

Of course, there will not be limits on how often the API can be used to download an SBOM or VEX document. The supplier will upload every new SBOM or VEX document to the server, and the API will be able to retrieve the most recent version.

The situation is different for the two types of documents. In the use case discussed in this book, both the SBOM and the VEX document apply to a single version of a single product. However, there will usually only be one SBOM per product/version. This is because an SBOM will normally not be issued unless there has been a change in the code of the product (especially a change in a component, such as adding or removing a component or patching a component vulnerability). A code change will require both a new version number and a new SBOM.

However, as will be discussed in Part 2 later in this book, VEX documents will often need to be updated very frequently, perhaps daily. The end user's tool will check daily (or even more frequently) for a new VEX document; it will download it if it finds one.

While the API will make the user's work easier, it will make the supplier's work incredibly easier. SBOMs can be distributed via a portal, since they do not need to be re-issued very often. However, due to the frequency with which VEX documents need to be updated (and the fact that it is not possible to predict when an update will be required), a portal will not be a good option, because of the need to notify users, etc. With the Transparency Exchange API, the supplier will simply post each updated VEX document and SBOM once on the Transparency Exchange server, and the API will do the rest of the work.

SBOMs for patched versions

At first glance, it might seem that a patched version of the software – i.e., an existing version with no change other than a patch having been applied to it – should be treated no differently from any other version. However, the Director of Product Security (DPS) of a major US software developer pointed out to the author in 2023 that, at least for many software developers, requiring a new SBOM with every patch would impose an unacceptable burden on them. Here is his reasoning:

A patch is always released between versions of a product, since most developers "roll up" any current patches into the next version.

Often, multiple patches are released between one new version and the next. Since it is almost always up to the customer to decide whether to apply a particular patch, new patches are not usually "cumulative" – i.e., the second patch doesn't include the first one; the third patch doesn't include the first and second patches, etc.

If the supplier is going to release an SBOM for a patched version of the product, they will face a dilemma: Should they assume that all previous patches (since the last new version was released) have been applied before the new patch? Should they assume that some of them have been applied? Or should they assume that none have been applied?

At first, it may seem that the only good solution, if the developer is going to release SBOMs for patched versions of their product, is to release an SBOM for every possible combination of patches that might have been applied, so that every user will have an SBOM that accurately reflects the codebase installed in their environment.

However, the DPS calculated that the number of SBOMs needed to do that is equal to 2 raised to the number of independent patches that have been issued since the last update. If three patches have been issued since the last update, this means the supplier needs to prepare 8 (2 raised to the third power) SBOMs when they release a fourth patch.

Eight SBOMs might sound doable to some people. But how many SBOMs does the developer need to prepare if there have been five previous patches? That's 32 SBOMs. How about ten previous patches? That's 1,024.

Clearly, the developer cannot be expected to produce a new SBOM for every possible combination of previously released patches, whenever they release a patch. One compromise might be for the supplier to release two SBOMs with every new patch: one SBOM that assumes all previous patches (since the last new version) have been applied and one that assumes no previous patches have been applied. Of course, this is a question that will require the supplier to consult with its customers.

SBOM Types

There are multiple phases of the software production process at which a software supplier can produce an SBOM; the results will be different for each of these phases. The members of the CISA Tooling and Implementation workgroup developed a document titled "SBOM Types"[36] to describe these. The Types are Design, Source, Build, Analyzed, Deployed and Runtime.

---

[36] Available at https://www.cisa.gov/sites/default/files/2023-04/sbom-types-document-508c.pdf

Note there is an alternative SBOM classification system, called "Lifecycles", which was developed by the OWASP CycloneDX community. It is described on page 13 of the "Authoritative Guide to SBOM", published[37] by the community.

Which of these is the best Type? The answer to that question is an unequivocal... "It depends". Each Type has its advantages and disadvantages (described in the document), but in the author's opinion, the three most useful are:

Build (specifically, an SBOM created with the final build of the software). For many software suppliers, this is likely to be the easiest SBOM to create, since it often requires nothing more than checking a box before executing the final build. This will almost always be more accurate than an SBOM created at any earlier stage of the build process, or even from the source code repository.

Analyzed. This SBOM is created from the binary files distributed for the product, and will be subject to the limitations of any SBOM created using binary analysis (an SBOM created using binary analysis will almost never be as accurate as an SBOM created from the build process). However, for legacy products and products developed using older languages, this may be the only option.

Deployed. This is an SBOM created by analyzing the files that are actually deployed, including in some cases an installer, a container, shared libraries[38], runtime dependencies (i.e., software items that are required in order for the software product to run, even though they are not part of the product itself. They are downloaded at runtime), etc. This SBOM is also created using binary analysis, but it is important because the risks faced by the user organization are based not just on the software product itself, but on everything that is installed with it. This is the only SBOM Type that allows a user to learn about vulnerabilities applicable to the other files installed with the product, not just to the product itself.

For example, if the installer is left in place after the software has been installed, but it contains an easily exploitable vulnerability, its compromise can be just as consequential as would a compromise of the software itself. For this

---

[37] Available at https://cyclonedx.org/guides/sbom/OWASP_CycloneDX-SBOM-Guide-en.pdf

[38] Shared libraries are libraries that are distributed as part of the operating system. The user cannot normally control shared libraries. This means that, if a product utilizes a shared library and the supplier built the software (and created the SBOM) utilizing a different version of that library than a user has on their system, the user may experience problems with the software. To avoid this, the supplier may want to leave shared libraries out of their SBOM, or at least provide some warning to the user that there might be discrepancies due to version mismatch. However, if the software requires a particular version of the shared library to run, the supplier will either need to provide that version with the product or instruct their customers to download and install the correct version, after they have installed the software itself.

reason, if it is possible for the supplier to distribute a Deployed SBOM, their customers should request that. However, since this SBOM does not provide as accurate a picture as possible of the software as the Build SBOM, the supplier might want to distribute both Types. This question needs to be discussed between the supplier and their customers.

Installation options

Often, a software product will offer different installation options: i.e., the user does not have to install every capability in the product, if not all of them are needed. A user might decide not to install an option they do not need to install, for security reasons (since not doing so will reduce the "attack surface" of the product) or simply to reduce the complexity of the product.

However, whenever an option is installed that did not come as part of the "base package" (or an option in the base package is de-installed), the result is a product that is different from the base package. In theory, Product Y with Option A installed should be treated as a separate product – e.g., "Product Y with A" – from Product Y by itself. It should have its own SBOM and VEX documents, its own reported vulnerabilities, its own versions, etc. In fact, that should be done for each combination of independent options, when there are multiple options. Thus, if Options A, B and C are all available, there should be eight "products" altogether: Y, Y+A, Y+B, Y+C, Y+A+B, Y+A+C, Y+B+C, and Y+A+B+C.

Of course, this can get ridiculous very easily; for example, with five options, there will be 121 different combinations of options. With ten options, there will be about 3.6 million combinations. Clearly, the supplier needs to a) decide whether any of the options introduces enough variation into the product to be treated as a separate product, and b) if so, choose just a small number of combinations to treat separately.

Requests to suppliers

Even though contracts with provisions regarding SBOM or VEX should be out of the question now, it *is* important for end user organizations not to be shy about informally reaching out to software suppliers regarding steps they can take to help their customers mitigate software component vulnerabilities using SBOMs and VEX documents.

For this reason, the author recommends that end users develop good working relationships with their suppliers and reach verbal agreements on how the supplier will create and distribute SBOMs and VEX documents. This will allow them to make requests and get honest answers from the suppliers without needing to have lawyers on hand at every step of the way. It is very likely that whatever set of processes is agreed to early in the discussions will need to be modified later, as experience reveals the need for changes.

The following are requests related to SBOMs that end user organizations should consider verbally relaying to their software suppliers. Note that none of these are "mandatory". Also note that, since the author believes that low cost, commercially available tools that ingest SBOMs and VEX information and output information on exploitable component vulnerabilities, will not be available to software end users for at least several years, a lot of these requests will need to be relayed through third-party service providers that will execute the required SBOM and VEX "processing", and make the results available to the end user. The requests include[39]:

How often SBOMs will be provided for the product. Ideally, a new SBOM should be provided with the release of every major and minor version of the product. However, to start out, it might be better just to request that the supplier provide a new SBOM for each major version; few suppliers are doing even this today.

The format (SPDX or CycloneDX) and data representation language (JSON or XML) in which SBOMs will be provided. As an earlier discussion points out, an end user may prefer one or the other format, but if the SBOM is provided in the wrong format – e.g. it is not in the format supported by a tool utilized by the end user – it will usually not be hard for the supplier to translate it into the other format. Most suppliers will probably standardize on one or the other format, often dictated by the languages and development tools they utilize.

The fields that will be included in the SBOM (see the earlier discussion of this topic).

Whether the SBOMs and VEX documents will be delivered to the customer or to a service provider acting on their behalf. As discussed in Part 3, it is likely that service providers will be the "intermediaries" between suppliers and their customers regarding component vulnerability management. This will be true for at least the next 2-3 years, until true end user tools become available.

At which phase (or phases) of the build process SBOMs will be generated for end user utilization (see the "SBOM Types" in Chapter 4).

If the supplier modifies an open source component before including it in the product, how they will notify the end user of this fact and how they will track vulnerabilities in the component going forward.[40]

If the supplier intends not to patch vulnerabilities that do not meet certain criteria for being important (e.g., when the CVSS or EPSS score, or both, is below a certain level), what exactly those criteria are. There are no correct or incorrect criteria, as long as the customer is told what they are.

---

[39] It is likely the reader will not understand why one or more of these provisions is included. Some of them were discussed earlier in this Section, but others were not. Anyone with a question should feel free to email the author.

[40] CycloneDX has a "pedigree" field that can be used for this purpose. See https://cyclonedx.org/docs/1.5/json/#components_items_pedigree.

How quickly the supplier will patch vulnerabilities determined to be exploitable in a product, or at least how they will prioritize vulnerabilities for patching.

How the supplier will learn of end of life (EOL) status for commercial components included in the product, and how quickly the supplier will upgrade or replace an EOL commercial component in the product (see the Section titled "Identifying other risks to software arising from components" in Chapter 6).

How the supplier will learn of end of life status for critical open source components (e.g., by monitoring the health of the community that maintains the component to determine whether there is any danger that new patches will stop), and how quickly the supplier will upgrade or replace an EOL open source component in the product.

Whether the supplier will try to provide a purl identifier[41] for every open source component listed in the SBOM.

Whether the supplier will try to provide a *verified* CPE name for every proprietary component or hardware device listed in the SBOM.

How many "levels" should we ask for?

An SBOM's components are often represented in a "dependency graph" like Figure 1.

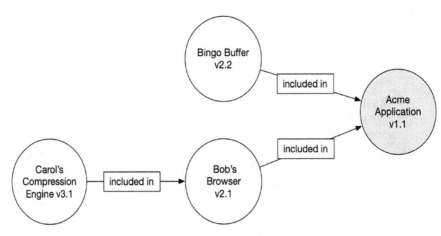

Figure 1: Dependency graph[42]

---

[41] See the chapter titled "The Naming Problem" later in this Part, for a discussion of why purl is so important, both today and even more so in the future.

[42] From "Framing Software Component Transparency, available at https://www.ntia.doc.gov/files/ntia/publications/ntia_sbom_framing_2nd_edition_2 0211021.pdf

A quick look at this graph shows there appear to be "levels" in an SBOM. That is, there are some components (two in this illustration – "Bingo Buffer" and "Bob's Browser") that appear to be "first level" components of the product, "Acme Application". There are other "second level" components (in this graph, there is only one, "Carol's Compression Engine", but that only means the developer of this dependency graph only knew of one component on the second level), and there are probably other "levels" of components beyond that.

The concept of "levels" in SBOMs is problematic. For example, there are often circular component references; that is, Component A is included in Component B, but a different instance of B is included in a different instance of A within the same product. Because of this, the CycloneDX SBOM format treats all components as being on the same "level" – that is, all components, components of components, etc. are listed, without reference to levels, under their single parent. However, the user can still build the dependency graph by utilizing the dependency relationships found in the SBOM.

As an example, the CycloneDX JSON fragment below (taken from the SBOM example listed earlier) states that "common-util version 3.0.0 is a component of "web-framework" version 1.0.0 (or equivalently, "web-framework" version 1.0.0 "depends on" "common-util" version 3.0.0).

```
"ref": "pkg:maven/org.acme/web-framework@1.0.0",
"dependsOn43": [
  "pkg:maven/org.acme/common-util@3.0.0"
]
```

A common question that comes up is, "How many levels of SBOMs should we ask our supplier for?" Of course, the answer to that question is, "As many as you can." Unfortunately, the risk posed by a vulnerable component like log4j does not diminish when it is found at "lower levels" of a product, although in some cases it may be harder for an attacker to "reach" it. It is always beneficial to know about as many components as possible in a product, regardless of their level.

What SBOM mandates apply to the private sector?

There is currently only one US government regulation that applies to the private sector in the US, which requires suppliers to produce SBOMs; this is from the US Food and Drug Administration (FDA). The FDA is charged with regulating the safety of medical products, including prescription medicines and medical devices that are sold in the US; in fact, FDA approval is a precondition for those items to be marketed in the first place.

---

[43] If a product "depends on" another product, it means the latter is a component of the former. This is why the words "dependency" and "component" are almost synonymous.

Introduction to SBOM and VEX

In 2017, the FDA announced that they intended to require SBOMs for medical devices marketed to hospitals in the US (the biggest category of these devices is infusion pumps). However, they required Congressional authority to mandate cybersecurity measures for medical devices (including a measure for SBOMs). This was finally granted by Congress at the end of 2022, in the Omnibus Reconciliation Act of 2022.

In October 2023, the FDA released a long-awaited document[44]: "Cybersecurity in Medical Devices: Quality System Considerations and Content of Premarket Submissions". Many people in the medical device industry were sure that it would be a "game changer" for SBOMs, but it proved to be anything but that[45].

The document included a requirement for just a single SBOM with every "premarket submission" (the packet of documents on safety that the FDA requires to approve any medical device to be sold in the US). Like the other documents in the packet, the FDA will not distribute the SBOM to any other party, including customers of the device (usually hospitals, of course), as some hospitals had hoped. The FDA's new document did not require the supplier to regularly distribute SBOMs to their customers, although it highly recommends the practice.

Given that the FDA Premarket Submission guidance only requires one SBOM and that it be delivered only to the FDA - not to customers - it is safe to say there are still no mandatory requirements for software or intelligent device suppliers to deliver SBOMs to US customers, other than federal agencies if requested due to Executive Order 14028.[46]

What are the prospects for such requirements in the near future (i.e., the next 2-3 years)? The author believes they are somewhere between slim and nonexistent. There are several reasons for this:

First, other than for safety reasons, the FDA is the only federal agency the author knows of that has authority to regulate suppliers to an industry, not just the industry itself. If there were ever to be regulations that apply to other software or device suppliers in the US (whether requiring SBOMs or anything else), this would require that some agency be given authority by Congress to impose such

---

[44] https://www.fda.gov/media/119933/download

[45] See this blog post: https://tomalrichblog.blogspot.com/2023/10/did-fdas-new-guidelines-require-any.html

[46] Some people were expecting that the upcoming EU Cyber Resilience Act would require that "product" suppliers (i.e. suppliers of software products or intelligent devices) regularly deliver SBOMs to their customers. However, the almost-final version made available in January 2024 (at https://eur-lex.europa.eu/legal-content/EN/TXT/PDF/?uri=CONSIL:ST_17000_2023_INIT) only requires the supplier to "draw up" an SBOM (p. 166), but not to distribute it to anyone else (it will be needed in the event of a successful attack on the software, although it will not be very useful if a new SBOM is not created for each new version of the software).

regulations. Needless to say, there is not currently any discussion in Congress of that happening, let alone any pending legislation known to the author.[47]

Second, regulations are almost always instituted because an industry is rapidly growing (or has already matured), and there is concern about either actual or potential abuses that need to be controlled (witness the current serious discussions in Congress about regulating the AI and cryptocurrency "industries").

Regulations are almost never instituted for the purpose of bringing a new industry into existence, and it is questionable whether it would even be possible to do that. While SBOMs are now being used heavily by software suppliers to manage security risks in their own products, there is no need to regulate that activity; only when SBOMs start to be distributed in significant quantities across organizational boundaries, for example from suppliers to end users or from upstream (component) suppliers to downstream (product) suppliers, will it even be necessary to consider regulations. Of course, that is currently far from being the case.

Third, regulation is only possible when the practices of an industry are well established and agreed upon; again, this means the industry is either mature or rapidly growing. Of course, almost no practices are well established in the SBOM "industry". For example, since SBOMs are not being regularly distributed in any industry for cybersecurity purposes,[48] there is no agreement on when and to whom they should be distributed, as well as under what conditions (e.g., with or without a non-disclosure agreement). All of these practices need to be worked out by the market participants (the suppliers and end user organizations) among themselves, before there can be any regulations imposed on top of those practices.

For example, suppose a law were to be passed that a software supplier must distribute a new SBOM with every new major version of their software. In the author's opinion, that would be a reasonable start. However, other questions would immediately arise, like what constitutes a "major" version. Of course, then there would have to be another regulation defining what a major version is (which also entails defining minor versions, patch versions, new builds, etc.).

---

[47] The Cybersecurity and Infrastructure Security Agency (CISA), part of the US Department of Homeland Security (DHS) has the power to require other federal agencies to take security measures; in fact, it exercises that power regularly. However, neither CISA nor any other federal agency is empowered to regulate private sector entities, absent specific authorization by Congress.

[48] The exception is the German auto manufacturing industry, where four or five major OEMs like Volkswagen are receiving SBOMs regularly from suppliers of the many devices that go into a car. However, this exchange is driven by the open source licensing use case (due in part to a rigorous German law regarding open source licensing), not software vulnerability management.

The problem with mandatory requirements, especially for an industry that is in the embryonic stage like the SBOM "industry", is that each requirement immediately points to the need for two or three more requirements. This is just an illustration of how, if industry practices are not already well-defined and a regulation, law, directive, or policy is imposed, the regulations, laws, directives, or policies will not be able to succeed until a lot of other practices are defined and codified. If the industry is already well established, of course, that will not have to happen.

The author highly recommends that anyone who thinks that SBOM regulations, laws, directives, or policies are inevitable (and there seem to be many people that think that way, including not a few founders of startups that seem to have built their business models on that idea) revise your thinking as soon as possible. Regulation of SBOMs will not happen for at least 5-10 years. First, we need to build up the SBOM "industry". Then, we can think about regulating it.

5. SBOMs and vulnerability management for intelligent devices

It is a fact that almost all the documents that have been written about software bills of materials only discuss SBOMs for software, not SBOMs for intelligent devices[49]. This is even though the need to have SBOMs for medical devices was one of the main drivers of the NTIA and CISA SBOM initiatives. However, even though the SBOMs produced by device manufacturers do not differ greatly from those produced by suppliers of user-managed software (i.e., almost everything we normally refer to as "software"), the vulnerability reporting responsibilities, and especially how they are implemented, differ significantly.

It is important to keep in mind the reason why SBOMs are needed by non-developers, whether for devices or for user-managed software: the user organization (or a service provider acting on their behalf) needs to be able to identify exploitable vulnerabilities in third-party components included in the software or device that, if not patched or otherwise remediated, pose a risk to the organization. What is needed for the user organization to achieve this goal, and how can the device manufacturer help their customers achieve it? There are four important types of actions the manufacturer can and should take to help their customers.

Reporting vulnerabilities in devices

Vulnerability management, for both intelligent devices and software, is only possible if there is a way for the user to learn about vulnerabilities found in the

---

[49] The author defines an intelligent device as a hardware device with one or more microprocessors, which execute code delivered in software and/or firmware. The device is usually delivered as a sealed package, meaning the user cannot open it themselves and therefore cannot directly update software or firmware.

device or software product. Of course, vulnerability databases are repositories for this information. But how does the information get into the vulnerability database? In most cases, information about vulnerabilities and what they apply to gets reported to CVE.org[50], an agency within the US Department of Homeland Security (DHS) that maintains the CVE database. This database was previously known as "MITRE", since it is operated by the MITRE Corporation. MITRE contractors still maintain the database, but they now operate under the management of the board of the nonprofit CVE.org. This board is comprised of representatives of government agencies like NIST and CISA, as well as MITRE and other private-sector organizations.

CVE information is entered into the CVE.org database by means of "CVE reports", which describe a vulnerability and the product or products it applies to. The reports are prepared by "CVE Numbering Authorities" (CNAs). These are usually software suppliers authorized by CVE.org. The CNAs prepare CVE reports both on their own behalf (i.e., describing vulnerabilities they have found in their own products) and on behalf of other suppliers that are not CNAs; as of early 2024, there are over 300 CNAs. Each CNA has a "scope" that indicates the types of suppliers it will assist in preparing CVE reports. A scope can comprise a country, an industry, etc.

The important thing to keep in mind is that information on a vulnerability (including the product or products affected by it) almost always gets entered in the CVE.org database by the supplier of the product. Obviously, this system relies heavily on the good faith of software suppliers. Fortunately, most larger software suppliers take this obligation very seriously, although the record is spotty for the smaller software suppliers.

Are device manufacturers also doing a good job of vulnerability reporting? Unfortunately, they could do a lot better. In fact, many major intelligent device manufacturers seem to have never reported a single vulnerability to CVE.org.[51] This can be verified by entering the name of the manufacturer in the "CPE Search"[52] bar in the National Vulnerability Database. If the search comes up empty (and the user has also tried a few variations on the manufacturer's name), this probably means the manufacturer has never reported a vulnerability for any of their products (it is possible to say this because a CPE name for a product is only created - by NIST - when a CVE report is filed that lists the product as

---

[50] https://www.cve.org/

[51] A leading firmware security expert, Tom Pace of NetRise, told the SBOM Forum in 2022 that he had examined one networking device (used in the military and in critical infrastructure) that had never had a vulnerability reported for it (in fact, none of the 50-odd devices made by the same manufacturer had ever had a vulnerability reported for it). He identified the major open source components found in the device's firmware and, based on his knowledge of the number of vulnerabilities found in each of those components, estimated that the device contains 40,000 unpatched firmware vulnerabilities!

[52] https://nvd.nist.gov/products/cpe/search

vulnerable to the CVE in the report. If there are no CPE names that include the name of the manufacturer, that probably indicates the manufacturer has never filed a CVE report).

The author recently checked this assertion by searching the NVD for the top ten medical device manufacturers (whose devices are sold in the US). The results[53] were, frankly, appalling:

Four of the manufacturers were not listed in the NVD at all, meaning they had never reported a vulnerability for any of their devices (one of those four manufacturers is the employer of a friend of the author's, who is a product security manager at that manufacturer. He told the author last year that his employer had never reported a vulnerability for any of their devices; the search confirmed his statement. This is one of the top medical device makers worldwide).

Four of the manufacturers had only a small number of vulnerabilities listed for their devices (one of these manufacturers had only reported two vulnerabilities across all their devices).

The remaining two manufacturers are part of very large, diversified companies that have reported many vulnerabilities. Because it would require a huge effort to determine which if any of those vulnerabilities apply to medical devices, the author cannot make any statement about them.

What is most disturbing about these results is that medical devices have the most stringent cybersecurity regulations of almost any other devices or software (this includes regulations imposed by the US Food and Drug Administration or FDA. Most other countries regulate medical devices as well). Yet, it seems medical device makers seldom report vulnerabilities in their devices.

For all practical purposes, this situation makes it close to impossible for hospitals to learn about vulnerabilities in the devices they use, without investing large amounts of time to do that (see the discussion later in this Chapter).

One defense the author has heard from device manufacturers, when asked why they are not reporting vulnerabilities for their devices, is to point out that devices do not have vulnerabilities; rather, the software and firmware products installed in the device have vulnerabilities. Without the software and firmware, the device is simply an empty box made of sheet metal or plastic. It is up to the developers of the software and firmware products installed in the device to report vulnerabilities in their products; it isn't the device maker's responsibility.

There are three problems with this argument. First, to learn about vulnerabilities this way, users of the device would need to know all the software and firmware products currently installed in the device; that is, they would always

---

[53] Reported in this blog post: https://tomalrichblog.blogspot.com/2024/01/how-will-fcc-construct-their-iot-device.html

need an up to date SBOM for the device. Yet, it is doubtful that many device manufacturers are providing a new SBOM to their customers whenever the software in the device is updated (one exception to this statement is probably Cisco™).

Second, even if users always had an up to date SBOM, tracking each software or firmware component in the device would be a huge job. Some devices have hundreds or even thousands of software and firmware components installed in them. For the device customer to track vulnerabilities in all those components, the supplier of each component would need to report vulnerabilities regularly to CVE.org. To say the least, that is not likely to be the case now.

Third, why should every user of the device be responsible for tracking all vulnerabilities in the device, when the manufacturer should be (and hopefully is) doing that as well? After all, the manufacturer will never know about vulnerabilities in their device unless they track vulnerabilities for every software and firmware product installed in the device. If there are 10,000 customers of a device, does it make sense that each of those customers would need to be constantly checking for vulnerabilities in every component, when the manufacturer could simply share the results of the analysis they are already doing?

Clearly, it makes no sense for device manufacturers to require their customers to bear the burden of learning about vulnerabilities for all the software components in the device. The manufacturer needs to monitor those vulnerabilities themselves (which they should be doing anyway, of course) and report each of them to CVE.org, using the CPE name *of the device*[54] (Cisco does this today for their networking devices). That way, assuming a device has 100 software or firmware components installed in it, their customers will be able to learn about vulnerabilities found in all those components with a single lookup in the NVD, not 100 lookups for individual components.

Patching vulnerabilities in devices

Like software suppliers, an intelligent device manufacturer should never report a vulnerability to CVE.org – or even to their own customers - unless they have already made a patch for the vulnerability available to their customers. Is it possible this is the reason why device manufacturers are for the most part never reporting vulnerabilities in their devices – that they never develop patches for vulnerabilities?

---

[54] More specifically, the supplier needs to report all current vulnerabilities in any of the software components in the device to the CPE name for the current *version* of the device. Because device manufacturers usually update the software in their devices (including application of security patches) in a single periodic update package, each update should be treated just like a new version of a software product. That is, each update should have its own version number, SBOM and VEX documents, and CPE name.

It is not true that device makers are not patching vulnerabilities! A device maker's regular updates to their devices include both functionality updates and security patches. Then, why wouldn't the device maker also report each vulnerability after it has been patched? The friend who works for a large medical device maker told the author in 2023 that the reason why his employer does not report vulnerabilities is they would never report them before they are patched – but once they have been patched, they are no longer vulnerabilities.

This might make sense, until one considers that software suppliers are often doing a good job of reporting vulnerabilities after they have issued a patch for them, yet the fact that a patched vulnerability is no longer a vulnerability[55] is just as true for a software product as it is for an intelligent device. Why are software suppliers reporting vulnerabilities, while device makers are mostly not reporting them?

The author believes this anomaly is due to how patching happens in software vs. in a device. Usually, when a software supplier develops a security patch for one of their products, they notify their customers about it right away, at the same time as they notify them of the vulnerability (they will presumably also notify CVE.org of the vulnerability and provide the information about the patch or other mitigation).

The software customer then needs to make the decision to apply the patch. Sometimes, they may not apply it right away, due to some concern about impacting performance (for example, operators of power plants often hold all patches until they are able to schedule an outage for the plant. They are concerned that an unexpected "side effect" of applying the patch might cause a serious problem if the plant were running when it is applied). But, since the software customer does have the option not to apply the patch, it is even more important for the supplier to provide them the information on the vulnerability, so they can decide whether the vulnerability poses enough of a risk that the need to apply it outweighs other concerns (this was probably the case with log4j).

However, device makers often give their customers little or no choice as to whether or not to apply a patch: since the patch comes as part of an update that fixes other vulnerabilities and at the same time increases the functionality of the device, the customer will often not want to block the update from being applied; in fact, for many household devices like baby monitors and smart thermostats, the manufacturer remotely installs the update without even notifying the user that this is happening.

---

[55] Unfortunately, this is not always the case. Many patches prepared by device and software suppliers turn out not to patch the vulnerability they were intended to address, at least not completely.

So, an important difference between a patch for a software product and a patch for an intelligent device is that application of the patch is almost completely under the customer's control in the case of a software product. However, that is much less likely to be true in the case of an intelligent device. For the moment, let's assume the device customer has no control at all over whether the patch is applied – that all devices are like baby monitors, where each update is installed without any pre-notification of the customer.

If we make this assumption, then it might make sense for the device maker never to report a vulnerability to CVE.org, or even to their customers. After all, since the update has just been applied to all customer devices without exception, the vulnerability has ceased to exist anywhere in their customer base. There is therefore no reason to report the vulnerability now.

But there are two problems with this argument. The first is that, since device makers often give customers the option not to apply an update immediately – and this is especially true with more critical devices like medical or industrial devices – many of them will not apply it right away; moreover, they may decide to hold off indefinitely. Plus, if the update was pushed out but the customer's device was offline at the time, it also will not have been applied.

If the device maker does not notify both their customers and CVE.org of the vulnerability once the update has been applied, all the devices that didn't receive the update will be vulnerable without knowing it. If a customer has postponed applying the update, that does not mean they should not know about a serious vulnerability that is patched in the update. This is because they might want to take some alternate measure to mitigate the vulnerability in the device – e.g., removing the device from the network altogether – during the time between when the update (including the patch for the vulnerability) became available and when they felt they could finally apply the update.

If the vulnerability isn't announced when the update is released, a customer that does not immediately apply it may be exposed to a serious vulnerability they don't know about. Just as bad, new customers may buy the device without knowing about the vulnerability, because an NVD search on the device will not find it (and as stated earlier, it is likely that the search will not find any vulnerabilities at all, assuming the manufacturer does not report vulnerabilities for the device).

This situation is made more poignant by another fact that the author learned in his discussion with the large medical device manufacturer in 2023: that manufacturer only performs a full device update once a year[56]. This means that in some cases, a serious vulnerability might go unpatched in customer devices for hundreds of days, without the customers even being informed that the vulnerability is present in the device. Again, if customers knew of the

---

[56] Given this manufacturer's leading position in their market, it is possible that other medical device manufacturers follow the same policy and only update the software in their devices annually. In fact, the author has heard that medical device makers update the software in their devices between every six months and every few years.

vulnerability, they might apply alternative mitigation like removing the device from their network.

Contrast this with what usually happens when a large software supplier learns of a serious vulnerability in one of their products. In most cases, the supplier will not immediately inform their customers of the vulnerability. However, they will usually start to work on a fix for the vulnerability as soon as they learn of it. When the fix is available, they will post it for customers to download (or in some cases, the supplier will advise customers to upgrade to a patched version of the software); at the same time, they will report the vulnerability in their software to both their customers and to CVE.org.

Why do device manufacturers and software developers approach vulnerabilities in their products so differently? The author suspects that there are two reasons for this:

Software users expect their suppliers to fix vulnerabilities soon after they are discovered, and will not long tolerate a supplier that doesn't do that; and

The vulnerability management practices of intelligent device suppliers are much less visible than those of software developers, for the very reason described earlier: it is hard for a customer even to learn about vulnerabilities in devices they use, since many device manufacturers never report a single vulnerability to CVE.org.

The author's opinion is that device manufacturers should move to a model like that of the software developers. Here are some suggested best practices:

If a manufacturer does not do a full device update at least every quarter, they should schedule regular "security updates" at least once a quarter, in which all outstanding security patches are applied. They then need to decide with their customers on criteria for when a patch needs to be made available immediately vs. waiting for the next security update.[57]

Upon learning of a serious vulnerability in one of their devices, they should immediately develop a patch. As soon as the patch is ready, they should make it available to their customers, along with reporting the vulnerability to their customers and to CVE.org.

If a new vulnerability does not meet the criteria for making the patch available immediately, the manufacturer should not report the vulnerability to CVE.org or to the customers of the affected device. Instead, they should schedule the patch for the next quarterly security update. With the update, they should notify both

---

[57] The criteria might include some combination of the CVSS (https://nvd.nist.gov/vuln-metrics/cvss) and EPSS (https://www.first.org/epss/model) scores, as well as whether or not the vulnerability appears in CISA's Key Exploitable Vulnerabilities, or KEV (https://www.cisa.gov/known-exploited-vulnerabilities-catalog) catalog.

the customers of the product and CVE.org of the vulnerability. They should do this for every vulnerability that was patched in the update.

What have we learned?

There are three main problems we have discussed regarding vulnerability management practices of intelligent device manufacturers:

1. Device manufacturers are in many or most cases not reporting vulnerabilities in their products to CVE.org. While many software suppliers are also not reporting vulnerabilities, this appears to be a much bigger problem for device manufacturers.

2. Except in the case of very serious vulnerabilities like log4shell, most device manufacturers do not immediately release a patch for a new vulnerability in one of their devices. Instead, they include the patch in the next full update, which might be up to one year later.

3. With the full update, they likely will include notification of the vulnerability in the patch notes. However, they seldom if ever also report the vulnerability to CVE.org.

The author recommends these practices to address these problems:

1. Device manufacturers should put in place procedures to report future vulnerabilities to CVE.org (including making sure they understand how the process works, contacting a CNA who can help them when they need to report a vulnerability, etc.).

2. Device manufacturers that do not provide at least quarterly full updates to their products should schedule at least quarterly security updates, during which all outstanding security patches are applied to the device.

3. Each manufacturer needs to consult with its customers to determine appropriate criteria[58] for deciding whether a newly discovered vulnerability in a device should be considered urgent and patched immediately, or whether the patch can wait for the next security update.

4. When a patch for a vulnerability is made available to customers, either on an urgent basis or as part of a scheduled quarterly security

---

[58] Perhaps including some combination of the vulnerability's CVSS and EPSS scores, and whether it is on CISA's Key Exploitable Vulnerabilities (KEV) list.

update, the manufacturer should report the vulnerability both to the customers (as part of the patch report) and to CVE.org.

Update

Shortly before publishing this book, the author had a long conversation with two product security staff members from a major medical device maker, as well as a security leader for a major hospital organization. He learned that this device maker is exploring adding a quarterly "security update". This means that all patches will be applied within three months at the latest, rather than one year – as is the case now, since this manufacturer only develops a full update for their devices once a year.

He also learned that the main reason why device manufacturers have been so slow to regularly apply security patches packages is that the devices were never engineered in a way that would permit that; enabling regular patching will require a fundamental re-engineering of each device. However, the manufacturers also understand that the situation described above is untenable; they are committed to changing it. This alone was encouraging news.

6. Advanced: How can SBOMs be used to reduce software risk?

There are many documents that discuss production and distribution of SBOMs (mostly from the developer point of view), but there are few that discuss how SBOMs can be utilized by an end user organization to reduce software cybersecurity risk. This Chapter discusses the four most important cybersecurity use cases[59] for SBOMs.

The role of SBOMs in vulnerability risk management

A vulnerability is a flaw in a software product's code that provides an avenue for an attacker to perform unauthorized actions. These can include a) gaining control of a software product or even an entire device, b) stealing important stored information such as credit card numbers, c) manipulating data including financial data, or d) causing a change in physical processes that may result in damage to machinery, to a process like the flow of electric power, or even to human beings.

It is important to understand that vulnerabilities are seldom inserted in software code by a malicious developer or by a malicious party that has penetrated the development process, although the consequences can be catastrophic when this occurs; undoubtedly the most devastating software supply chain attack was the huge and very well designed 2019-2020 compromise of the SolarWinds Orion™ platform by Russian government-backed operatives (Microsoft estimated that about 1,000 people were involved in executing those attacks)[60].

---

[59] As opposed to open source license management use cases.

[60] This campaign allowed the attackers to insert the Sunburst malware in seven updates of the SolarWinds Orion platform, using methods that were (at the time) undetectable by SolarWinds. This 15-month campaign, discovered in December

Instead, almost all vulnerabilities appear in one of three ways:

A software developer, or the organization they work for, did not follow current best development practices or decided to take a shortcut. Thus, they inadvertently created code that was known at the time to contain a vulnerability, although probably this was not known by the developer.

Even if the developer(s) followed best development practices, often years later a researcher might discover that what had previously been thought to be vulnerability-free code in fact contains a vulnerability that can be utilized by a hacker to compromise a software product by following a particular set of actions (this set of actions is known as an "exploit"). Any software product that contains this code may be susceptible to that exploit; therefore, it contains the vulnerability. It makes no difference if the vulnerable code was created one minute or ten years ago; it is still susceptible to the exploit.

A previously unknown vulnerability was discovered by a hacker or a nation-state, who used it to attack one or more organizations (a so-called "zero day" attack). Of course, this is the worst way for a new vulnerability to be "discovered".

In the first case, it is possible that the vulnerability could have been discovered in the product before the software was delivered to customers, since it might have been detected with a vulnerability scanning tool. However, in the second and third cases, the vulnerability could never have been found in the product until the vulnerability itself was discovered and became publicly known, and a "signature" for the vulnerability was incorporated into scanning tools.

In other words, any software used by an organization can "develop" new vulnerabilities, even though it may previously have been thought to be vulnerability-free. Even if the software was vulnerability-free at time of procurement, most software will develop vulnerabilities over time, as the vulnerabilities are discovered by researchers or hackers. If a developer follows the best development practices, their software will be less likely to develop vulnerabilities later, but it may do so all the same. It is likely that every software product will develop one or more vulnerabilities over its useful life; the more lines of code in the product, the more likely it is to develop vulnerabilities[61].

Because all software can develop vulnerabilities at any time, any organization that uses software (which is nowadays almost any organization, public or private, on the planet - even if the software just runs on a smartphone) needs to implement

---

2020, was probably, along with the Stuxnet attack on an Iranian uranium enrichment facility (discovered in 2010), the most elaborate cybersecurity attack ever. A good description of the SolarWinds attack can be found here: https://www.crowdstrike.com/blog/sunspot-malware-technical-analysis/.

[61] The author thanks Jean-Baptiste Maillet for this insight.

a software vulnerability management program appropriate for the software they are running and their degree of sophistication. The simplest program might be, "Hire someone we trust and make sure they apply every patch we receive from our software suppliers." However, most organizations will need a more sophisticated program.

Any organization that has access to up to date SBOMs for software products they utilize can take advantage of broader vulnerability management capabilities than can an organization that does not have SBOM access. We will discuss both cases.

First, in the absence of access to up to date SBOMs, a vulnerability management program can be summarized as:

1. For every software product/version or intelligent device version utilized by the organization, monitor a vulnerability database for newly identified vulnerabilities in the product/version.[62] When a user enters the name and version number of one of those products in the vulnerability database, they may see a listing of vulnerabilities that are found in the software.[63]

2. Whenever a serious vulnerability appears, contact the supplier to find out when they will patch the vulnerability, unless the supplier has already provided a patch for it. If needed, keep up the pressure until the supplier has patched the vulnerability.[64]

3. Apply the patch as soon as it is received.[65]

4. Continually repeat steps 1-3.

---

[62] Jean-Baptiste Maillet points out that the best way to find product/versions for which a new vulnerability has been listed is to monitor creation of CPEs. This is because, as will be explained later, when a new vulnerability is identified in a product/version, NIST employees will create a CPE name(s) for the product(s) in which the vulnerability was reported. Only if a vulnerability has already been identified in the same product/version will no new CPE name be required.

[63] Often, it is not easy to look up a particular software product or intelligent device in a vulnerability database, due to the lack of an identifier for the software that is supported by the vulnerability database. The only two identifiers that are supported in vulnerability databases today are purl and CPE. See the later chapter titled "The naming problem".

[64] Some large suppliers put out monthly "patch releases" for their software products, that include patches for vulnerabilities identified in the last month.

[65] Unfortunately, this advice is much easier said than done, since most organizations today have a backlog of patches to apply. This means the organization needs to have a scheme for prioritizing patch applications. Often, this is based on a score for the vulnerability, such as CVSS or EPSS, or on whether the vulnerability appears in CISA's Key Exploitable Vulnerabilities (KEV) catalog.

SBOMs add a new tool to the organization's vulnerability management toolbox. Because the greater part of the code in almost any modern software product is components written by third parties, it is more likely that new vulnerabilities will be due to a third-party component than to the code written by the supplier itself (the code written by the supplier is sometimes referred to as "first-party code").

As mentioned earlier, in 2017 a study[66] by Veracode found that only 52% of software suppliers patch third-party component vulnerabilities. While that percentage has almost certainly risen since 2017, the fact is that suppliers are more likely to monitor their own code for vulnerabilities than they are to monitor component code written by third parties; this is especially true for components incorporated in the product as compiled binaries, not source code. If the supplier does not distribute SBOMs to their customers, the customers will have no easy way to learn what components are in their products, and using that information, learn what vulnerabilities apply to those components.

When a user organization (or a third-party acting on their behalf) has up to date SBOMs for some or all of the software products they utilize, the above sequence of vulnerability management steps becomes the following[67] sequence (the first three steps are repeated from the above list, since they do not change. The steps listed in italics are made possible by having SBOMs, although they are subject to some qualifications and caveats. These will be described in the remaining chapters of this book):

1. For every software product/version or intelligent device version utilized by the organization, monitor a vulnerability database for new vulnerabilities.

2. Whenever a serious vulnerability appears for the product/version, contact the supplier to ask when they will patch it; keep up the pressure until that happens.

3. Apply the patch as soon as it is received.

---

[66] https://www.veracode.com/sites/default/files/pdf/resources/ipapers/soss-2017/index.html

[67] The italicized steps will almost always need to be performed by an automated tool, since the number of components in a software product can run into the hundreds, thousands, or even tens of thousands. As of the beginning of 2024, there are no easy to use, low cost and commercially supported tools available for this purpose. Moreover, given the need to address issues like the naming problem and confusion over what VEX is, the author believes these steps will be performed by third-party service providers, at least for the next few years. See Part 3 of this book for further discussion of how SBOMs will move forward.

4. *When the organization receives a recent SBOM from a supplier of a product they utilize, extract the list of components from the SBOM and look them up in a vulnerability database like the NVD.*

5. *Identify vulnerabilities that apply to the components. For each product and version utilized by the organization and for which the organization has an SBOM, create a component vulnerability list that includes all vulnerabilities applicable to any component listed in the SBOM. For example, if the product has 150 components and the vulnerability database lists a total of ten open vulnerabilities for those 150 components, the component vulnerability list will consist of those ten vulnerabilities (usually indicated with a "CVE" number). Note that the vulnerabilities on the list do not need to be connected to the components in which they were identified; that information is not usually needed after they have been identified, although it certainly can be retained if desired.*

6. *At least daily, utilize the Transparency Exchange API[68] to retrieve from a server maintained by the supplier (or by a third-party service provider acting on behalf of multiple suppliers) a VEX document containing the complete list of component vulnerabilities for a product/version utilized by the organization, along with an up to date exploitability status designation for each component vulnerability (Note: Unfamiliar terms in this Section will be explained in the second part of this book, "Introduction to VEX").*

7. *At any time, the user will be able to obtain from the tool an up to date, formatted list of exploitable component vulnerabilities in a product/version used by the organization. This can be utilized to confirm that the vulnerabilities are present in the product/version, as well as to coordinate with the supplier regarding when any exploitable vulnerabilities will be patched. This list will ideally be*

---

[68] https://github.com/CycloneDX/cyclonedx-transparency-exchange-api This API is currently under development by the CycloneDX project. It will allow component vulnerability management tools to retrieve up to date SBOMs and VEX documents from a central server. This API will support both major SBOM formats and both major VEX formats. See the Section titled "The Transparency Exchange API" in Chapter 4.

provided in the format required by the vulnerability or asset management tool(s) utilized by the organization.

8. This formatted list should include the name and version string of a product in use by the organization, the CVE number (or other identifier) of each vulnerability in the product version, and the exploitability status of each vulnerability in the product version (i.e., "affected", "not affected", "under investigation" or "fixed"). This should allow the vulnerability management team to find the product, verify the presence of the vulnerability (or determine it is in fact not present), and apply a patch if available.

9. Contact the product supplier to find out when they will patch all the exploitable vulnerabilities on the list[69]; keep up the pressure until the supplier has either patched or otherwise mitigated all exploitable component vulnerabilities, that match criteria for being "patch worthy". These criteria should be announced in advance by the supplier.

10. Apply each patch as soon as possible after it is received, or according to the organization's overall patch prioritization program.

11. Repeat steps 1-10 continually, while the product/version is still under support.

The result of the above steps will ideally be that, for every product/version for which the user organization regularly receives and processes SBOMs, the organization will always know what the exploitable component vulnerabilities are. Moreover, they will always have verified the presence of each vulnerability in the product in question, as well as confirmed a date by which the supplier will provide a patch. This applies both to vulnerabilities in code written by the supplier itself and to vulnerabilities that are due to a third-party component.

Note that providing a list of exploitable vulnerabilities that can be ingested by a vulnerability management tool does not imply that the tool itself "understands"

---

[69] A software supplier should not feel obligated to patch every vulnerability that is found in one of their products; there are many cases in which a component can truly be considered so inconsequential that it does not need to be patched. However, the supplier should establish definite criteria for when they will not patch a vulnerability, and make sure their customers understand those criteria from the start of their relationship with the supplier.

SBOMs, or even that it understands the general idea of product components. As of this writing, no major supplier of tools for vulnerability, asset or configuration management has announced direct support for SBOMs.

Fortunately, if the end user can obtain lists of exploitable component vulnerabilities for the software products they operate from their component vulnerability management tool (like the tool described earlier and in Part 3 of this book), it is not necessary that the vulnerability management tool itself understand SBOMs. All vulnerability and asset management tools understand product names and vulnerability identifiers, which the above process can provide.

Identifying other risks to software arising from components

There are many other areas of risk to software arising from components used in the software, that are not "vulnerabilities" in the same sense as CVEs. Analysis of SBOMs can help identify these risks. Unlike true vulnerabilities, these risks cannot be remediated through application of a patch. In most cases, mitigating the risk requires changes to one or more practices of either the software supplier or the end user organization.

Some of these risks are listed below. Note there is usually not a clear line that allows an organization to determine whether these constitute serious risks. The exact parameters of most of these risks will need to be determined by the user organization (hopefully aided by discussions with their software suppliers), as they design their software vulnerability management program. Whatever parameters the organization identifies will need to be flexible, since most of these problems cannot be parameterized. Listed below are *types* of risk that need to be considered by the organization, not the specific risks themselves or their mitigations. Note that none of these risks lend themselves to an automated solution.

1. "End of life" components. In the software world, a product, or a particular version of a product, is considered to be in end of life (EOL) status if its supplier has announced it will no longer support the product/version after a certain future date.[70] "Support" refers to assistance from the supplier's help desk for problems with using the software, but it also refers to patching. If a supplier supports their product, this usually means they are committed to providing patches when

---

[70] Usually, a product itself will not be in end of life status, but one or more versions of the product may be. This is a normal occurrence. Suppliers usually do not want to support out-of-date versions of their products forever, and thus set end of life dates for the versions they will no longer support. As long as the supplier provides sufficient notice to their users when a particular version of their product will become EOL, their customers will be able to take the steps necessary either to upgrade the product to a supported version or to remove it from their network(s).

vulnerabilities are identified in the product; this commitment ends when the product is no longer supported.

Of course, software components are "products" in their own right, and they can also be declared EOL by their suppliers. If the supplier of a software product learns that one of the components in their product will soon be in EOL status, they should remove the component altogether or upgrade it to a supported version. Leaving an out-of-support component in a software product (without upgrading it) long term means that, if a serious vulnerability is discovered in the component, it will possibly never be patched.

End users should ask their suppliers for their policy with respect to EOL components. Normally, the discussion will be about when the supplier will notify customers of product components for which an EOL date has been announced (since the supplier is the "customer" of the component's supplier, they will presumably receive any EOL notices, which are not always made public).

The author's opinion is that the supplier should notify their customers as soon as they learn that a component is going EOL. What actions the supplier takes after that may need to be discussed with their customers on a case-by-case basis. Sometimes, replacing an out-of-date component may be more disruptive to the product than not removing it from the product, although the supplier still needs to commit to "backport"[71] patches for serious future vulnerabilities like log4shell[72].

Information on end of life components is not easy to find, since it might or might not be posted on the component supplier's website, and in any case, it is currently not posted in any standard machine-readable format. Obtaining this information may require contacting the component supplier (which may be an open source community) directly. It is the author's opinion that doing this should be the responsibility of the product supplier, since they introduced that component into their product; the product supplier needs to take responsibility for mitigating

---

[71] A "backported" patch is a patch for a dangerous vulnerability, that a supplier applies to an otherwise unsupported version of one of their software products. The supplier does this in a case in which the opprobrium they would incur by not providing the patch outweighs their natural inclination to use the vulnerability as an incentive to get users of the unsupported version to upgrade. A good example of this was the WannaCry (https://en.wikipedia.org/wiki/WannaCry_ransomware_attack#:~:text=WannaCry% 20is%20a%20ransomware%20cryptoworm,WanaCrypt0r%202.0%2C%20and%20 Wanna%20Decryptor) ransomware attack, in which Microsoft provided backported patches for users of Windows XP and Windows Server 2003, both of which were in EOL status.

[72] This blog post discusses this issue further: https://tomalrichblog.blogspot.com/2023/04/its-time-to-retire-candy-bar.html

risks associated with the component, even when the component is in end of life status.

2. EOL open source components. When it comes to open source components, "end of life" usually means something different than it means in the case of proprietary software products. In the latter case, there is an identifiable supplier (usually a company, but sometimes an individual) that commits contractually to certain terms and duration of support. However, open source products are maintained by an online community of developers, who are not usually paid directly for their efforts (although their employer may include supporting open source projects in their job description). This means there is not usually an identifiable "supplier" for open source components. A request for support usually needs to be emailed to the community. There is no guarantee when, or even if, the sender will receive a response.

With open source components, usually no person or organization makes any legally binding commitment to patch future vulnerabilities[73]. However, if the community that supports the component is large and active, it is often safe to assume that both updates and patches for the component will be made available in the future. Therefore, unless that community has issued a statement that a particular version of their component is in EOL status, the product supplier can probably assume that patches for the component will continue for the time being.

However, there are many open source communities that are not large. If the community diminishes to a small number of maintainers, it is possible it will "peter out" without notice. This means that at some point, nobody will be left to support the product.

Of course, this leads to the same risk already discussed for proprietary software components that become EOL: security patches will no longer be available for the component.[74]

This means that the supplier of a product that contains open source components (and about 90% of software components are open source) needs to conduct some surveillance of the online communities that maintain those components, to determine whether they are still active. They can look for such red flags as:

Whether there have been any "commits" to the project within, for example, the past six months. Any change at all to the software requires a commit, so the

---

[73] There are some for-profit companies that take it upon themselves to support and patch open source products. The most prominent example of these is Red Hat™. Because they provide a binding support and patching commitment (as well as indicate when a product is going into EOL status), the author considers these companies to be the equivalent of suppliers of proprietary software, at least for purposes of what EOL means for them.

[74] Jean-Baptiste Maillet points out that, if anything, commercial suppliers are more likely to discontinue support for a product without notice than are open source communities. In fact, he has seen that happen only once for an open source product.

lack of commits may indicate that none of the previous maintainers are touching the software anymore.[75]

Whether any patches or updates to the software have been released in the past six months to one year.

Whether the online notes among the project maintainers have stopped, or whether they indicate that most of the maintainers are no longer involved with the project.

If the product supplier discovers that an open source component raises one of the above red flags (or similar red flags), they should treat the component as if it were an EOL proprietary component: that is, they should replace or upgrade it within, for example, three months. Of course, the supplier of the product should conduct this surveillance; the responsibility for doing so should not be left to the customers of the product that contains the component.

3. "Single maintainers". Sometimes, the online community supporting an open source product will have dwindled to a single individual; at other times, the "community" will always have consisted of one individual. While this individual may well be the most brilliant software developer in the world, the fact that there is just one individual poses the risk that they will be hit by the proverbial bus; thus, nobody will be left who understands the code for the product and can develop patches and upgrades.

Of course, in some cases another individual might be recruited to take the first person's place, in the event they can no longer participate in the project. However, it would never be a good idea to plan on this happening. Whenever the supplier of a software product learns that one of the open source components of the product is maintained by a single individual (even if this has always been the case), they should treat the component as if it were EOL and make plans to replace it within a certain amount of time.

4. Components with longtime vulnerabilities. As was stated earlier, all software products develop vulnerabilities over time; this means it is unrealistic to expect any software to be "free from vulnerabilities". However, it is realistic to expect that suppliers will patch any serious component vulnerabilities within a certain period, perhaps three months or less. If that does not seem to be happening, the user should have a conversation with the supplier (for a proprietary product) or the open source community that supports the product.

5. "Long in the tooth" components. Even if it does not contain any serious vulnerabilities, a component should never remain in a software product for many

---

[75] Jean-Baptiste Maillet also points out that the one exception to this rule is for cryptographic components, since cryptographic algorithms do not change often, if ever.

years, except in certain circumstances.[76] Since knowledge of secure coding practices has improved markedly in recent years, the older a component is, the more likely it is to have been developed when there was much less understanding of secure coding.

6. Outdated components. Often, a component in a product, which is discovered in an SBOM for the product, is many versions behind the current version of the same component. While it is impossible to specify a hard and fast rule for when and how a component should be upgraded to a newer version, a supplier with a seriously out-of-date component in their product should at least explain to customers why it is there and promise to patch any serious vulnerabilities that may develop in the component later, if they do not upgrade or replace it.

It is important to note that, while there are often good reasons for not replacing a component whenever a new version comes out (since sometimes the new version turns out to have problems that were not present in the earlier version), if a component in a product is multiple major versions behind the current version, this probably means there are vulnerabilities that are patched in the current version, that are not patched in the version of the component that is now in the product. The supplier should promise to update product components with some frequency, perhaps at least every 1-2 years, or at least provide a reason why they are unable to do so.

7. Excessive number of unpatched component vulnerabilities. As already discussed, all software develops vulnerabilities over time, even if it may have been close to "vulnerability-free" when it was delivered. If a component contains unpatched vulnerabilities, this does not in itself constitute a risk. This is especially true if the vulnerabilities are of low severity.

However, it *is* a risk if there are an excessive number of unpatched vulnerabilities in a particular component and they have been there more than perhaps one year. For example, if one component in the product has 20 unpatched vulnerabilities but none of the other components has more than one or two, the product supplier needs to explain why they have left this component in the product, as well as what plans they have either to replace it or to patch the unpatched vulnerabilities.

It is important to note that there are, as of early 2024, no readily available databases that include data needed to measure any of the above seven categories of risk. For example, while there are a number of open source projects that maintain lists of end of life products, they are all very limited in their coverage. This does not mean that someone trying to find out, for example, how far behind the current version a component listed in an SBOM is, will not be able to obtain an answer; but it does mean they may need to devote some time to doing so.

---

[76] One reason why some software products may contain a large number of out-of-date components is the "tight coupling" problem described in this blog post: https://tomalrichblog.blogspot.com/2023/04/its-time-to-retire-candy-bar.html

There are some risks that are unique to open source components, including:

1. Suspicious activity in an open source project. Attackers know that 90% of software components are open source.[77] Because of this, the attackers are becoming more creative all the time. In one type of attack used recently, a malicious organization monitored open source projects for long term inactivity, then swooped in to commit malicious code to the project. The malicious code contained a backdoor that the attackers could "open" after the project had been incorporated as a component of other software.

Software suppliers can protect from this kind of attack by not using any open source component for which a long period of inactivity has ended with a new commit from an individual that previously had no involvement with the project.

2. "Poisoned" open source package repositories. Because open source software code repositories are – as the name applies – open to everybody, they are subject to attacks that proprietary software repositories are not subject to. Two recent examples of this are:

Python library attacks, in which "attackers uploaded 12 malicious libraries using typo-squatting techniques by creating libraries titled "diango," "djago," "dajngo," and others to trick developers who searched for the popular "django" Python library. Unsuspecting developers downloaded these libraries and integrated them into applications under development, which then compromised users.

RubyGems.org attack, in which "an attacker uploaded 11 libraries which contained a backdoor that allowed attackers to use pre-chosen credentials to remotely execute commands of their choice on infected servers."[78]

Attacks like these do not directly affect most software using organizations, since only software developers are likely to download open source libraries. However, the RubyGems attack resulted in backdoored software components being included in software products provided to end users, and the Python library attacks could easily have done the same. This would leave users of the poisoned software in the same situation as the SolarWinds customers who loaded the poisoned Orion updates on their networks: offering a wide-open door to attackers, without having any idea they were doing that.

Of course, it is probably impossible to prevent attacks like these altogether, since there are so many ways they might happen. One important measure a supplier can deploy, to lower the likelihood that an employee will download a poisoned component and include it in a software product, is to train their

---

[77] Source: https://www.sonatype.com/resources/white-paper-state-of-the-software-supply-chain-2020

[78] *Ibid*

employees on how to recognize these attacks, including by scrutinizing the name of the file being downloaded and the URL from which it is being downloaded.

Another important measure is to compare a hash value of any component they have just downloaded with the hash of the component in its authoritative repository. This would not have short-circuited the Ruby Gems attacks, since the main repositories themselves were compromised. But typo-squatting attacks like those on the Python libraries might have been discovered, since in those cases the library used was not the authoritative one.

3. Vulnerabilities in open source components. A consideration that is especially applicable in high-assurance use cases has to do with open source components: The vulnerabilities found in vulnerability databases such as the NVD are based on analysis of the source code of open source components, as found in source repositories such as GitHub.

However, in some cases a supplier downloads components as binary objects from a package manager, not as source from the repository. The package manager adds to the component other binary objects that are not part of the component itself, but which are required to run the component; these are known as "runtime dependencies".

The result of these two facts is that the vulnerabilities listed for some open source components in the NVD do not include any vulnerabilities found in runtime dependencies. This means that an end user, just by looking up a software component in a vulnerability database, may not learn of all vulnerabilities that affect the component as it is implemented in the software product they are using.

One possible solution to this problem is for the supplier to "enhance" their SBOM (which will usually be produced as part of the "final build" of the software, before the runtime dependencies are added by the package manager) by including the runtime dependencies in the SBOM – meaning the user will be able to learn about all sources of vulnerabilities in the software they use. One very large software and services company has indicated they plan to take this approach.

Identifying risks from vulnerabilities in procured software

Whenever an organization is procuring software, they should request SBOMs from all suppliers being considered. This is true, whether the organization is comparing multiple suppliers of a certain type of product and wishes to use data provided in an SBOM to learn about the security of the competing products, or the organization has already chosen a particular product and is just trying to determine what risks they may face after they have procured it and put it into use.

Just as an organization needs to learn about vulnerabilities identified in components of software that is currently in use, it needs to learn about vulnerabilities found in components of software that is being procured or considered for procurement. The organization should request an SBOM[79] from the supplier or suppliers whose product(s) are being considered for the procurement and make it clear that the failure to provide an SBOM is likely to weigh against the supplier in the procurement.

What can the organization learn about software risks from a single SBOM? They can learn about two types of risk: those due to the product and those due to the supplier of the product.

Product risks

It might seem strange to speak about risks due to a software product, since the supplier presumably created the product in the first place. Aren't even product risks also due to the supplier? They usually are, but product risks are essentially "built in" to the product. That is, it was the supplier's actions or lack of action in the past that created the product risk. However, it is no longer possible to change these at the time of procurement. The organization needs to learn about risks included in the product they will buy; an SBOM is one of the most important tools for learning about those risks.

All the risks listed in Chapter 6, in the Section titled "Identifying other risks to software arising from components" are examples of product risks. These risks might be evaluated by analyzing a single SBOM from a product supplier as part of a procurement.

Supplier risks

There are also risks that are directly due to the supplier of the software product. These have to do with actions the supplier will perform - or will not perform - throughout the time that the customer organization utilizes the product. Because a number of these risks have to do with how the supplier handles components and the vulnerabilities introduced by those components, an SBOM is an essential tool for learning about supplier risks as well.

---

[79] It would be better to request all SBOMs, going back a year or whatever the supplier will provide. However, given the current situation in which the buyer will be lucky to receive any SBOM at all, a supplier should not be penalized if they cannot (or will not) provide any SBOM beyond a current one (of course, the SBOM provided should match the software version that the buyer is considering for procurement; that should be a firm requirement).

As an example of an evaluation of supplier risks, consider the following results from an analysis[80] of a single SBOM for a single software product (which happens to be a well-known cybersecurity tool):

- 141 vulnerable components were found in the product, out of 699 total components.
- 77 unique vulnerabilities were found in the product, which of course is a lot (this means, on average, each vulnerability was identified in about two different components).
- What's worse is the fact that the average elapsed time since the initial disclosure of the vulnerabilities was *2,978 days*, which is more than 8 years.[81]
- Vulnerabilities were grouped by severity, based on their CVSS score category: low, medium, high or critical. The analysis found:
- There were 5 low-severity vulnerabilities. Their average age was 2,801 days or 7.67 years.
- There were 61 medium-severity vulnerabilities, whose average age was 2,987 days or 8.18 years.
- There were 9 high-severity vulnerabilities, whose average age was 3,058 days or 8.37 years.
- There were 2 critical vulnerabilities, whose average age was 3,447 days or 9.44 years.

It is interesting that the most serious vulnerabilities were the oldest, with the average serious vulnerability having been identified 9 ½ years ago. The person who performed this analysis had no explanation for that fact.

Here are some informal conclusions from this data (drawn by the author, not the service provider that analyzed the SBOM):

---

[80] The analysis was conducted by Fortress Information Security. These results are condensed from this blog post: https://tomalrichblog.blogspot.com/2022/08/9-years.html.

[81] The analysis did not address the question of exploitability of vulnerabilities. It is certain that at least some of these vulnerabilities are not actually exploitable in the product, meaning it might not be important to patch them initially. However, the author's opinion is that no component vulnerability should be left unpatched for more than say a year or maybe less, even if it is initially deemed not to be exploitable by the supplier. The reason for this is a future code alteration in the product might inadvertently change the vulnerability's status in the product from not exploitable to exploitable, if it is allowed to remain unpatched.

It is hard to understand how a supplier can allow 77 vulnerabilities of any severity, let alone of critical severity, to remain unpatched[82] after 7 ½ years (as is true for the 5 low-severity vulnerabilities), let alone for 9 ½ years (which is the case for the 2 critical vulnerabilities). If the organization doing a procurement is seriously considering purchasing a product from the supplier that compiled this record, they should have a discussion with them about the maximum time they will allow any vulnerable component to remain in a product, without either being patched or removed.

Of course, it is possible that some or all of the vulnerable components were obtained only recently, for example in the last year. In other words, a supplier might defend themselves by pointing out that a critical vulnerability was in the component for 8 ½ years before they introduced the component into their product a year ago. However, then the question becomes why the supplier even included such a component in their product in the first place, since they presumably should have known about the vulnerability before purchasing or downloading the component. More generally, a discussion of this problem should lead to a broader discussion of the supplier's supply chain risk management policies. Do they even check for vulnerabilities in components before they include them in their products? And if they do check for them, do they perform analyses of those vulnerabilities, such as those described earlier?

Just learning the above data from an SBOM should lead to the acquiring organization having a serious talk with the supplier before they finalize the procurement. They need to discuss the supplier's component acquisition policies, as well as their component vulnerability management policies. Moreover, the procurement contract might well include the requirement that the supplier patch certain component vulnerabilities, or even replace the vulnerable components altogether.

Are we affected?

As use of open source software components has steadily increased in the last decade, more and more serious vulnerabilities have been discovered in components that were in widespread use, but which also were – until the

---

[82] It is important to note that, if the supplier of the product had patched the product to mitigate a component vulnerability, it would not have been apparent in this analysis, since the component/version itself would still appear as vulnerable in a vulnerability database. Of course, if the supplier were issuing both SBOMs and VEX documents for their products, they would have been able to notify customers through a VEX that the vulnerability in the component had been patched (i.e., "fixed") in their product.

vulnerabilities were discovered – almost completely unknown to software users. These components include OpenSSL, Apache Struts, log4j and others.

Whenever one of these vulnerabilities has become known, the first question on the mind of IT managers in almost any organization is, "Is our organization affected?" Of course, just knowing the names of the software products installed on their networks does not help them answer this question; a component name is almost never included in the name of the product it is installed in.

To answer this question, an organization needs to have SBOMs for the software products they utilize, which include as much detail as possible. Just as importantly, each SBOM needs to be re-issued (not revised) with each new version of the product.[83] However, it will be many years before detailed SBOMs are available for most products, and before they are re-issued with every new version.

Does this mean that software users should give up hope of being able to find every instance of, for example, a vulnerable log4j version on their networks? As of this writing, the vulnerabilities in the log4j library have been well known for over two years, yet a significant number of vulnerable instances remain in place and may never be found.

Frankly, it will be decades, if ever, before the average software user (i.e., an organization whose main activity is not software development) will be able to state with certainty that they know of every instance of a vulnerable component that is in use anywhere in their networks.[84]

Does the "level" matter?

The author used to believe that it is important for the user to know at what "level" a vulnerable component is found in a product they use. In other words, he

---

[83] The NTIA "Minimum Elements" document states that a new SBOM should be issued whenever the code of the product has changed; this used to be the author's opinion as well. However, in the early stages of SBOM availability, it is unreasonable to expect suppliers to issue a new SBOM with every code change. Initially, if a supplier is willing and able to provide a new SBOM for every major and minor version of their product (or at least every major version), this should be a cause for rejoicing, not despair.

[84] The author cringes whenever he hears either SBOM novices or experienced practitioners talk about how SBOMs will allow users to find every instance of a vulnerable component in their environment. Currently, the only true statement that can be made is that users will learn about more instances of a vulnerable component if they receive and analyze SBOMs for as many products that they use as possible, than if they do not receive and/or analyze any SBOMs. Unfortunately, the idea that software users (not developers) will ever be able to push a button and learn about every instance of a component like log4j that is found anywhere in their network environment (or on their desktops) is fantasy. Promoting ideas like this does a disservice to the cause of SBOMs.

believed that a vulnerable component found on the first "level" – i.e. a direct dependency of the product – is more dangerous than the same vulnerable component found on, for example, the tenth "level".

However, multiple discussions with experts who are in a much better position to answer this question have assured the author that this opinion is wrong: a vulnerable component like log4j on the tenth "level" is just as dangerous as the same component on the first level.

An important implication of this fact is that the component "dependency graph" – i.e., the diagram that can be used to identify the "level" on which a component is found in the product – is not helpful in comparing relative risk posed by components on different "levels". An SBOM that lists all components in alphabetical order contains almost as much useful risk information as a detailed dependency graph.

Can SBOMs provide a "roadmap for the attacker"?

One of the most common objections to SBOMs is that they will provide a "roadmap for the attacker"; this objection is usually deployed by software developers who do not want to distribute SBOMs to their customers. The argument usually runs something like:

If an attacker can get their hands on an SBOM for a particular product/version, they will be able to look up the vulnerabilities for the components in the NVD or another vulnerability database.

Knowing those vulnerabilities, they will be able to exploit them to attack the product/version when they run across it on a network they are trying to penetrate.

However, this objection doesn't hold water, for four reasons:

It assumes that SBOMs will in some way be made publicly available. Of course, for open source software, that is likely to happen – there is no good way to avoid that. But the entities that are most likely to raise this objection are developers of proprietary software. The author frankly has not yet run across any developer of proprietary software that intends to distribute SBOMs to their customers without requiring them to sign a non-disclosure agreement (NDA). True, an NDA does not provide an ironclad guarantee that the SBOM will not be distributed outside of its intended audience, but requiring an NDA is certainly much better than making the SBOM publicly available.

The "bad guys", just like the "good guys", have access to open source and commercial binary analysis tools. These allow them to generate their own SBOM for a product if they have access to the binaries. So, they already have a "roadmap".

Given that the bad guys probably have SBOMs already, the least the supplier can do is provide SBOMs to their users, so they are able to defend themselves properly. In other words, SBOMs are just as much an "essential tool for the defender" as they are a "roadmap for the attacker".

The most important reason why this objection doesn't hold water is that most software vulnerabilities are reported by the supplier of the product. Knowing what is good for them (as well as their customers), very few suppliers will ever report a vulnerability for their product unless a patch is already available (in fact, most CVE reports include patch or upgrade information). For vulnerabilities that have been reported and for which a patch has been quickly issued, an organization that patches serious vulnerabilities as soon as the patch is available should be safe.

Unfortunately, the last statement contains three assumptions that will not always be true:

If the vulnerability is being actively exploited in the wild before the supplier reports the vulnerability in their product and develops a patch, the patch may arrive too late to do any good.

If the user organization has fallen behind in applying patches they have received from their suppliers (and this is true of most organizations) and does not have a good method for prioritizing patches (beyond "First in, first applied"), they may never apply the patch until they have already been compromised.

Even if the organization does have a good method for prioritizing patches (e.g., utilizing some combination of CVSS score, EPSS score, and presence on KEV list), that will never be foolproof. If a CVE receives a low priority using that method, organization-specific circumstances (e.g., the mix of devices and software within the organization) may still lead to the CVE having a big negative impact on the organization.

7. What is the current state of SBOM use?

As discussed in Chapter 1, software bills of materials have been produced and utilized since about 2010, although not always under that name. As of the writing of this section (early 2024), it can truthfully be said that SBOMs have achieved significant success in the software developer community yet are barely visible at all among organizations whose main activity is not software development.

How have SBOMs been successful? How have they not been successful?

The first machine-readable SBOM format was SPDX, which was created to help software developers address the very real risks posed by open source software licenses (although SPDX has for years also addressed the cybersecurity risk management use case). Even though software developers can download any open source component "for free", the component always comes with a license. Different licenses impose different restrictions on how the developer can utilize the component, so it is important that developers and device manufacturers know about the license that comes with every open source component in their products.

In fact, for at least several years, large European auto manufacturers ("OEMs") and suppliers have intensively exchanged SPDX SBOMs for the approximately 50 intelligent components included in the average new automobile. This is, to the author's knowledge, currently the largest active exchange of SBOMs between end users (which in this case means the auto manufacturers) and their suppliers (the large component suppliers like Bosch™) in the world.

The OEMs require SBOMs from their device suppliers, because each of those devices includes open source software components; the OEMs are quite concerned about having to conduct a recall because of an open source license management problem.[85] Of course, that would be very expensive.

---

[85] This is especially important for the German OEMs, due to provisions of German law regarding open source licenses.

However, almost all the current discussions of SBOMs (including this entire book) relate to their use in cybersecurity risk management. Where have SBOMs found success in that use case? There are two "branches" of the cyber risk management use case for SBOMs: software developers looking for vulnerabilities in software they develop and software end users looking for vulnerabilities in the software in use on their networks.

"End users" includes organizations whose main activity is not developing software. This includes commercial, nonprofit, and governmental organizations. It also includes the "business side" of software developers, since developers rely on third-party software to run their businesses, just like any other organization.

Today, SBOMs are widely used by software developers to manage the cyber risks posed by the many components (approximately 90% of which are open source[86]) that they include in their products. In fact, the Dependency Track[87] open source tool already mentioned was developed more than ten years ago, specifically to allow software developers to identify and monitor the vulnerabilities found in the components (dependencies) included in a software product. It is currently used over 500 million times every month (i.e., 17 million times a day) to identify or monitor vulnerabilities present in open source components found in a software product[88]; of course, these components are identified in an SBOM for the product.

Besides Dependency Track, there are many other tools, mainly used by software developers, that ingest an SBOM (or produce it themselves), then look up each component in a vulnerability database to identify vulnerabilities linked to the component. These tools, usually classified as Software Composition Analysis (SCA) tools, also track the same components for new vulnerabilities as time goes by, even multiple times a day - as does Dependency Track.

While it is not true that all, or even a majority, of software developers utilize SBOMs for their products to learn about component vulnerabilities, a significant minority of them do this now. These are often the suppliers that utilize the most advanced development tools, since modern tools often produce an SBOM as an automatic by-product of every software build. By generating SBOMs for a product as it is being built and monitoring for vulnerabilities in the components currently included in the product, the developer may take steps to manage software risks, including[89]:

---

[86] https://www.sonatype.com/resources/white-paper-state-of-the-software-supply-chain-2020

[87] https://dependencytrack.org/

[88] https://tomalrichblog.blogspot.com/2023/12/500-million.html

[89] None of these steps should be considered "mandatory", although they might be considered "best practices". The OWASP Software Component Verification Standard (https://scvs.owasp.org/) is widely acknowledged as the best set of guidelines for management of software components by developers.

- Patching component vulnerabilities before the product is made available to customers;
- Replacing a component that contains a serious vulnerability that cannot easily be patched;
- Replacing a proprietary component that has been declared end of life by its supplier;
- Replacing an open source component that no longer seems to be under active development, leading to the possibility that security patches for the component will not be readily available (or available at all) in the future;
- Replacing a component whose provenance is questionable or unknown; and
- Replacing a component that contains serious vulnerabilities that are more than a year old, which have never been patched by the component supplier.

Because there are so many risks that can be avoided by doing this kind of analysis, and because software supply chain security has become such a huge concern after the SolarWinds and Kaseya attacks, more and more software developers are taking steps such as the above.

Thus, there is not much question that SBOMs have already proven to be a great success with software developers. Is that also true for software end users?

Unfortunately, there the story is very different. The author knows of only a small number of medium-to-large software suppliers that regularly distribute SBOMs to customers – i.e., for every major or minor version of their product (there may be some small suppliers that also do this). And there are few medium-to-large organizations that *regularly* (i.e., with each major version of the product) obtain SBOMs from at least a few of their software suppliers and use those for the purpose of managing vulnerabilities in software or intelligent devices deployed on their networks.

Whose fault is this – that of the suppliers or that of the end users? As just described, at least a large minority of software suppliers – and especially the larger ones – regularly produce SBOMs for their own use, perhaps more than one a day for every product that is in development. Is the fact that these are seldom if ever being regularly distributed to their customers due to the suppliers' reluctance to distribute them or to the fact that their customers are not requesting them? The answer to both parts of this question is Yes. As of early 2024, suppliers are generally reluctant to distribute SBOMs, while at the same time users are hardly ever requesting them.

While this book discusses both use cases – the use cases of software developers and of software end users - the focus is primarily on the end user case. The question driving this book can be summarized as follows: Why, given that developers are using SBOMs heavily for their internal product risk management purposes, are they being used very little by end users for third-party software component risk management purposes?

Why aren't suppliers distributing SBOMS? Why aren't users asking for them?

As of the writing of this book in the beginning of 2024, there is still very little utilization of SBOMs by end users, although there is no question that developers are using them heavily. On the other hand, it is also certain that use of SBOMs among suppliers is still just a fraction of what it ultimately might be. SBOM use by suppliers is still in its early stages, despite the impressive numbers already logged.[90]

On the other hand, there is no question that end users also need the data from SBOMs. They need it for the purpose of securing the software they rely on to run their businesses, nonprofit organizations, and government agencies. Suppliers who are asked why they are not distributing SBOMs to their customers almost always point to the fact that their customers are not asking for them. Why are software customers not asking for SBOMs from their suppliers?

In the author's opinion, there are three main reasons for this:

Very few, if any, product suppliers are making SBOMs regularly available to their customers. By "regularly available", the author means an SBOM is updated with every new version of each software product or intelligent device.[91] Some suppliers to the federal government have provided one or two SBOMs to federal agencies in response to Executive Order 14028[92] (hereinafter the EO), which mandated that all US federal agencies start requiring SBOMs from their suppliers of "critical software". However, for an SBOM to provide benefit to an end user, it must be for the version of the software the user is currently running. An SBOM for any previous version will almost never provide a list of components that corresponds to the components in the user's version. Thus, the supplier needs to provide a new SBOM whenever a new version of their product is released.

---

[90] As of early 2024, the open source tool Dependency Track is used more than 17 million times a day to look up a component listed in an SBOM in a vulnerability database. Almost all this use is by developers.

[91] Hereinafter in this book, the term "product" will collectively refer both to software products and intelligent devices. In the small number of cases where it will be important to distinguish between the two, the reason for doing so will be made clear.

[92] https://www.whitehouse.gov/briefing-room/presidential-actions/2021/05/12/executive-order-on-improving-the-nations-cybersecurity/

There are no commercially supported, easy-to-use and "complete"[93] component vulnerability management tools currently available - i.e., tools that ingest SBOMs and VEX information for the product/versions utilized by a user organization and output daily updated lists of exploitable component vulnerabilities, usually in a format supported by the user's vulnerability, asset or configuration management tool(s).

There are currently no third-party services available that ingest SBOMs and VEX information for the products utilized by the customer organization and output daily updated lists of exploitable component vulnerabilities. In the author's opinion, these services are likely to appear much sooner than end user tools. See Part 3 of this book for a discussion of how they may appear, perhaps in the near future.

However, there is another mystery: Given that suppliers are using SBOMs very heavily to manage vulnerabilities encountered while developing and updating their own products, why aren't they encouraging their customers to start using them – rather than waiting for the customers to request them? After all, it will be to the suppliers' benefit if their customers are able to utilize SBOMs and VEX information to secure their products. If they can make effective use of SBOMs to manage component vulnerabilities in the software products they utilize, end users will be both more inclined to say good things about their suppliers' products and less inclined to tie up the suppliers' help lines with complaints about unpatched vulnerabilities that turn out to be false positives.[94]

There are five main reasons why suppliers are not distributing SBOMs, even though a lot of them are using SBOMS very heavily to manage vulnerabilities in their own products:

First, some suppliers simply do not want to air their dirty laundry. For example, it is likely that a lot of suppliers are ashamed about old and/or vulnerable components in their products, which they are unable to replace for any number of reasons[95]. How can such a supplier release an SBOM to their customers, if it is likely to be met with ridicule or outrage or both?

The best answer to this question is that a supplier should not feel obligated to list every component they know of in their SBOM and end users should not press the suppliers to do so. Instead, if a supplier either does not have the required information for a component or they do not want to release the information, they

---

[93] For a description of a "complete" tool, see Part 3 of this book.

[94] The reason for this statement will become clear when we discuss VEX in the second part of this book.

[95] One important reason why suppliers are reluctant to replace old components in certain software products is discussed in this blog post: https://tomalrichblog.blogspot.com/2023/04/its-time-to-retire-candy-bar.html

should either enter "omitted" in CycloneDX or "NOASSERTION" in SPDX. The supplier does not have to explain to the customer the reason for leaving a field empty.

At this stage, where distribution and use of SBOMs are still in their infancy, there is a big danger that users will let the perfect be the enemy of the good and demand that complete information about every component of a product be listed in the product's SBOM. The result of that will not be that the supplier will suddenly fill in every empty field in their SBOM, but that they will not release the SBOM at all. Their customers need to take the "glass half full" attitude, in which they're happy they're getting any information on software components at all, and not be angry that they aren't getting everything, since the great majority of software users are not currently receiving component information at all.

Second, the "naming problem" (see Chapter 6 later in this Part) dictates that producing SBOMs for end users requires a manual and potentially time-consuming process of finding purl or CPE identifiers (or preferably both) for all components listed in the SBOM. Until the naming problem is at least on the way to being solved (which the author believes it is), some suppliers will simply not want to get involved with SBOMs.

Again, the "solution" to this problem for the time being is for the supplier not to include a purl or CPE for some components, if finding one is initially too difficult or too time-consuming (the supplier should always leave some "placeholder" information for a component, even if they have no other information than that). As time goes on and both the supplier and their customers become more educated on how SBOMs can help them mitigate risks due to software vulnerabilities, the supplier will become more comfortable with including purls or CPE names in their SBOMs, while their customers will start asking for them more regularly.

Third, many suppliers do not even want to think about releasing SBOMs to their customers unless they have confidence that they will also be able to provide VEX data to them[96]. Currently, in large part because there are literally no end user tools that make proper use of VEX information, there are almost no VEX documents being produced regularly. Unfortunately, "no VEXes" ultimately means "no SBOMs". Currently, the OWASP SBOM Forum[97] is working on this problem. To learn more about that effort, see Part 3 of this book.

Fourth, It is no secret that there is tremendous uncertainty regarding SBOMs, and close to 100% uncertainty regarding VEX; this is because (as of early 2024) there has been close to no distribution to and use by non-developers of SBOMs, and even less of VEX documents, for the purpose of software component vulnerability management. Again, the last part of this book will provide some

---

[96] The reason for this statement will be discussed at length in Part 2, "Introduction to VEX".

[97] https://owasp.org/www-project-sbom-forum/

perspective on this problem, as well as discuss how the OWASP SBOM Forum is addressing this problem.

Fifth, most commercial software suppliers have legal departments (or outside counsel) that need to approve all sales contracts; one red flag for them is the presence of undefined or vaguely defined terms in the contract. What are the chances that, even when a software product manager feels they are ready to release SBOMs and VEX information for their product, the legal department will be willing to sign a sales contract that includes provisions regarding SBOMs and VEX documents – unless there is a body of experience and case law that they can draw on to determine whether the terms they are agreeing to are clear enough to be enforceable?

The author believes that point is still years away, but that does not mean that SBOMs cannot move forward anyway. Part 3 of this book describes the idea of a big "proof of concept" (PoC), in which many software suppliers and end users collaborate to produce and utilize SBOMs as a group learning exercise, with no contracts or other legal encumberments that might prevent this from happening at all.

Why are many suppliers reluctant to distribute SBOMs to end users?

There are two groups of reasons why many suppliers are reluctant to distribute SBOMs for their products. The first group is what might be called "normal business reasons", including:

Reluctance to invest in producing SBOMs for customers, given uncertainty about what the demand for them will be. Even though a large percentage (although probably not a majority) of suppliers are producing SBOMs for their own use now, that does not mean they could easily start producing them for their customers. There are a lot of steps that a supplier might omit in creating an SBOM for their own use, that they would never omit when creating one for customer use.

Concern about how and whether the supplier will be able to recover their cost of producing and distributing SBOMs. These costs are unlikely to be high, but given the unknown elements – especially regarding distribution of SBOMs and VEX documents – it is understandable that many suppliers would want to have more certainty regarding costs before they plunge into distributing SBOMs to customers.

The supplier's competitors are not distributing SBOMs for their products, so the supplier does not feel pressure to do so themselves. This is undoubtedly one of the biggest reasons at work today: There is a "vicious circle", in which one supplier's failure to distribute SBOMs to customers reinforces other suppliers' reluctance to distribute them. The good news about this is it could easily be replaced with a "virtuous circle", in which the "bandwagon effect" causes suppliers to fear being left behind by their competitors in distributing SBOMs (the author apologizes for mixing metaphors here). In fact, the author believes this will ultimately be what is responsible for SBOMs succeeding (it has undoubtedly already been a major cause of suppliers becoming heavy users of SBOMs for internal risk management purposes).

Concern about revealing intellectual property if they distribute SBOMs to customers. Since creating an SBOM does not reveal any of the supplier's code, at first glance it is hard to understand how intellectual property could be a concern. However, there are some industries, especially automobile manufacturing, in which the identity of useful open source components is itself considered to be a trade secret. Of course, the auto manufacturers need to provide SBOMs to their customers, but they are concerned that they will end up falling into their competitors' hands as well.

The second group of reasons why suppliers are not distributing SBOMs to their customers is "SBOM-specific" reasons, including:

Concern by developers' legal departments that the organization will be sued for making an inadvertent error, especially given that there are currently no agreed-upon best practices for producing and distributing SBOMs. Examples of these concerns are inadvertently misidentifying a component, mistakenly saying a vulnerability was not exploitable in a VEX document, etc.

Concerns about old or vulnerable components that cannot be removed because of product stability concerns, yet which will inevitably make the supplier look bad if included in an SBOM.[98] The solution to this problem is for the supplier not to reveal any piece of information they do not want to reveal, but instead insert NOASSERTION (in SPDX) or "omitted" (in CycloneDX) in its place. However, many suppliers, and especially their legal departments, will be hard to convince on this issue. They will need to see competitors including a lot of empty fields in their SBOMs, before they will be willing to do this themselves.[99]

Concerns about the large amount of time and resources the supplier is likely to spend mitigating naming problems in their SBOMs (see the chapter titled "The naming problem" later in this Part).

Uncertainty over which of the six SBOM Types[100] is appropriate for a supplier to produce, for particular customers or in certain situations. It will be hard to

---

[98] The author discussed this problem, referred to as "tight coupling" of components, in this blog post: https://tomalrichblog.blogspot.com/2023/04/its-time-to-retire-candy-bar.html.

[99] Unwarranted concerns like this (and others described in this Section) will hopefully be alleviated in the large-scale Proof of Concept described at the end of Part 3. All participants in the PoC will be required to sign an NDA saying they understand that the exchange of SBOMs is purely for educational purposes, and they will not utilize the SBOMs they receive in the PoC to make business decisions.

[100] https://www.cisa.gov/sites/default/files/2023-04/sbom-types-document-508c.pdf

compare SBOMs of different Types, especially if they are from different suppliers.

For a supplier starting to create VEX documents, concern about being able to prove that a vulnerability is not exploitable in one of their products, since that requires proving a negative.

Concerns that users are not going to be able to utilize VEX documents to "whittle down" the list of component vulnerabilities found in their products to only those that are exploitable, meaning the suppliers' help desks will be overwhelmed with support calls about non-exploitable vulnerabilities.[101]

Lack of consistency in tools for producing SBOMs, meaning that an SBOM prepared with one tool will sometimes be incompatible with an SBOM for the identical product, which was prepared with a different tool.

Questions about how to create an SBOM for an intelligent device. See the previous chapter titled "SBOMs and vulnerability management for intelligent devices".

The two "showstopper" problems

While there are many reasons why software suppliers are not distributing SBOMs to their customers, the author has frequently heard from suppliers that software customers are not asking for them. Why aren't the customers doing this?

SBOMs are not tools in themselves. Rather, they are a source of important information that is required to learn about risks arising from third-party components in software that an organization utilizes to run its operations. When SBOMs first started to be discussed seriously in the NTIA Initiative, it seemed that just by learning about vulnerabilities and other risks that arise from components, user organizations would have all the information they need to protect themselves from those risks.

However, early in the NTIA Initiative, some people who were working on component vulnerabilities came to realize there were two important problems with this narrative. First, the naming problem meant that only a small percentage of component names in an SBOM, which was generated through some automated process, will appear with identifiers that can be used to look up the component in a vulnerability database and find vulnerabilities applicable to that component.

CPE and purl are the only two software identifiers that are used in vulnerability databases. CPE is the only identifier supported by the National Vulnerability Database (NVD), the most widely used vulnerability database

---

[101] In the author's opinion, this is the basis for one of the two "showstopper" problems (the other being the naming problem) that is inhibiting distribution to and use of SBOMs by non-developer organizations.

worldwide, while purl (which stands for "package URL") is by far the most widely used identifier for open source software components in vulnerability databases like OSS Index[102] and OSV[103] (for further discussion of CPE and purl, see "The naming problem" later in this Part).

If one of these identifiers is not listed for a component in an SBOM, it will normally be hard for an end user to learn about vulnerabilities found in the component. Ideally, before distributing an SBOM to customers, a software supplier would verify that every component listed in the SBOM has either a CPE or purl identifier.

Finding a purl identifier for an open source component should usually be easy, since purl has no central database. As long as the supplier preparing an SBOM knows the repository from which they downloaded the open source component (usually a package manager) and the name and version number of the component in that package manager, they should be able to create a proper purl.[104]

However, finding a CPE is not easy, because the great majority of them do not exist, and a lot of them are wrong. Pages 4-6 of the OWASP SBOM Forum's 2022 white paper[105] on the naming problem go into detail on the major problems with CPE.

When a supplier cannot find a CPE or purl for a component listed in an SBOM, they can still list the other information about the component. They can also remove all information about the component, although they should still leave a "placeholder" for the component identifier – either "omitted" in CycloneDX or "NOASSERTION" in SPDX.

The second major problem, which has proven even more serious than naming, is the problem of exploitability of component vulnerabilities.[106] Early on during the NTIA Initiative, people who were identifying and testing component vulnerabilities were struck by the fact that only a small percentage of the component vulnerabilities they were able to identify in a vulnerability database proved to be exploitable in the product itself.

---

[102] https://ossindex.sonatype.org/

[103] https://osv.dev/

[104] See Chapter 8, "The naming problem".

[105]

https://owasp.org/assets/files/posts/A%20Proposal%20to%20Operationalize%20Component%20Identification%20for%20Vulnerability%20Management.pdf

[106] The discussion below, continuing through the end of this Section, necessarily overlaps with some parts of the second part of this book, "Introduction to VEX". However, unlike the discussion in that part, this discussion focuses on the fact that confusion over what VEX is - and the resulting lack of end user tools - is one of the two major reasons why SBOMs themselves are not being distributed to organizations whose main purpose is not developing software. A reader who is having trouble understanding this discussion may want to read Part 2 of the book first, then return to this Section.

In other words, for the great majority of component vulnerabilities, scanning and other tests of the product itself could not confirm that a vulnerability was present in the product, even though testing of the component separately from the product would confirm that the vulnerability was present in the component. The reason for this fact is that in most cases, how the component is installed in a product mitigates the vulnerability.

The general consensus in the software security community is that the percentage of non-exploitable component vulnerabilities in the average software product is over 90%. In other words, if a tool like Dependency Track[107] ingests an SBOM for a product (or creates one itself) and identifies 100 component vulnerabilities in a major vulnerability database, on average, fewer than ten of these vulnerabilities will be exploitable in the product itself (and many people in the developer community will tell you that the actual number is fewer than five vulnerabilities).

At first glance, this might appear to be a good thing – and it is, on one level. If a software product was found at first to contain 100 component vulnerabilities, but was then found to be affected by only ten of those, that means the level of component vulnerability risk has dropped below 10% of what it was at first believed to be.

However, the problem is that the user will initially not know which are the exploitable component vulnerabilities and which are not exploitable. The main reason why a user should want to learn about exploitable component vulnerabilities is these are the ones they need to be concerned about. For each exploitable component vulnerability, they should a) do their own testing to confirm that the vulnerability is in fact present in a product they utilize and b) coordinate with the supplier's help desk to learn when a patch will be available for it.

What is the consequence if a user of a software product, who is concerned about risks arising from components in that product, is not able to learn which component vulnerabilities are exploitable and which are not? In that case, the prudent course is probably to treat every component vulnerability as if it is exploitable and spend large amounts of time on the phone or emailing the supplier's help desk, trying to get them to commit to specific dates to patch each component vulnerability they have identified. The user will be frustrated by the amount of time they have to devote to these activities and by the fact that the help desk staff seems to be dismissing most of their concerns as unwarranted.

The help desk staff will have a very different experience, but an equally frustrating one. They will have to tell caller after caller that yes, they know that Component ABC in the product is listed in the NVD as affected by CVE-2023-

---

[107] https://dependencytrack.org/

12345 and yes, they know this vulnerability has caused a lot of concern in the software community recently. However, the supplier's own testing shows it is not exploitable in their product, even though Component ABC is listed on the SBOM for the product.

Help desk staff usually find a lot of job satisfaction in helping people solve problems. But they receive no satisfaction from telling caller after caller that they don't really have a problem and that they should just calm down – which never seems to work, anyway.

The fact that this outcome seemed inevitable was quite alarming to the early participants in the NTIA Initiative, especially to a few very large software and device suppliers. They could see this would not be a sustainable situation. If software users get excited about obtaining SBOMs for the products they utilize, but then learn about a lot of component vulnerabilities and start trying to get their suppliers to patch them, frustration will quickly set in; they will probably decide that the "promise" of SBOMs is purely illusory, and there is no point in wasting any more time on them.

It was to address this problem that a working group within the NTIA Initiative decided that the best course of action was to develop a machine-readable document format, meant to be distributed through the same channels as SBOMs but not to be directly tied to them. The main purpose of the format is to inform a user tool, which ingests SBOMs and identifies component vulnerabilities in them, of the "exploitability status" of the vulnerabilities it has identified. This format was given the name VEX, which stands for "Vulnerability Exploitability eXchange" (although, as often happens, the acronym was arrived at before the group decided what it stood for).

Note that the VEX concept only makes sense if the document a) is machine-readable, and b) is read by an end user tool that also ingests an SBOM and identifies vulnerabilities applicable to components listed in the SBOM. While the first condition has been realized in principle, the second condition has not been realized at all.

Today, no software supplier that wishes to inform their customers of non-exploitable component vulnerabilities will realize any benefit from using a machine-readable format for the VEX, given there are no tools designed to ingest SBOMs and VEX documents and provide end users a list of exploitable component vulnerabilities; the supplier would be better off just putting the VEX information in an email in English and sending it to the customers of the product in question.[108]

---

[108] Indeed, the author has heard from more than one large software supplier that, when they give customers the option of machine readable or PDF SBOM and VEX documents, the customers almost always choose the PDF versions, since they do not have low-cost, *commercially-supported* tools to make use of the machine-readable documents, and they don't have time to assemble and operate various open source tools that might collectively achieve the desired end result.

See Part 3 of this book for a more in-depth discussion of this issue, as well as a discussion of how the OWASP SBOM Forum is now working to solve the problem.

When will a complete end user component vulnerability management tool appear?

The author admits to disappointment that, as of the beginning of 2024, no software security tool vendor has even announced they will develop something resembling a complete[109] SBOM/VEX consumption tool; a couple of years ago, he expected such tools to be available by now. However, the author also does not believe this is the fault of the tool vendors, since there has been little to no public discussion – other than hints in the author's blog – of the need for such a tool.

The author has come to realize in the last year that it was probably unrealistic to expect such an end user tool to be feasible at all for at least a few years, given the many open questions about SBOM and VEX (some of which have already been discussed and some of which, such as the naming problem, will be discussed later in this book).

This statement might seem to ring the death knell for use of SBOMs by end users. After all, SBOMs and VEX documents only make sense when utilized by a software tool. Otherwise, the supplier would be much better off putting whatever information they wish to provide in a PDF file and distributing it via email. If software users don't have a tool to read SBOM and VEX documents and make use of the information in them for vulnerability management purposes, they certainly will not demand that their suppliers provide SBOMs in the first place; in fact, this is the situation today.

The author believes it is unlikely there will be a complete, low-cost, easy-to-use, and *commercially supported* SBOM consumption tool for at least several years; yet a truly successful end user tool will need to be all of those. While in previous years the author said just the opposite, he currently suggests to startup and established tool vendors that a true end user SBOM/VEX consumption tool is not a worthwhile or realistic target for their efforts, given current obstacles like the naming problem.

Does this mean SBOMs are toast, at least as far as utilization for vulnerability management purposes by non-software developers is concerned? The answer is, "Definitely not!" Utilizing SBOMs for vulnerability management purposes will

---

[109] For a description of what a "complete" SBOM consumption tool would do, see Part 3 of this book.

probably be as beneficial for non-developers as it has already proven to be for developers.

However, saying that end users will not soon be able to directly utilize SBOM and VEX documents is not the same as saying that end users will not soon have access to *information* derived from those documents. Moreover, it is certainly not the same as saying that end users don't need to have the most important information that can be derived from SBOMs and VEX documents - namely, an at-least-daily-updated list of exploitable component vulnerabilities in software products/versions utilized by the end user organization.

How is an end user organization going to gain access to daily-updated lists of exploitable component vulnerabilities in software products they utilize, if they cannot track component vulnerabilities using tools they own and operate? This is two questions. The first is who will perform the required tracking and make the results available to end users. The second is who will pay for that service.

The fact that it is unlikely there will be a complete SBOM/VEX consumption tool available for years does not mean there will not be any such tool at all – just not an end-user-grade tool. The reason why an end-user-grade tool will not be available is that the requirements for such a tool are much more stringent than for a tool to be used by experts.

For example, while an end-user-grade tool would need to be built on the (dubious) assumption that all SBOMs it consumes will have already solved the naming problem – meaning that all or most of the components listed will include a valid CPE or purl identifier – a service provider using an expert-grade tool or tools (probably open source) would be able to get around this problem by utilizing *ad hoc* techniques to find CPEs or purls for the components in an SBOM. Software developers, and consultants that work with them, are already using a variety of such techniques. However, end users would never be willing to put in the work required to apply those techniques (especially because the techniques require a lot of trial and error).

For this reason, the author believes that service providers will arise (perhaps in 2024) that have built their own tooling to ingest SBOMs and VEX documents and output lists of exploitable vulnerabilities in products/versions used by end user organizations. Moreover, this tooling will be operated by people who have some experience with dealing with issues like the naming problem, who will be able to work around these issues.

The author believes that, even though the entire end user component vulnerability tracking process will probably never be fully automated, there will certainly be enough automation that the service providers who initially undertake this venture will over time enter a "virtuous circle" of automation. In such a circle, suppliers that initially utilize a basic level of automation will gradually ratchet up that level, as they figure out how to automate parts of the component vulnerability tracking process that previously required human involvement. This will allow them to gradually lower their prices, which will bring them more business, etc.

Anyone who doubts that this virtuous circle could happen in real life is referred to the numerous examples of exactly that in the history of computing, and especially of the internet. For example, there are numerous internet-based services such as voice transmission, movie streaming, language translation, malware detection, tax preparation, etc. that used to be relatively expensive and are now often totally free. This is because the cost of providing them has declined rapidly due to increasing automation. Even early email systems were expensive to buy and operate, whereas now they're mostly free for individuals.

While it is unlikely that SBOM-based component vulnerability management services will ever be completely free, the fact is there will ultimately be a huge market for them – and the "cost" of the services may ultimately be nothing more than the willingness to read a few ads on the screen. After all, just about every organization in the world utilizes software to run their business today; they all need to mitigate risks in the software they use. When the price of component vulnerability management declines to a level that they can afford, they will jump on the bandwagon – and that will further drive down the cost of delivering the services.

Who will pay for component vulnerability management services?

The author was lucky enough to be able to study with Professor Milton Friedman when he was an economics major at the University of Chicago. One important principle that Dr. Friedman often articulated was that one must always distinguish between the person who pays the bill and the person who writes the check (check being the dominant form of payment in those days!). What he meant by this was that you always need to analyze the economic forces at work in any transaction, which determine who bears the ultimate cost; you should never assume that the person who writes the check or hands over the credit card is the one who bears the cost in an economic sense.

An example of this principle, which is quite relevant to this discussion, is vulnerability patching services. The author remembers the time in the late 1990s when it became apparent that software vulnerabilities were not a rare event that could be treated as such (which had been the assumption previously), but a continually recurring problem that would require an ongoing solution. The first software suppliers to offer regular security patches for their products usually charged for them, either directly or by requiring that the customer pay for maintenance to have access to the patches.

However, as the number of discovered vulnerabilities continued to increase, along with attacks based on those vulnerabilities, the opinion quickly grew within the software user community that patches should not come with a charge. Perhaps as importantly, people realized that there is a type of "herd immunity" that comes into play when a large percentage of the users of a software product have patched a vulnerability. This is because hackers like to attack products in which serious

87

vulnerabilities are mostly unpatched, and they are discouraged from attacking products in which serious vulnerabilities are mostly patched. Each user of a software product benefits when every other user has access to free security patches.

As a result, today there are few if any software suppliers that charge for security patches, mostly because users have come to expect that the price they pay for the software comes with free patches. If a supplier suddenly announced they were going to start charging for security patches today, they might well be out of business tomorrow. In other words, while software customers 25-30 years ago usually bore the cost of developing security patches themselves, the supplier now bears it, since they no longer charge their customers separately for patching.

Let's look at SBOMs from the same analytical viewpoint. Moreover, let's assume the author is correct that the software component vulnerability tracking services required by customers will be provided by third-party service providers. Who will pay those providers, both in the short and the longer terms?

In the short term, it seems likely that software users will pay the service providers. After all, the dominant "economic model" that is behind both the NTIA and CISA SBOM initiatives is one in which software suppliers provide SBOMs and VEX documents to their customers, but analysis of those documents is their responsibility.

However, it is the author's opinion that the component vulnerability tracking (SBOM/VEX) services "market" will follow the trajectory of the software patching "market" in the late 1990s: Analyzing SBOMs and VEX documents to produce lists of exploitable component vulnerabilities will increasingly be seen as the responsibility of the suppliers – after all, the suppliers chose the components included in their products. More importantly, software users will increasingly require that component vulnerability management services be included in the price they pay for software, just as they did with patching services in the 1990s.

The author believes that an important difference between component vulnerability management services and patching services is that software suppliers have never outsourced patch development to any significant degree; after all, developing patches is just one form of software development.

However, component vulnerability management services are quite different from software development. While it is possible that a small number of software suppliers will try to provide these services on their own, it is unlikely that will prove to be a good investment – any more than would an investment in insourced janitorial or paycheck preparation services, which are mostly outsourced now. The economies of scale that can be gained by the service providers, since they will presumably have hundreds or even thousands of software suppliers as customers, will probably far outweigh whatever expertise the software supplier could bring to bear, if they tried to provide the service themselves.

So, the "final state" will be that software suppliers will gladly pay the costs of the service providers offering component vulnerability management services.

Meanwhile, the latter will compete with each other to make their services more efficient, and thus be able to charge lower prices to the suppliers.

Of course, there will always be some software end users who want to perform component vulnerability management themselves, simply because they enjoy doing that. But they will literally be paying for that enjoyment.

In the above discussion, we have still not addressed the most compelling reason why software suppliers should bear the cost of having third-party service providers perform software component vulnerability tracking: It makes no sense to force thousands or tens of thousands of customers to perform exactly the same set of steps that the supplier could perform on their own, and then distribute the results to their customers.

For example, suppose a software product has 10,000 users, all of whom are concerned about managing vulnerabilities due to components in the product. Does it make more sense for the supplier to track component vulnerabilities themselves and just distribute the results to their customers, or to leave it to the customers to perform this tracking themselves (even if they need to pay a third-party to do it)?

Let's suppose that performing the required component vulnerability tracking for one product for one year requires that an organization spend fifty hours in total. If all 10,000 users do this, the total cost to them will be 500,000 hours. Ideally, if they all work with the same information from the supplier (i.e., both the SBOM and the VEX documents), they will all end up with the same results: a list of exploitable component vulnerabilities in the product and version, which is updated daily to reflect new VEX documents received from the supplier.

Now, let's suppose the supplier performs the same tracking themselves, or pays a third-party to do it. They will spend fifty hours on this as well, and they will achieve the same result as each of their 10,000 customers. They will then make the results available to their customers (presumably using their customer portal).

Now, here's the hard question: Which is more, 500,000 hours or 50 hours? You're correct! 500,000 hours is more than 50 hours. In other words, if each of the customers must perform this analysis themselves, 499,950 hours of the customers' time will be "wasted" in an economic sense, since the supplier could just as easily have performed the work themselves and distributed the results to their users.

Here is the even harder question: How could it ever make sense for a supplier to require each of its customers to perform software component vulnerability tracking that the supplier could perform just as cheaply on its own, while simply distributing the results to their customers? The answer is this would never make sense from the point of view of total economic well-being. The supplier should perform this service themselves. This is why the author believes that, while end users may initially pay for component vulnerability tracking services, suppliers will soon pay for the services themselves – and be happy to do so, since it will bring them a lot of goodwill for a minimal investment.

Thus, the author believes the "steady state" software component vulnerability tracking ecosystem will, perhaps 3-4 years from now, consist of mostly third-party service providers providing this service to software customers, and usually being paid by the suppliers themselves.[110]

What have we learned about SBOM use by end users?

Here is a summary of the discussion so far in this chapter: While SBOMs can be helpful in procurement, license management and other use cases, the most important cybersecurity use case - and the one that is assumed in most of what is written about SBOMs, including Executive Order 14028 - is "component vulnerability management".

In that use case, information from SBOMs and VEX documents will be continually analyzed to produce a list of exploitable component vulnerabilities found in a particular version of a software product; the list will be updated daily, mainly to accommodate new VEX information (there will normally be only one SBOM per product version, which will stay the same during the entire time that version is in use. But there will be many VEX documents). Lists like this will continually be made available to end user organizations, so those organizations will at any time be able to learn what exploitable component vulnerabilities are found in the software they use to run their operations.

SBOMs are not currently being distributed to end users in any significant volume for supply chain cybersecurity risk management purposes. This is mostly because users are not asking for them.

The main reason why users are not asking for SBOMs is there are no easy-to-use, low-cost, and commercially supported tools available for them to identify and track software component vulnerabilities in software they utilize to run their operations.

Moreover, it is unlikely that such tools will be available for many years. Therefore, the author believes that third-party service providers will arise soon to track software component vulnerabilities using tools they have developed specifically for this purpose.

---

[110] Of course, there will be many cases in which the supplier will be either non-existent (as is usually the case for open source software) or unwilling/unable to pay for this service themselves. In those cases, the software users will need to pay. In the longer run, as more and more software end users come to realize that software component vulnerability tracking provides substantial benefits to them, suppliers that are unwilling or unable to pay for this service may lose market share, just as any supplier that does not develop security patches for their products today will almost certainly lose market share.

The service providers will be able to provide lists of exploitable component vulnerabilities in both a "generic" format and in formats that can be ingested by specific tools that can utilize the information, including vulnerability scanning, patching and configuration/asset management tools.

Because the responsibility for performing this analysis will ultimately be seen to reside with the suppliers, after a few years, the suppliers will usually pay the service providers to do this work for them and make the results available to customers who use their products.

There are three "showstopper" problems that currently seriously inhibit regular provision of SBOMs to end users (meaning provision of a new SBOM with every new version of a software product). Neither of these problems needs to be completely "solved" before SBOMs can be regularly distributed to end users, but there is progress being made toward solving both:

The naming problem (described in the next chapter).

Uncertainty about what VEX is, including the lack of specifications on which completely interoperable producer and consumer tools can be based (discussed in Parts 2 and 3 of this book).

Another important problem is the current lack of "complete" (see Part 3 for an explanation of what that means) end user tools for component vulnerability management. This problem is not fundamental, but is a result of the two "showstopper" problems. In fact, it may be addressed for one very important use case in the near future (see Part 3).

SBOMs for SaaS

It is no secret that more and more software has moved to the cloud, if it has not been there since it was "born". Moreover, this trend is accelerating. Today, many organizations utilize exclusively SaaS (which stands for "software-as-a-service", meaning cloud-based software) to run their businesses. Some people have wondered whether and how they will be able to receive SBOMs for the SaaS they use.[111]

The purpose of SBOMs is to enable the software user to learn about the risks they face by using their software, which are due to the third parties that created the components included in the software. This concept assumes that a software product is installed in a user organization's on-premises infrastructure; once installed, it doesn't change until the user either upgrades or patches it. When that happens, it means the version has changed; the supplier should provide their customers with a new SBOM based on the new version.

---

[111] In fact, as of early 2024, there is a CISA workgroup working on the question of software transparency for SaaS (see the table later in this Section).

However, SaaS is quite different from on-premises software. A SaaS application is often upgraded multiple times a day, meaning that a user at 9 AM will use a different product than a user at 1 PM, who will in turn use a different product than a user at 6 PM. In order for each of those users to have an SBOM that describes the software they are actually using, the SaaS provider would need to develop a new SBOM every few hours and would need to provide it to all users of the SaaS product immediately – so they can make a decision whether or not to use the SaaS that day. In a few hours, that SBOM will be out of date and a new one will be needed.

Needless to say, this is not feasible. The "traditional" concept of an SBOM – an inventory of the components within the software (i.e., "software within software") at a point in time – does not work with SaaS. Of course, this doesn't mean that risks from software components disappear when the software is in the cloud – they are still there. But the end user will probably never be able to have an up-to-the-minute SBOM for a SaaS application (let alone VEX documents, which are also needed).

This means users can't track SaaS component risks on their own, as they will be able to do for on-premises software when SBOMs and VEX documents are widely available. The best that can be done regarding third party component risks is to require the SaaS provider to attest that they regularly produce SBOMs for their product, and that they use them to learn about and mitigate risks in the product.

However, there is another type of third party risk that is quite relevant to SaaS: that is risks from third party *services* used by the SaaS product. On-premises software uses components to save the effort that would otherwise be required to code functions that have already been coded by others – after all, why reinvent the wheel? Similarly, SaaS uses third party services (some free, others for cost) that perform specialized services that a typical SaaS provider would not find easy to provide on their own. Some examples include:

- Authentication services
- Storage services
- News feeds
- Access to specialized databases

Just as in the case of third party software components, third party services all carry risks, which they often transfer to the product itself. For example, if a SaaS product uses a third party authentication service and it goes down, does that mean that nobody can access the SaaS itself? In some cases, it may mean that, but in others it may not. An organization that is choosing a SaaS product for an application like payroll should ask each SaaS provider that they are considering to provide an inventory of the services they use. The organization might require that the inventory be listed in the CycloneDX "SaaSBOM" format.[112]

---

[112] https://cyclonedx.org/capabilities/saasbom/

As of early 2024, the CISA SBOM Cloud working group is drafting a document[113] called "Service Transparency". On page 6, the document includes a table titled "Data Fields for Service Transparency". These are suggested fields to be included in a SaaSBOM:

1. *Service identifier:* A unique identifier for the service such as a URL, pURL, URI or IRI. A service endpoint will also do as an identifier.

2. *Service provider:* The unique identifier of the entity, person, or organization providing the service. E.g., Alphabet, Google, cloud.google.com, googleapis.com

3. *Service functions:* The types of functions the service provides. E.g. identity, authentication, certificate authority, CNA, load balancing, etc.

4. *Service location:* The geographical location where the service is hosted. Cloud Providers list these as us-east, brazil-south, etc. Multiple locations may be listed here.

5. *Service protocol:* Communication protocol used by service endpoints, e.g. http, https, mqtt.

6. *Service agreement:* The text from or link to the Terms of Service agreed to by the consumer of the service.

7. *Service status:* A link to the status page showing service uptime information.

8. *Data flow:* Uni-directional or bi-directional.

9. *Data classifications:* The classification of the data being ingested by the service. E.g. PII, PHI, confidential, public.

Each one of the above fields corresponds to an area of risk for third party services. For example, if "Data Flow" is bidirectional (meaning the primary service will both receive and transmit data with the third party service), the risk is greater than if it is unidirectional, since some data from the primary service will need to be shared with the third party. Controls will need to be in place to prevent inappropriate sharing of data.

Third party services can have dependency relationships, just as software components do. That is, third party service A may depend on service B, which in turn depends on C, etc. In some cases, an outage of C may cascade down to B and A. Of course, it would not be feasible for an end user to require that the SaaS

---

[113]

https://docs.google.com/document/d/1ZpTtsY0H2SwfNRq6qUzLMiWLQ8OwlhmJeg_M0cxrOiQ/edit

operator provide information on all the service dependencies of their direct service providers; just a list of the latter will be a good start. However, it is feasible for the customer to require the primary service provider to provide evidence that they are at least tracking those dependencies themselves.

Probably the biggest obstacle to an end user organization being able to assess risks due to SaaS providers used by the organization is finding the data required to assess the risks. Unlike with software components, there is no central database of vulnerabilities like the NVD; in fact, there is currently no standard taxonomy of service vulnerabilities, playing an equivalent role to CVEs for software vulnerabilities.

However, there are certainly data sources that can help in evaluating third party services. For example, if the SaaS provider can furnish their customers with legal names of the organizations that provide their third party services, the customers can often find those names in various databases. They can check on risk concerns such as headquarters country, past bankruptcies, enforcement actions by regulators such as the Federal Trade Commission, etc. Given the constantly growing importance of SaaS, it is likely there will be databases of service vulnerabilities in coming years.

SBOMs are already successful

Given the tone of many of the statements so far, the heading of this Section might seem anomalous at best. However, it is true: Even though outside of the software developer community, SBOMs are not being distributed or utilized in any volume at all, it is possible to say they have already had a great deal of success. How could that be?

To understand this, it is important to understand the fundamental purpose of SBOMs in the supply chain cybersecurity use case. That purpose is *not* to empower end users to secure the software they operate by their own efforts; this is simply not possible. Securing software requires being able to patch vulnerabilities. Other than in exceptional cases, end users cannot develop their own patch for a product they did not write themselves; having SBOMs does not change this situation.

So, why do end users need SBOMs (or at least the data from them)? What good does it do to provide users with lots of information on what makes up the software they operate, if they can't directly use that information to improve their level of security? And, even if the end user could improve their security if they had SBOMs, the two previous parts of this book have shown that end users have so far had access to just a trickle of SBOMs and a dry creek bed of VEXes. How could SBOMs be said to be successful?

The author stands by his statement. The fundamental purpose of distributing SBOMs to end users of software was never to empower them to fix vulnerabilities due to third-party components on their own. Instead, it was so the end users could put pressure on suppliers to fix the vulnerabilities by patching them[114]. Even more importantly, the suppliers can feel the pressure without receiving a single phone call from a user. Just knowing that their customers will soon know a lot more about the risks posed by third-party components in their software (due to SBOMs, of course) is probably already having a huge impact on suppliers' interest in making their products as secure as possible, both before they ship them and afterwards.

The author has already pointed out multiple times that SBOMs are being heavily used by software suppliers to manage vulnerabilities in the products they are developing. In fact, the open source tool Dependency Track is now being used over 17 million times a day[115] to look up vulnerabilities in components found in an SBOM; that figure has grown 150% since April 2022.

What is driving that growth? Of course, a large part of it is simply more awareness – and a more receptive attitude – among software suppliers of the need for better supply chain security. But the author believes that the mere fact that awareness of SBOMs and their benefits among end users is also growing quickly, and that the required formats, best practices, etc. are being at least discussed by end users, has already inspired many software developers (especially the larger ones) to pay much more attention to the security of the third-party components in their products.

---

[114] A 2017 study by the software security company Veracode said, "A mere 52 percent of (software development) companies reported they provide security fixes to components when new security vulnerabilities are discovered. Despite an average of 71 vulnerabilities per application introduced through the use of third-party components, only *23 percent* reported testing for vulnerabilities in components at every release." (the author's emphasis)

[115] https://tomalrichblog.blogspot.com/2023/12/500-million.html

8. Advanced: The naming problem

As has already been mentioned, one of the two biggest impediments to widespread distribution and use of SBOMs is the naming problem. Briefly stated, this term refers to the fact that software products often are identified using different names, which leads to a lot of confusion; in most cases, there is no single arbiter or database that can resolve these discrepancies.

What makes the naming problem so important in the field of software security, and especially in SBOMs, is that it is very hard to learn about vulnerabilities associated with a software component without knowing how the component is named in a vulnerability database.

If the user looks up the wrong software name in a vulnerability database, they are likely not only to miss information but to receive false information, since the user will normally not have a way to determine if the response they received actually refers to the product they intended. For example (using common names, not actual software identifiers), suppose the user is looking for a product they know as "Uncle Charlie's whiz-bang operating system". When they enter that in the vulnerability database's search bar, they receive these two responses:

"Uncle Charlie whizzer operating system"

"Mr. Charlie's whiz-bang O/S"

Obviously, neither of these is a 100% match for what the end user searched for. Suppose the user guesses that the first response is the correct match and learns that this product is loaded with serious software vulnerabilities. The user might drop everything and start removing this operating system from its network (which would not be an easy job, of course). However, they might then learn that the product with so many vulnerabilities isn't in fact the one they use, meaning all this work will be wasted. Do they really want to take that chance?

On the other hand, suppose the user guesses that the second response is the right one and learns there are no vulnerabilities at all associated with that product. Does this mean they shouldn't worry at all about their operating system? Only if they're sure they guessed correctly. But how can they ever know that with certainty? And how can they be sure that the problem isn't that both of these responses are for different products than what they were searching for, while the software they know as "Uncle Charlie's whiz-bang operating system" isn't listed in this vulnerability database at all?

The naming problem manifests itself in two important ways (although there are others as well). The first is through the "aliasing problem". This problem is not specific to any vulnerability database, although it is much more significant for proprietary software than for open source software.

Examples of the aliasing problem include:

A product has been transferred from Supplier A to Supplier B, due to a merger or acquisition; moreover, the name of the product changed from "Sawdust" to "Happy Dust" after the transfer. Of course, software products are acquired and renamed all the time. If a user acquired the product when it was owned by Supplier A and they look up Sawdust today in a vulnerability database, it is likely they will never learn of *any* vulnerabilities that were reported for the product after it was acquired by Supplier B. By the same token, if the user bought the product (Happy Dust) after the acquisition by Supplier B, they will often not be able to learn of vulnerabilities that were reported for Sawdust by Supplier A before the acquisition, because they know the product only as Happy Dust.

Suppose the supplier of a product changed the method by which they represent versions in the product in 2019; for example, they moved from alphanumeric version strings such as "14A, 14B, 15C", etc. to a purely numeric string, as in the "semantic versioning[116]" scheme: "2.5.0, 2.5.1, 2.6.3", etc. When the supplier changed the versioning scheme, they set 2.5.0 as the first version in the new scheme. In 2024, an end user that is searching for previously identified vulnerabilities in that product, and searches for vulnerabilities reported before version 2.5.5 (the version they use), will probably just see vulnerabilities reported in versions after 2.5.0; versions that are before that will not be found in the search, since the versioning scheme changed. Thus, the user will probably never learn of vulnerabilities reported before 2019.

If the name of a product changed after version 3.4 (for example), a user of v3.4 might believe they have the latest version (meaning they are likely to have the most recent patches, etc.), since they won't find any versions later than v3.4 in a vulnerability database. There may have been six more versions issued under the new name, which that user will not normally see in their search.

All three of the above problems are aggravated by the fact that the end user will usually have no way of learning about what they are missing, since there is currently no authoritative source to learn of supplier name, product name, or versioning scheme changes.

---

[116] https://semver.org/

Steve Springett, leader of the OWASP Dependency Track and CycloneDX open source projects, has proposed a scheme called Common Lifecycle Enumeration, in which "lifecycle events" such as name changes, acquisitions, versioning scheme changes, etc. will be recorded in an online "ledger" by the entities responsible for those changes.

For example, if Supplier B has acquired Supplier A's Sawdust product and renamed it Happy Dust, they will record that fact in the ledger that includes Happy Dust. Thus, Happy Dust users that wish to learn about vulnerabilities that were identified in the product before it was renamed will be able to learn the previous name in the ledger.

Steve has started an online group[117] that is working on this problem. All interest and participation are welcome.

The second way that the naming problem manifests itself has to do with the National Vulnerability Database (NVD). This is the most widely used vulnerability database in the world; therefore, its problems are felt in many ways all over the world. The NVD's naming issues are mostly due to the idiosyncrasies of the identifier that the NVD is based on, Common Platform Enumeration (CPE)[118], as well as on how the NVD responds when a search doesn't turn up any records.

In early 2022, the author formed an informal group called the SBOM Forum (now the OWASP SBOM Forum), which meets weekly to discuss problems that are preventing SBOMs from being widely used, as well as to identify solutions to those problems. Early on, the group converged on the idea that the most important problem to address was naming – specifically, the naming problem in the NVD. Very few people who have been working in software vulnerability management, and especially SBOMs, have not been frustrated by problems with CPEs in the NVD – although all agree that the NVD is a valuable resource that needs to be sustained.

In September 2022, the SBOM Forum published a white paper containing a "proposal"[119] for addressing this problem. This paper has since received a lot of attention.

The proposal speaks for itself, although the author admits it is not an easy read. The centerpiece of the proposal is the purl identifier, which was briefly discussed earlier. Even though purl was only developed in the last 10-15 years, it has quickly become the paramount identifier of open source software.[120] This is

---

117

https://docs.google.com/document/d/1sRMS1IX0r7ZkYthDR0VY1bYyvp_6K_xw4 sR1vZwla8E/edit#heading=h.ja4fvxtw8jqu

[118] https://www.ipa.go.jp/en/security/vulnerabilities/cpe.html

[119] It is available at
https://owasp.org/assets/files/posts/A%20Proposal%20to%20Operationalize%20Co mponent%20Identification%20for%20Vulnerability%20Management.pdf.

[120] A somewhat more readable discussion of purl is in this blog post:
https://tomalrichblog.blogspot.com/2022/11/the-purl-in-your-future.html

why it is no exaggeration to say that CPE and purl are the only two software identifiers in use by major vulnerability databases today. The NVD and a few derivative databases based on the NVD utilize CPE; almost all other vulnerability databases utilize purl.

The most important feature of purl – and what is undoubtedly the hardest feature to understand – is that it requires no centralized database. Purl is based on the concept of a "download location". Open source projects are found in repositories, usually source code repositories and package managers. While there are other fields available in purl, the only three that are essential are the download location, the project name in that download location and the version number in that download location.

For example, a user searching a vulnerability database for vulnerabilities applicable to version 1.9.1 of the "batik-anim" package, which they downloaded from the Maven package manager, can follow the purl specification to learn that the purl for this package is "pkg:maven//batik-anim@1.9.1". Note that the user does not have to do a lookup to a central database, as is the case with CPE. Simply by knowing the purl syntax and using the three pieces of information mentioned above, they can construct the purl for this package.

Moreover, the user can be reasonably sure that any vulnerabilities that have been identified for that package will have been recorded against the same purl (as shown in the OWASP SBOM Forum white paper just referenced, this is definitely not the case for CPE, since even the NIST staff members responsible for assigning CPE names often violate the specification in doing so – meaning that simple searches for that name, based on the CPE specification, will often not be successful).

The OWASP SBOM Forum white paper provides a lengthy discussion of the advantages of "intrinsic identifiers" – those that don't rely on a central database, but instead can be constructed from information the user already has – vs. "extrinsic identifiers", which rely on a central database. This is the heart of the argument the paper makes for the superiority of purl over CPE, although there are other unrelated reasons why CPE is simply not a reliable identifier (see pages 4-6 of the white paper).

The white paper focuses on changes that could be made to the NVD to address this problem. The most important of these changes would be to allow vulnerabilities in a product to be identified by searching on a purl for the product, not just on a CPE (although CPE would not go away). However, this will require a previous change by the NVD[121], which itself may not happen for 3-4 years.

---

[121] Before the NVD can accept queries using purl, it must adopt the CVE JSON 5.1 specification, which allows both purl and CPE software identifiers to be included in CVE reports. However, before the NVD can adopt the 5.1 spec, they first need to

While the OWASP SBOM Forum wants to see the NVD adopt purl when it is able to do so, we also feel there needs to be a single vulnerability database that the entire world looks to as an authoritative source – a lot like the NVD is looked to today. Moreover, unlike the NVD, this database should not be tied to any one country.

Instead, this database should ultimately be run by a truly international organization like IANA[122] (which currently assigns IP addresses and runs DNS worldwide), which we have preliminarily named the Global Vulnerability Database (GVD); however, it will probably initially be developed by a group of private and public sector organizations from all parts of the world.

One big advantage of the GVD is that it could include other vulnerability identifiers than just CVEs. There are many other types of vulnerability identifiers, mostly tied to various open source repositories. The OSV[123] vulnerability database gathers together many of these identifiers; probably the best known of them is the GitHub Security Advisory (GHSA)[124]. Thus, besides supporting multiple software identifiers (at least CPE and purl), the GVD would support multiple vulnerability identifiers as well.

In fact, the Global Vulnerability Database[125] might very well not be a single database at all, but rather more of a "switching hub" among multiple vulnerability databases (including the NVD). The GVD would field queries referring to CPE and purl software identifiers, as well as to CVE and other vulnerability identifiers, and route them as appropriate among various vulnerability databases. Moreover, the answer to a query might combine results from multiple databases.

The existing vulnerability databases would remain as they are and be maintained independently. This means that the data in them would not need to be collected to a central point and "harmonized"; that would be quite expensive and perhaps completely unnecessary.

As of early 2024, all the above discussion is purely speculative. However, the naming problem continues to exact a big toll on the software security industry, including by making complete automation of SBOM production and consumption impossible. Given that fixing the naming problem in the NVD will take years and likely never be "complete", the easiest way to address the problem (but certainly not "solve" it, which may never happen) will be to design a new

---

adopt the 5.0 spec; they are currently having problems doing that. Since a lot more work will be required after the NVD adopts the 5.1 spec, this means it will probably be *at least* three years before the NVD can be said to support both purl and CPE identifiers. In the author's opinion, that is too long to wait, given what the naming problem is costing the software industry today.

[122] https://www.iana.org/

[123] https://osv.dev/

[124] https://github.com/advisories

[125] https://tomalrichblog.blogspot.com/2023/11/the-global-vulnerability-database-wont.html

vulnerability database from scratch, which includes everything that we know today should be included in such a database. Moreover, it needs to be a truly global database, meaning that public and private organizations worldwide (including the NVD, of course) will be able to contribute expertise and resources, and all organizations will be able to use the database.

If your organization would like to get involved with the Global Vulnerability Database effort and/or support it financially, please contact the author at tom@tomalrich.com.

Part Two: Introduction to VEX

9. Why do we need VEX?

VEX, which stands for "Vulnerability Exploitability Exchange", is a much-discussed concept in the SBOM community, but as of the beginning of 2024 it remains just a concept. There is no agreement on what VEX should be, and the few documents that have been published on VEX by the NTIA and CISA workgroups are incomplete and not consistent. Moreover, there are only a small number of software suppliers that regularly produce documents called "VEX" for distribution to customers, or that have even produced a demonstration VEX document. As of today, those documents are not based on a standard specification (which has not yet been developed).

Given that fact, why is the SBOM community even talking about VEX? They are doing this because VEX was intended to address an acutely perceived need: As suppliers started producing SBOMs for their own use and looked up vulnerabilities that applied to components in the SBOM, they realized that the great majority – probably at least 90% - of those component vulnerabilities were not exploitable[126] in the product itself – meaning that an attacker would not be able to utilize the vulnerability to compromise the product, even though the component, when considered as a separate product, was indeed affected by the vulnerability. The suppliers realized that, when they started regularly delivering SBOMs to customers, their help desks would start receiving huge numbers of calls and emails regarding what were in effect false positive vulnerability findings. This would be a big source of dissatisfaction for both help desk personnel and customers.

The suppliers decided there needed to be a way to proactively notify customers, after they had looked up vulnerabilities for the components shown in an SBOM in the NVD or another vulnerability database (using a tool like Dependency-Track or Daggerboard[127]), which of the component vulnerabilities they had identified were exploitable and which were not exploitable; these two designations (and two others, to be discussed later) are referred to as the "exploitability status" of a vulnerability.[128]

---

[126] For a discussion of "exploitability", see the Section titled "The concept of exploitability" immediately below.

[127] https://www.youtube.com/watch?v=zRLTXEObvas

[128] The Director of Product Security for a very large US software supplier, who was one of the three people who advocated for the VEX idea in the early days of the

The suppliers knew that if they could do this, their customers would know which component vulnerabilities pose a risk to them and which do not; that way, the customers could just pay attention to the former (and not bother the help desk about the latter, of course).

The suppliers also realized that, given the huge number of components that would be found in some software products – and the huge number of likely false positive vulnerability findings for those components – the notifications needed to be automated. Finally, the SBOMs and VEX documents would need to be incorporated into an automated component vulnerability management workflow.

Figure 2 below illustrates this workflow:

1. The user's tool ingests a new SBOM provided by the product's supplier. It includes a list of all the components in a particular version of the product.

2. The tool looks up each of the components in a vulnerability database like the NVD and makes a list of all the component vulnerabilities in this version of the product (we will refer to this as a "product/version" from now on).

3. The supplier issues a VEX document that refers to the product/version and provides the exploitability status of each component vulnerability.[129]

4. The tool ingests the VEX document and utilizes it to identify the component vulnerabilities that are not exploitable in a report. The user doesn't need to be concerned about those vulnerabilities.

5. As the supplier issues new VEX documents (which should be done whenever the exploitability status of any component vulnerability changes in the product/version), they will be ingested. The report will be reissued (or updated online) to reflect the current status

---

NTIA, points out that their need for VEX is somewhat different, although practically it amounts to the same thing: Since they patch all vulnerabilities in components of their products already, customers will not tie up their help desk lines demanding that those vulnerabilities be patched; they already know they will be patched.

However, because patches are available for all component vulnerabilities, customers are likely to waste a huge amount of time applying patches when they're not needed, unless they can be quickly notified which component vulnerabilities are exploitable and which are not. Using the 90% figure for non-exploitable component vulnerabilities, this means that, if a customer spends 20 hours applying patches, 18 of those hours will be wasted. This supplier would like to help their customers avoid this outcome.

[129] The status of some, or even most, vulnerabilities will initially be "under investigation", if the supplier has not yet determined their exploitability status.

designations (e.g., a vulnerability that was previously "under investigation" will now be determined not to be exploitable). This might be done daily.

6. Normally, the SBOM will not change until the version of the product changes. When that happens, the above process will restart from step 1.

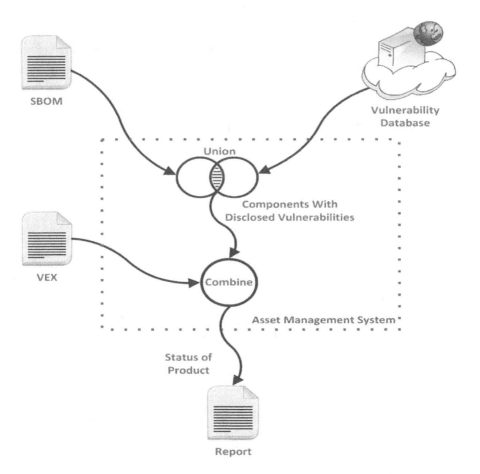

Figure 2: The first VEX use case [130]

As of the beginning of 2024, there are at least three machine-readable formats for VEX notifications, but there are no low-cost, commercially supported tools available that will ingest VEX information and incorporate it into an SBOM-based vulnerability management workflow, as shown in the diagram above. Perhaps for this reason, suppliers report minimal demand from customers (if any at all) for VEX notifications. After all, end users can't be expected to request VEX documents if they can't do anything useful with them.

---

[130] Taken from an unpublished document of the NTIA VEX working group, "VEX Overview", available at https://docs.google.com/document/d/10n3LA1wfD8MBwC-Od5INhd2OBStuW_dXmMoDiWL2rX4/edit

Today, the consensus in the software industry is that at least 90% of component vulnerabilities are not exploitable in the product itself[131], usually because of how the component was incorporated into the product. For example, a library may have four modules. However, the supplier of the software might have only needed to use one of them, so they did not install the other three. A serious vulnerability might be identified in one of the three uninstalled modules, but because the NVD will normally just list the library, not its modules, a search on the library's identifier will indicate that the library is vulnerable. Users may get upset because they believe the product is susceptible to the vulnerability, when in fact that is not the case.

Another reason why a vulnerability might not be exploitable in a product/version is that the supplier edited the vulnerable code out of an open source component before installing it in their product. Of course, the vulnerability databases have no way of knowing about that; they simply answer the question whether component ABC, when considered as a standalone product, is affected by CVE-12345. Only the supplier knows that they have edited the code of component ABC before installing it in their product.

Many security professionals may, when confronted with the above statistics, argue that the fact that only 3-10% of component vulnerabilities are exploitable is a good thing, not a bad thing. After all, this means the product's attack surface is 90 to 97% less than they might have thought originally. How can this be bad?

This would be a valid argument, were it not for one fact: The user doesn't know which component vulnerabilities constitute the exploitable 3% and which constitute the non-exploitable 97%. Without some way of learning this information, a prudent security professional should treat every component vulnerability as exploitable. What other choice do they have, except to possibly leave their organization unprotected when the next log4j incident occurs?

Of course, there are some organizations – those with high assurance needs, like hospitals and military contractors – that will go out of their way to treat *every*

---

[131] At the 2019 RSA Security Conference, Chris Wysopal of Veracode presented the results of a study that company did of customer codebases. The study found that only a small percentage of vulnerabilities in open source projects in languages like Java and Python are exploitable in the product itself. The slides from that presentation are here: https://www.rsaconference.com/library/presentation/usa/2019/how-understanding-risk-is-changing-for-open-source-components.

Also, a 2022 study indicated that 97% of identified component vulnerabilities in a software product are not in fact exploitable (the study used the word "attackable"): https://www.google.com/url?q=https://www.darkreading.com/application-security/open-source-software-bugs--attackability&sa=D&source=docs&ust=1661359395521475&usg=AOvVaw1syPSfjdlR6krnp_CvVP-9.

component vulnerability as exploitable. And there is good reason for that, since in some cases the supplier's judgment that a particular vulnerability is not exploitable in their product might be mistaken. It is also possible that a future code change in the product will inadvertently change the status of a component vulnerability from "not affected" (not exploitable) to "affected" (exploitable).

Of course, if organizations like this are going to consider every vulnerability to be exploitable, in theory they shouldn't need VEX documents; they just need to receive SBOMs and look up component vulnerabilities using a tool like Dependency Track – then press the supplier to fix every vulnerability[132].

However, it is safe to say that most end user organizations are already suffering under a big backlog of unpatched software vulnerabilities. They will be pleased to hear that at least 18 of every 20 component vulnerabilities they learn about are not exploitable in the product itself (although learning that requires the supplier to distribute VEX documents regularly, which is not usually happening now).

It is the author's opinion that SBOMs will never be widely distributed or used among any organizations besides software developers, until there is an automated and secure way for the developer to notify customers (or a service provider acting on their behalf) which component vulnerabilities are exploitable, and which are not exploitable, in a product/version they use. This is why it is imperative to find a way to make VEX work.

The concept of exploitability

VEX is based on a different concept of exploitability than what many security professionals think of when they hear that term. The more common use of the term "exploitable" refers to a probability: the probability that a particular vulnerability will be used to exploit software products in general. In this sense, exploitability depends on multiple factors, including whether exploit code is available, whether it is being actively used, etc.

The main use for this concept of exploitability is to prioritize how the organization patches vulnerabilities in the software it utilizes. The higher the likelihood that a vulnerability can be exploited, regardless of the system involved, the higher the priority that should be assigned to patching (or otherwise mitigating) the vulnerability wherever it is found on the organization's networks.

Note that this sense of "exploitable" is usually meant to apply to all products. That is, if the vulnerability (CVE) is highly exploitable in one product, it will be

---

[132] The Director of Product Security for one very large software supplier says his company patches every vulnerability, including component vulnerabilities, in their products; they do this because they have certain high-assurance customers who insist they do his. Even when his organization can prove to the customer that the vulnerable code is not even present in the product (e.g., the SBOM mistakenly listed a vulnerable component as being present in the product, when that was not the case), they insist on this – saying they need this for internal compliance purposes.

# Tom Alrich

highly exploitable in many other products in which it is found, unless mitigations have been applied to those products that make the vulnerability less exploitable. The EPSS score (Exploit Prediction Scoring System133) and CISA KEV Catalog (Known Exploited Vulnerabilities134) are based on this concept of exploitability.

By contrast, exploitability in VEX refers to the status of the vulnerability in a single version of a software product or intelligent device. It asks a single question: Can the vulnerable code (which is the source of a component vulnerability) be successfully attacked to take control of, or otherwise harm, the software product? This is equivalent to asking whether the product/version discussed in the VEX document is affected or not affected by the component vulnerability being considered. The answer to this question is referred to as the "status" (or the "exploitability status") of the vulnerability in the product/version.

However, it is somewhat misleading to describe the status of a vulnerability in a product/version as either "affected" or "not affected"135, with no middle ground possible. This is because there are environmental variables that will be specific to the network on which the application is deployed, or even to the desktop environment in which it is deployed; these environmental variables will be the final determinants of whether, in practice, a user experiences the vulnerability's VEX status to be the same as what the VEX document states. This is because, by necessity, the VEX document does not take account of anything unusual in the user's environment.

For example, a VEX document may indicate that a vulnerability is exploitable in a product/version, yet a common firewall setting (e.g. closing a particular port) may make the vulnerability not exploitable. If the firewall setting is considered a normal best practice by cybersecurity professionals, the supplier may instead want to list the vulnerability as not exploitable in a VEX document for the product/version, while at the same time reminding users about the need for this setting.

Therefore, while "affected" and "not affected" are valid status designations for a vulnerability in a product, they both need to be understood to be based on

---

[135] It is somewhat confusing that the two most important status designations in VEX – "affected" and "not affected" – refer to the status of the product with respect to the vulnerability (e.g., "Product A Version X is affected by CVE 12345"), whereas VEX is designed to answer a question about the status of the vulnerability with respect to the product/version (e.g., "CVE 12345 is exploitable in Product A Version X"). In the author's opinion, "exploitable" and "not exploitable" would have been better terms to use, and he can attest that the NTIA VEX working group considered using those terms early on. However, the group could never agree on a good definition of "exploitable" for VEX.

particular assumptions. While some standard assumptions do not need to be explicitly stated by the supplier (e.g., the user's version of Windows or Linux receives regular updates), other less standard assumptions do need to be stated.

The exploitability finding in VEX is used to determine whether the supplier needs to patch the vulnerability in the software product (or intelligent device) that the VEX notification applies to. If the vulnerability is exploitable in the product, it should normally be patched.136 If the vulnerability is not exploitable in the product, the supplier may not normally feel obligated to develop a patch, unless some customers require that this be done.

In most cases, the party producing the VEX document (indicated in the "author" field) will be the supplier (also called the developer) of the product. The supplier is usually the only entity that can make a binary assertion regarding exploitability, which is required by a VEX document. This is because a VEX assertion (or denial) of exploitability needs to be based on knowledge of the code in a product and how it works; it is very hard for an outside party to make a VEX assertion about a product, even if they have access to the source code.

While the "exploitability" discussed in this book refers to the VEX sense of the word, the common use of the term is probably more important for the average user organization. It is safe to say that the vulnerability management team at the average medium-to-large-size organization is overwhelmed with vulnerabilities to investigate. It is less important for them to know whether a particular vulnerability is exploitable in a particular product (the information that VEX provides them) than it is to know which vulnerabilities are most likely to be exploited, across all products installed on their network (i.e., the more common use of "exploitable").

In other words, the number one concern of these teams is triage: deciding which vulnerabilities they will prioritize in their patching efforts and which vulnerabilities do not need to be prioritized. VEX information does not help in triage, since it is absolute and therefore not subject to prioritization. Exploitability information in the common sense, such as EPSS scores and the KEV catalog, is much more helpful for prioritizing patching efforts. Once it is decided in the triage that a particular vulnerability should be next in line for patch application across all devices on the network, VEX information could then be considered, since a "not affected" VEX status for a particular software product or device means that product does not need to receive the patch for the vulnerability in question.

This table compares the two types of exploitability:

---

136 If the supplier of the product has already agreed with end users that vulnerabilities (CVEs) that have for example a CVSS or EPSS score below a specified threshold (or that meet some other criterion or criteria) do not need to be patched, the supplier may not patch vulnerabilities that do not meet this threshold, even if they are exploitable in the product in the VEX sense. However, these criteria need to be at least announced in advance; they cannot be revised with every new vulnerability.

Type of Exploita-bility	Absolute or Percent	Applies to Vulnerability or Product	Question answered	Possible answer values	Main use
Common (e.g. in EPSS or KEV)	Percentage	Vulnerability	How likely is it that this vulnerability can be exploited in products in general?	0-100%	Prioritization of patching efforts
VEX	Absolute	Product	Can this vulnerability be exploited in this particular product and version?	Yes or no	Determining whether a component vulnerability poses any risk at all to the user of a product, and therefore whether the supplier should develop a patch for it.

Who can determine exploitability in the VEX sense?

While it may sometimes be necessary to have a party other than the supplier determine whether a component vulnerability is exploitable in the full product, it is certainly true that the person or organization that developed the code for the product will be able to make the most informed decision on that subject.

However, in many cases, including most open source projects, there is no single individual responsible (and compensated) for determining whether component vulnerabilities are exploitable in the project/product or not; thus, it is likely there will be no authoritative information available about exploitability of component vulnerabilities in the software, and no VEX documents will be released.

In such cases, probably the best course of action is for the user to assume that all component vulnerabilities are exploitable in the product itself, then remove from this list of exploitable vulnerabilities all that do not meet the organization's current prioritization criteria (for example, EPSS or CVSS score that is below a certain level).

In making an assertion about whether a vulnerability can be exploited in their product, the supplier normally makes several standard assumptions. If the supplier has not made these assumptions in a particular case, it is important for them to inform the user of that fact, usually in a text field or even in a separate note. These assumptions may include:

The attacker is of average skill. If a vulnerability is only exploitable by a super-hacker who knows every trick in the book, it is not exploitable in the VEX sense. If super-hackers were the norm, then almost every vulnerability would be exploitable in any product. Of course, users with high assurance use cases, like large hospitals, critical infrastructure providers and military contractors, will often assume they face primarily super-hackers. But even for these users, there are some component vulnerabilities that can safely be ignored. See the discussion of Status Justifications later in this Part.

The attacker will not use "chained" or "side-channel" attacks. These are attacks that start with exploit of a different vulnerability, then move "laterally" within the product to exploit the vulnerability addressed in the VEX. Because it is impossible to enumerate every possible side-channel attack, a definitive assertion regarding VEX exploitability would never be possible if these attacks had to be considered. Again, a high assurance user might well assume they will face skilled hackers who will be able to utilize these more complex attacks, but other users may not need to make that assumption.

The software product has been installed in the configuration recommended by the developer. This includes the configuration of the software itself, as well as recommended network configuration, especially whether it should be connected to the internet. For example, if the attack can be blocked by not connecting the device to the internet, this does not mean the vulnerability is not exploitable in the VEX sense. Rather, the vulnerability *is* exploitable, and disconnecting the device from the internet is a mitigation for the vulnerability. However, if the supplier normally recommends that the device on which their software is installed not be connected to the internet, then the supplier might identify the vulnerability as not exploitable in a VEX document.[137]

---

[137] There is one caveat to this caveat: The supplier should never include in their documentation a recommendation not to attach a device to the internet, when they know it will be difficult for the device to be used properly if it is not connected. A supplier might do this so they can use it later as a "Get out of jail free" card in the event their product is hacked, e.g., "We told you not to connect it to the internet!" This gambit probably would not work from a legal point of view, but more importantly, it is a terrible trick to pull on their customers.

Status designations

Vulnerabilities listed in a VEX document need to have one of these four status designations:

- "affected" (the vulnerability is exploitable in the product/version),
- "not affected" (the vulnerability is not exploitable in the product/version),
- "under investigation" (the supplier has not yet determined whether the vulnerability is exploitable in the product/version), and
- "fixed" (the vulnerability has been patched in the product/version, meaning it is no longer exploitable).

Note that, when a supplier fixes a vulnerability in Version 1.0.0 of a product, the number of the fixed version will be different, perhaps 1.0.1. This is because, since the code has been changed from what was in version 1.0.0, the version number should change as well. Version 1.0.0 should retain the "affected" status with respect to the vulnerability in question, since the fix was not applied in that version. This serves as a notification to anyone in the future who still uses an unpatched version 1.0.0, that they need to download and apply the patch as soon as possible.

The status designations of component vulnerabilities in a product/version need to be continually updated. That is, whenever the exploitability status of any vulnerability in the list changes (for example, a vulnerability that was previously "under investigation" is now determined to be "affected"), this change should immediately be reflected in the list of component vulnerabilities[138] and a new VEX document should be provided to customers. Thus, the user should always be working with the most recent information.

Just as a status justification is required whenever the status of a vulnerability is "not affected", a "mitigation" is required whenever a vulnerability has an "affected" status. This is a short text field that describes a mitigation that the user should apply to the vulnerability. The two most common mitigations are "Apply patch ABC, available at (URL XYZ.com)" and "Upgrade to most recent

---

[138] Not only should the list be continually updated with changes in exploitability status of vulnerabilities, but it should also be updated whenever a new vulnerability is identified for one of the product's components. In other words, the user's tool (or the third-party service provider's tool) should check at least once a day to learn if there are new vulnerabilities listed for either the first-party product/version or for third-party components included in the product/version. Any new vulnerabilities should be added to the list for the product/version. Component vulnerabilities should initially be assigned a status of "under investigation", but the supplier should act as quickly as possible to determine whether the status of each vulnerability is "affected" or "not affected".

supported version" (or perhaps "Upgrade to version 4.2"). If a longer description of the mitigation than will fit in the field is required, the field can contain a URL pointing to the description.

Status justifications

When a supplier decides that a component vulnerability is not exploitable in the product/version and lists the status of that vulnerability as "not affected", they should provide a "status justification" for this statement. A status justification is simply a supplier's statement of the reason why they consider a vulnerability not to be exploitable in the product/version that is the subject of the VEX document. For a good discussion of status justifications, see the 2022 CISA document, "Vulnerability Exploitability Exchange (VEX) - Status Justifications".139

In 2021, the CycloneDX (CDX) VEX format was the first to include status justifications, although they are called "justifications" in CDX. There are nine possible justifications, all of which are machine-readable. They are:

- requires_dependency = exploitability requires a dependency that is not present.
- code_not_present = the code has been removed or tree-shaked[140].
- code_not_reachable = the vulnerable code is not invoked at runtime.
- requires_configuration = exploitability requires a configurable option[141] to be set/unset.
- requires_environment = exploitability requires a certain environment which is not present.
- protected_by_compiler = exploitability requires a compiler flag to be set/unset.
- protected_at_runtime = exploits are prevented at runtime.
- protected_at_perimeter = attacks are blocked at physical, logical, or network perimeter[142].

---

139 https://www.cisa.gov/sites/default/files/publications/VEX_Status_Justification_Jun22.pdf

[140] https://developer.mozilla.org/en-US/docs/Glossary/Tree_shaking

[141] The configurable option should not be part of the supplier's normal configuration recommendation.

[142] This justification is only valid if the supplier has instructed the user to take particular measures during installation of the product, such as blocking a particular firewall port. Absent such instructions, the user cannot be expected to have taken whatever steps are required, unless they are considered to be a universal best practice, such as requiring authentication for remote access. If the supplier has not provided those instructions, the state of the vulnerability should be listed as "affected" in the

- protected_by_mitigating_control = preventative measures have been implemented that reduce the likelihood and/or impact of the vulnerability.

The CISA document explains the concept of status justifications and provides a detailed discussion of five specific justifications. After the CISA document was developed in 2022, these five status justifications were included in the CSAF format, so they can be included in VEX documents prepared using CSAF (they are not referred to as "status justifications" in the CSAF specification, but "flags"). The five status justifications and their CycloneDX (CDX) equivalents are:

- Component_not_present *(equivalent of "requires_dependency" in CDX VEX)*
- Vulnerable_code_of_component_not_present *(equivalent of "code_not_present" in CDX VEX)*
- Vulnerable_code_cannot_be_controlled_by_adversary *(there is no precise equivalent in CDX VEX, but the "protected_by_compiler", "protected_at_runtime", and "protected_at_perimeter" justifications in CDX provide a more fine-grained coverage of this concept)*
- Vulnerable_code_not_in_execute_path *(equivalent of "code_not_reachable" in CDX VEX)*
- Inline_mitigations_already_exist *(equivalent of "protected_by_mitigating_control" in CDX VEX)*

If none of the nine "justifications" (in CDX VEX) or the five "status justifications" (in CSAF VEX) corresponds to the reason why the supplier asserts that a vulnerability is not exploitable in the product/version, both VEX formats provide the supplier the option of utilizing a text field to explain the reason for the "not affected" status. This field is called "detail" in CDX and "details" in CSAF.

Why is it useful for an end user organization to have a machine-readable status justification in a VEX document? One likely use case is found in an organization that believes it is subject to attacks by hackers with an above-average level of sophistication. Organizations like this might include hospitals, military contractors or electric utilities; this book calls them "high assurance users".

---

product/version, and any measures required to block exploitation of the vulnerability should be listed as mitigations.

Because these high assurance organizations believe (with ample justification, in many cases) that they are subject to more sophisticated attacks, they might decide that some of the status justifications don't apply in their case; as a result, if a supplier points to one of these justifications as the reason why they say the status of a vulnerability is "not affected", these organizations will instead treat the status as "affected".

In other words, these organizations will not take the supplier's word that a component vulnerability is not exploitable in their product; they will investigate it themselves. They may also press the supplier to patch the vulnerability, even though the supplier lists its status as "not affected". The machine-readable status justification will help them separate vulnerabilities they want to investigate from those they do not need to investigate.

For example, the CycloneDX "code_not_reachable" justification ("vulnerable code not in execute path" in CSAF VEX) indicates that, even though the code that implements the vulnerability is present in the product/version used by the customer, the supplier has determined that an attacker of average skill will not be able to reach it if they attack the product; therefore, the supplier has assigned this vulnerability a status of "not affected".

While this justification might be acceptable for most organizations, it might not be acceptable for a large hospital. The hospital might decide that the supplier's assurance that the code is not reachable by the average attacker does not in itself provide sufficient reason for them to ignore the vulnerability, since they have always assumed (with ample justification, given the large number of hospitals that have been hit hard by ransomware attacks in recent years, causing patient deaths in some cases) that they face above-average attackers. Thus, the hospital may still try to get the supplier to patch the vulnerability and – if the supplier will not do that – they may apply an alternative mitigation to the vulnerability, including possibly removing the vulnerable device from their network altogether.

On the other hand, if the supplier lists "code_not_present" as the justification for a "not_affected" state, the hospital might decide this provides sufficient assurance to them that they cannot be attacked using this vulnerability. This is because the vulnerable code isn't even in the product and therefore can't be exploited by any attacker, no matter their skill level. Thus, they might decide they do not have to investigate this vulnerability any further. The following table illustrates how a "typical" user organization and a large hospital might differ:

CDX "state" of vulnerability	"justification"	Typical user organization will:	Atypical user organization (e.g., large hospital) will:
"not affected"	"code_not_reachable"	Treat vulnerability as not exploitable	Treat vulnerability as exploitable
"not affected"	"code_not_present"	Treat vulnerability as not exploitable	Treat vulnerability as not exploitable

There are two CDX VEX justifications that are likely to be considered valid, even by a high assurance user:

- "code_not_present" ("Vulnerable_code_of_component_not_present" in CSAF VEX). In this case, the vulnerable code has been removed from the product, perhaps because the supplier removed it from an open source component that normally contains the vulnerability.
- "requires dependency" ("Component not present" in CSAF). In this case, a vulnerable component that was listed in the SBOM was later found not to be in the product after all (perhaps because it was misidentified to begin with). Therefore, the vulnerability is not in the product.

In both cases, one can say there is no possibility that the vulnerability in question can be exploited to attack the product. Therefore, when a high assurance user encounters one of these two justifications, they might leave the status of the vulnerability at "not affected". However, if the same user encounters any of the other justifications, they might consider the status of the vulnerability to be "affected".

When tools are developed to ingest SBOMs and VEX documents and output exploitable component vulnerabilities, they will hopefully allow the user to decide for themselves which justifications they consider to be inherently valid (e.g., "requires dependency") and which they consider inherently invalid (e.g., "code not reachable"). In the former cases, the status of the vulnerability would remain as "not affected", while in the latter cases, the tool would change the vulnerability's status from "not affected" to "affected".

10. Advanced: The two principal VEX use cases

There are two principal use cases for VEX. The first is more important and is the one that the VEX concept was developed for. In this use case, a supplier has released an SBOM for one of their products to customers of that product; some of their customers have used a tool like Dependency Track[143] or Daggerboard[144] to identify vulnerabilities that affect components listed in the SBOM. They are now requesting that the supplier patch all the component vulnerabilities they have identified.

The supplier knows that most vulnerabilities in third-party components included in a software product are not exploitable in the product itself. The supplier wishes to prevent both customers and the supplier's own staff members from wasting huge amounts of time discussing, and in some cases patching, component vulnerabilities that are not exploitable in their product. The supplier wishes to inform their customers which vulnerabilities are exploitable[145] in their product and which are not exploitable; the supplier believes it is safe for the customers to ignore the latter vulnerabilities.

However, it is often quite hard to determine whether a vulnerability is exploitable in a software product. For that reason, especially immediately after an SBOM has been released, there will be many component vulnerabilities for which the supplier can only notify the user that the vulnerability is "under investigation". As time goes on, the supplier will determine whether at least some of the "under investigation" vulnerabilities are exploitable and will provide updated information to their customers (along with patches for exploitable component vulnerabilities).[146]

---

[143] https://dependencytrack.org/

[144] https://www.youtube.com/watch?v=zRLTXEObvas

[145] In general, a supplier should never notify their customers of an exploitable vulnerability in their product without first having developed a patch and made it available to their customers (or at least recommended an upgrade strategy to a version of their product which is not affected by the vulnerability). At the same time as they inform their customers of an exploitable vulnerability, they should file a CVE report with CVE.org.

[146] Of course, there needs to be a limit to the supplier's deliberations. If, after a certain period (perhaps three months?), the supplier still has not determined the exploitability status of a component vulnerability in a version of one of their products, they should either patch the vulnerability or replace the component with a new or upgraded component that is not affected by the vulnerability. This requirement should

There are two types of vulnerabilities that the user must be told about:

Component vulnerabilities that are exploitable in the full product. It might be said that the main purpose of analyzing an SBOM for vulnerability management purposes is to derive the list of component vulnerabilities that are exploitable in the product. As soon as they have developed a patch for an exploitable component vulnerability, the supplier should report the vulnerability to their customers, along with information on patching the vulnerability or upgrading to a patched version of the product. The supplier should also report the vulnerability to CVE.org.

Component vulnerabilities that are not exploitable in the product/version, or that are still under investigation. At first, it might seem odd to say that the user needs to learn about both exploitable and non-exploitable component vulnerabilities in a product/version; after all, the only vulnerabilities that pose a threat to the user are those that are exploitable.

However, not only does the user need to know more than just the list of component vulnerabilities that the supplier believes to be exploitable in the product/version; they need to know about the *total set* of vulnerabilities that the supplier considered in the first place. After all, if a supplier missed some component vulnerabilities when they looked for them in the NVD, they may have never known about a serious vulnerability that could turn out to be exploitable in the product/version.

How can the user learn which component vulnerabilities the supplier considered? They can review the set of vulnerabilities shown in the most recent VEX document for the product/version under consideration and compare that to the set of vulnerabilities identified by Dependency Track or another tool, based on the SBOM received for the product/version. Do the two sets have approximately the same number of vulnerabilities? If so, the supplier probably did not "miss" many component vulnerabilities.

But what if the supplier's list (shown in the VEX document) is much smaller than the list shown by Dependency Track? The user should then send the comparison to the supplier and ask why the supplier identified so many fewer

---

be enforced by customers, although trying to use contract language for this purpose, when there is still so much ambiguity about SBOM and VEX, would be a useless exercise and would likely more than offset any benefit derived from it.

Software customers also need to understand there are some vulnerabilities that pose so little risk to their organization that requiring the supplier to patch them will cost more than any benefit derived from doing so. If customers and suppliers agree on criteria for determining which vulnerabilities to patch and which ones not to patch, the supplier should be allowed to follow those criteria and not be pressured to patch every vulnerability, regardless of its importance.

component vulnerabilities – and suggest the supplier start tracking the status of these vulnerabilities as well.[147]

Addressing the first VEX use case

Given that the average software product has close to 150 components[148] and each component can have vulnerabilities, this means the VEX list for a particular product/version may change regularly, perhaps daily. This means suppliers may need to distribute a VEX document daily for every supported version of every software product or intelligent device that they produce.

Needless to say, distributing updated VEX documents daily for all supported product versions of all products would require a lot of work on the part of suppliers. Is there a way that suppliers can provide their customers the near-real-time information on the exploitability of component vulnerabilities that they need, without having to distribute a huge volume of documents to those customers every day? Indeed, there is (or rather, will be). Please see the Section titled "Transparency Exchange API" in Chapter 4 above.

The first VEX use case is essentially the same as the use case identified originally by the NTIA Software Component Transparency Initiative in 2020, when discussion of the VEX concept began. However, at that time, the NTIA initiative believed that VEX documents would consist mostly of negative vulnerability notifications like "CVE-2023-12345 is not exploitable in Product A Version X" and not positive vulnerability notifications like "CVE-2023-12345 is exploitable in Product A Version X. Please apply patch ABCD to Version X as soon as possible." The author now believes that a VEX document should provide exploitability status information for all component vulnerabilities identified using the SBOM for a product/version.

To summarize, a VEX document intended to address the first VEX use case should contain the following information (note that these items will be contained in different fields in CycloneDX VEX than in CSAF VEX). This information is all specific to one version of one product:

- Metadata required by the format;
- Name and identifier for the product[149] (the identifier needs to allow lookup in a vulnerability database, meaning it must be either a purl or a CPE name);

---

[147] When available, the user tool will perform this comparison automatically and notify the supplier about any discrepancy.

[148] Source: https://www.sonatype.com/resources/white-paper-state-of-the-software-supply-chain-2020

[149] To avoid confusion initially, the author recommends that only one product/version be discussed in one VEX document. Later, as use of VEX increases and consumption tools improve, this recommendation might be relaxed.

- Version string(s) for the product;[150]
- Component vulnerabilities that are exploitable in the full product (i.e. their status is "affected")[151];
- Component vulnerabilities that have been determined by the supplier not to be exploitable in the full product (status is "not affected");
- Component vulnerabilities that are "under investigation" or "fixed";
- For each "not affected" status designation, a status justification;
- For each "affected" status designation, a mitigation;
- As required, information on a vulnerability, such as CVSS score, EPSS score, CWEs[152], etc.

Consuming VEX documents in the first use case

Consuming – or using – VEX documents needs to be tightly integrated with the process of consuming SBOMs and vice versa. While both SBOMs and VEX documents need to be consumed by an automated process, it is possible to describe this process in a non-automated fashion, as below. Note that the discussion below also serves as the discussion of the component vulnerability management use case for SBOMs. Both SBOMs and VEX documents are needed for proper component vulnerability management, and the use cases for both document types are tightly intertwined.

It is best to think of the process of utilizing SBOMs and VEX documents for software component vulnerability management purposes as one of developing and maintaining lists of component vulnerabilities in one or more software versions which are in use by an organization; these are stored in a database and

---

[150] A single VEX document can address multiple versions of the product, as well as multiple version ranges.

[151] Of course, in general there should never be a statement that a product is affected by a vulnerability, unless there is a notification of a patch available for that vulnerability, or another mitigation. Note that when the patch is applied, the version string will change. This means the original version retains the "affected" status, but the version with the patch applied has a different version number. The "mitigation" field in the VEX document should contain information on how to download the patch, a fixed version to which the user should upgrade, or another mitigation for the vulnerability.

[152] CWE stands for "Common Weakness Enumeration" (https://cwe.mitre.org/).

updated daily (i.e., as new vulnerabilities are identified for components in the SBOM for the product/version[153]).

Each component vulnerability needs to have a status designation. When the vulnerability is first identified, its status will be "under investigation". The database of component vulnerabilities will contain all the fields in a VEX document. As new VEX documents arrive from the supplier for the same product/version, the consumption tool will insert any new or changed information into the database, including any revised status designations (e.g., changing the status of a vulnerability from "under investigation" to "affected" or "not affected").

The database will contain the most recent information on vulnerabilities found in a product/version, including their current status designations. The user organization should be able to retrieve from the database, for a particular product/version, an up-to-date list of all vulnerabilities, a list of all vulnerabilities with "affected" or "not affected" status, etc. The list can be retrieved in a format necessary for ingestion into a vulnerability or asset management tool.

Below are the main steps for populating and updating the database:

The consumption process begins with parsing an SBOM and loading into the database the name and version string of the product, as well as other information about the product, such as a CPE or purl identifier.[154]

Whenever a new SBOM is provided for the same product, it will have a different version number and its own set of components. Even if the components in one version of a product are identical to those in another version, the two versions still need to be maintained separately. In other words, *there needs to be a unique list of component vulnerabilities for every version of the product that is included in the component vulnerability database*, even for minor and patched versions (of course, not all versions of a product need to be included in the database – just those versions that are in use by the organization).

Either simultaneously or subsequently, another process will look up each of the components of the product in the NVD or another vulnerability database, to find vulnerabilities that apply to them. These are loaded into the database. The "status" of each of these vulnerabilities will default to "under investigation" until one or more VEX documents are received from the supplier, that change status designations of vulnerabilities.

---

[153] There should be a one-to-one correspondence between product versions and SBOMs. Any change in the code or components of the product should be designated a new version with its own SBOM. This means that an SBOM for a product/version will usually never change; when the code changes, the version number will change and a new SBOM should be generated.

[154] Information about the components listed in the SBOM can be loaded into the component vulnerability database as well. However, since it is not necessary to have a list of components in order to create or use a VEX document, this should be an optional step, not the default. Note that neither of the two VEX use cases described in this chapter requires information about the components themselves to be present.

For each product/version in the database, the tool will regularly (presumably daily) monitor the NVD (or another vulnerability database or databases) for new component vulnerabilities that have appeared. Whenever a new vulnerability is identified for a component of that product/version, it will be added to the list for that product/version, with an initial status of "under investigation".[155]

Additional information on the status of component vulnerabilities in the product/version will be received in VEX documents. There can be at least four results of this process:

The component vulnerability is not exploitable ("not affected") in this product/version. The supplier enters a status of "not affected" for the vulnerability in the VEX database. The supplier must also enter a status justification, using one of the nine CycloneDX VEX "justifications" or one of the five CSAF "Status Justifications".

The component vulnerability is exploitable ("affected") in the product/version. Normally, the supplier will not change the status of a vulnerability to "affected", unless they have released a patch for the vulnerability. When the user applies the patch, the version number of their instance of the software should change to that of the patched version. The supplier will issue a new VEX document for the patched version which lists the vulnerability as "fixed" or "unaffected", but they should leave the status in the vulnerable version at "affected", along with listing the URL to download the patch in the "mitigation" field. This will serve as a reminder to any user that has not yet applied the patch, that they need to do so as soon as

The component vulnerability is exploitable in the product/version, but it does not meet the organization's threshold for riskiness; therefore, it will not be patched. In this case, the supplier needs to set the status to "affected", but enter in the "mitigation" field something like "Will not fix. Does not meet (Supplier Name)'s criteria for risk[156]."

The component vulnerability in the product and version specified has been patched. If the supplier has already patched the vulnerability in question, there is

---

[155] When a user discovers a new component vulnerability that the supplier of the product/version has not been tracking so far, the consumption tool should notify the supplier of the newly identified vulnerability and confirm whether the supplier will track the vulnerability. Normally, the supplier should reply in the affirmative, and will initially assign the vulnerability the status of "under investigation". The supplier will later determine whether the status is "affected" or "not affected".

[156] The supplier needs to establish and publish for its customers what its criteria are for determining the degree of risk posed by a vulnerability, as well as make clear the threshold below which the supplier will not patch an exploitable vulnerability. The supplier should never change the criteria without notifying customers beforehand.

obviously nothing more to be done, except for the user to apply the patch or upgrade to a patched version. The patched version of the product will have the status "fixed".

At any time, the database should contain the most recent status information for all component vulnerabilities in each product/version in use by the user organization. The end user organization should be able to retrieve that information at any time.

The user organization will be able to use this information to:

1. Search on their networks for the exploitable vulnerabilities in the product/version(s) in which the vulnerabilities are found, using a vulnerability or asset management tool. The searches will verify that the vulnerabilities are in fact present in their environment;

2. Coordinate with the suppliers of the products used by the organization by phone or email, to determine when exploitable vulnerabilities will be patched; and

3. Apply patches to the proper devices.

It is important to note that having a list of exploitable vulnerabilities in various product/versions does not in itself provide any information on prioritization of the organization's vulnerability and patch management activities.

Since VEX information only applies to a particular version of a particular product, it is not useful for coordinating vulnerability and patch management activities across an organization, because such coordination must be enterprise wide. EPSS or KEV information, which applies to the exploitability of individual vulnerabilities across *all* products, is much more useful for prioritization of vulnerability and patch management activities.

To summarize the first VEX use case, it provides a user organization with a regularly updated list of all component vulnerabilities that are present in a software product/version that they utilize, along with the current exploitability status (as well as the status justification and mitigation, where applicable) of each component vulnerability. The user organization can retrieve the current list at any time and utilize it in their vulnerability management activities, as described above.

VDR

In early 2022, the National Institute of Standards and Technologies (NIST) published a three-sentence paragraph in an appendix to the new version of SP 800-161, which reads:

Enterprises, where applicable and appropriate, may consider providing customers with a Vulnerability Disclosure Report (VDR) to demonstrate proper and complete vulnerability assessments for components listed in SBOMs. The VDR should include the analysis and findings describing the impact (or lack of impact) that the reported vulnerability has on a component or product. The VDR should also contain information on plans to address the CVE.

VDRs are now considered by some to be superior to VEX, for two reasons:

VDR includes both exploitable and non-exploitable vulnerabilities, whereas the original VEX idea was that it would primarily include the latter. However, as discussed earlier, the author believes that VEX should include both exploitable and non-exploitable component vulnerabilities.

VDR includes a) a description of the impact of the vulnerability on the product, as well as b) the supplier's plans to address the vulnerability. Of course, b) just refers to the "mitigation" field in a VEX document, which is filled in when the status of a vulnerability is "affected". a), "the impact of the vulnerability on the product", is not a field that is addressed in the VEX formats. It would most likely need to be addressed in a text field, or the supplier might communicate this to their customers in a non-machine-readable context like email.

The author's opinion is that it is important for the user to learn of both exploitable and non-exploitable vulnerabilities found in a software product they rely on; it is also important for this list to be updated at least daily, as new component vulnerabilities are identified or as the supplier changes their judgment of the exploitability status of vulnerabilities that are already included in the list. Whether the document is called VEX, VDR or something else is less important than what it does.

The second VEX use case: vulnerability and patch notifications

The first VEX use case answers the questions, "What component vulnerabilities are found in a software product and version that I operate?" and "What is the exploitability status of each vulnerability?" These questions arise when a software user has received an SBOM from the supplier of the product and identified component vulnerabilities using a tool like Dependency Track.

As described earlier, the answer to these questions is a list of component vulnerabilities in the product/version described in the SBOM[157] and the exploitability status of each one: "affected" (along with a mitigation), "not affected" (along with a status justification), "under investigation" or "fixed".

It is instructive to consider the characteristics of this first use case:

It applies to a single version of a product – the one that the user operates. If the user happens to operate multiple versions of the same product, they need to

---

[157] An SBOM always refers to a single version of a single product.

receive separate VEX documents for each version. In this use case, it makes no sense to address more than one version of a product at a time.

The purpose of the first use case is to provide software users with a complete list of the vulnerabilities found in the components in a product/version that they utilize, along with the exploitability status of each one.

The information provided in this first use case is urgently needed by the user. This is because, if a user does not know which component vulnerabilities are exploitable in the product and which are not, the prudent course is for them to assume they are all exploitable. Then the customer may contact the supplier's help desk about each component vulnerability. Since at least 90% of those vulnerabilities on average will prove not to be exploitable, this will result in a big waste of both the customer's and the help desk's time.

The purpose of the second use case is to notify customers of one or more exploitable component vulnerabilities that have been patched in a product (in most cases, if a component vulnerability is exploitable and has not yet been patched, the supplier should not release any information about it until a patch or alternate mitigation is available). Because any change to the code of a software product, including application of a patch, requires that a new version number be created for the patched version, this use case always involves at least two versions of a product, and sometimes more than that.

The simplest example of the second use case is the following statements in a VEX document (which might be called the "basic patching use case"). The document notifies the customer that version 3.2.0 of Product ABC is affected by CVE-2023-12345.

The status of CVE-2023-12345 is "affected" in version 3.2.0 of Product ABC (i.e., version 3.2.0 is affected by this vulnerability).

The user's mitigation is to apply the patch available at URL patchID.suppliername.com or to upgrade to the patched version 3.2.1.[158]

When the patch was applied to version 3.2.0, the patched version was designated as 3.2.1 (this follows the rules for semantic versioning, in which the first two integers designate the major and minor versions respectively, and the third integer designates the patch level). Therefore, the status of CVE-2023-12345 is "fixed" in version 3.2.1 of Product ABC.

A more generalized version of the second use case is:

One or more supported versions of Product ABC are "affected" by CVE-2023-12345. Other versions are "not affected".

---

[158] When a patch is applied to for example version 5.1 of a product, application of the patch should increment the version number of the user's installed instance of the product to the patched version number, say 5.15. However, if the version number does not change after the user applies a patch to their instance of the product, it is up to the user to record that their instance of the product is now the patched version number, in case the user needs technical support later.

The supplier develops a mitigation for every affected version, either a patch or an upgrade to a patched version.

The patched versions all have a different number from the corresponding versions before they were patched. Their status is "fixed".

For an example of a VEX document for the generalized second use case, see the Section titled "C. Single Product, Multiple versions, Single Vulnerability, Multiple Statuses" in Chapter 15.

Comparing the first and second VEX use cases

The table below compares the two VEX use cases just discussed:

Use Case	Number of Products	Number of versions	Number of vulnerabilities	Purpose of Use Case
1	1	1	No limit	Maintain continually updated list of all component vulnerabilities in the product, along with exploitability status of each.
2	1	2 or more	1 or more (1 preferred)	Identify versions affected by the vulnerability and list a mitigation (usually a patch or an update) for each. Identify updated versions.

11. Fields in a VEX document

There are currently two formats in which a VEX document can be created: CycloneDX and CSAF[159]. In a later Section, we will discuss these two formats in general terms and provide examples of both CycloneDX[160] and CSAF VEX documents. This Section describes the fields that need to be included in a VEX document, regardless of which format is used.

In 2022, the VEX working group, operating under CISA's auspices, published a document titled "Vulnerability Exploitability Exchange (VEX) Use Cases".[161] This document included (on pages 2-3) a section titled "Minimum Data Elements". Of course, this document has no regulatory force, but the "data elements" (more commonly called "fields") listed are all sensible ones. All of them are included in the list below, although with some slight modifications.

A VEX document that can be used to meet both the first and second VEX use cases should include the following fields. Some of these fields are required for the document to be useful; the other fields are optional. Any tool for producing or consuming VEX documents in either CycloneDX or CSAF format will need to support at least these fields:

---

[159] In 2023, a new VEX format called OpenVEX (https://github.com/openvex/spec/blob/main/OPENVEX-SPEC.md) was introduced. This format was designed to address the use case of removing non-exploitable vulnerabilities from results generated by a vulnerability scanner. Since that is not the use case discussed in this book and OpenVEX does not support product versions as an independent field (which, in the author's opinion, is essential for a VEX format), this format will not be discussed further here.

[160] The reader may have noted that CycloneDX is also an SBOM format. In fact, the CycloneDX "engine" can be the basis for at least 11 different document types: https://cyclonedx.org/capabilities/

[161] Available at https://www.cisa.gov/sites/default/files/publications/VEX_Use_Cases_Aprill2022.pdf

Metadata

The VEX document needs to include the VEX Format Identifier, the Identifier string for the VEX document, the Author and the Timestamp. Of course, these are different in the two formats.

Product or component name

This is the name by which a product or component that is referred to in the VEX document is commonly known. Since vulnerability databases are indexed on specific identifiers for products (CPE or purl), not common names, this field is included primarily so that a casual user reading through the document will be able to understand what the VEX is about.

The author's opinion is that a VEX document should normally only refer to one product, although it will often refer to multiple versions of that product. This is not because there is something wrong with producing a single VEX for multiple products, but rather because this guideline will initially make it much easier to create both supplier and consumer VEX tooling. Later, this guideline can be relaxed.

Product or component version string

The purpose of listing versions of a product is for there to be an objective way to track any changes that have been made in the code of the product. This includes changes in included components or first-party code, new patches or upgrades, etc. While in theory a new SBOM is required for every change in the code of the product, probably the best that can be hoped for at the current time is a new SBOM for every major version and minor versions if possible.

There are many possible formats for version strings, and a product or component supplier (which may be an open source project team) has complete freedom to use any versioning format they want. However, if the supplier wants to be able to specify a version range in a VEX document, they will need to choose a versioning format for which there are rules that will always place multiple versions in the order in which they were created. For an in-depth discussion of version ranges and how they are implemented in CycloneDX, see the Section titled "Version Ranges" later in Chapter 16.

Product or component supplier name

This is the common name for the supplier of the product. Normally, a supplier name (like a product name) can be the source of a lot of confusion, since often people who work for the same company will refer to it by different names, e.g. "Cisco", "Cisco, Inc.", "Cisco Europe", etc. Because of this, it is hard to identify the supplier of a software product with any precision (this is especially true for open source products), and full automation of this field is close to impossible.

The fact that the supplier field is difficult to automate might not seem to cause a huge problem, were it not for the fact that the NTIA "Minimum Elements.." document refers to this as one of the seven minimum fields in an SBOM. Since the Minimum Elements were intended to facilitate automation, the fact that this one field inhibits automation is unfortunate.

In general, software customers should be very careful about requiring their suppliers to include all the NTIA "minimum fields" in their SBOMs. Since neither of the two types of software identifiers found in vulnerability databases – CPE and purl – requires the user to know the supplier of a software product they are looking for, not requiring it should not cause problems, and in fact may avoid some problems.

Product identifier(s)

In the first and second VEX use cases, the purpose of VEX is to describe the exploitability status of one or more vulnerabilities identified in one or more versions of the product. Vulnerabilities are identified by searching for an *identifier* for the product or component in the National Vulnerability Database[162] (NVD) or another vulnerability database (although some tools do this automatically for the user, once an SBOM has been ingested and parsed). Perhaps the most widely used of these tools is the open source Dependency-Track[163], which is currently used more than 17 million times every day to look up vulnerabilities for the components listed in an SBOM.

While there are many identifiers used for software products and software components, the two most important of these, when it comes to the first and second VEX use cases, are CPE and purl. CPE is currently the only identifier supported by the National Vulnerability Database (NVD). CPE names are assigned by NIST (the National Institute of Standards and Technology, which is part of the US Department of Commerce).

CPE includes the product name, supplier name and version string for the product/version in question. Since CPE is the only identifier supported by the NVD, it currently plays a huge role in the worldwide software vulnerability management ecosystem. On the other hand, it is widely understood that there are a lot of problems with CPE.

The OWASP SBOM Forum, an informal group formed by the author at the beginning of 2022 to discuss issues that are preventing widespread distribution and use of SBOMs, early on identified the problems with CPE as one of the most important inhibitors to distribution and use of SBOMs. The group produced a

---

[162] Described at https://nvd.nist.gov/
[163] Described at https://dependencytrack.org/

high-level "proposal"[164] in September 2022 to address the CPE problems in the NVD; these problems are described on pages 4-6 of the proposal.

Another identifier, that is just as important as CPE and rapidly becoming more important, is purl, which stands for "product URL".[165] Purl has already become the leading identifier for open source software. This is because it requires no centralized database or assignment of identifiers, yet at the same time it provides a mechanism by which a user of an open source software product (or, more frequently, an open source component of a software product) can reliably learn of vulnerabilities that apply to it. This is possible because the leading open source vulnerability databases (including Sonatype's OSSIndex[166] and Google's OSV[167]) are all based on purl.[168]

The OWASP SBOM Forum's proposal advocates incorporating purl as an identifier in the NVD, along with the existing CPE identifiers. This will ultimately make it much easier to find vulnerabilities applicable to open source components in software products (which is significant, since around 90% of components, in both open source and commercial software products, are open source[169]). The proposal also describes how purls can be used to identify commercial products and components, which will ultimately alleviate a lot of the problems involved with finding commercial products and components in the NVD.[170]

The best advice for suppliers creating either SBOMs or VEX documents is to assign either a CPE or a purl to every product or component referred to in the document, since these are currently almost the only two software identifiers used in vulnerability databases worldwide. For proprietary products and components as well as intelligent devices, CPE is currently the only naming option. For open source products and components, purl is by far the preferable option, since the open source vulnerability databases are all based on purl.[171]

---

[164] Available at
https://owasp.org/assets/files/posts/A%20Proposal%20to%20Operationalize%20Component%20Identification%20for%20Vulnerability%20Management.pdf

[165] Described at https://github.com/package-url/purl-spec

[166] Described at https://ossindex.sonatype.org/

[167] Described at https://osv.dev/

[168] Note that not all open source software can be identified using purl, for example, projects based on C or C++.

[169] Source: https://www.sonatype.com/resources/white-paper-state-of-the-software-supply-chain-2020

[170] The author admits that more work needs to be done regarding a method for identifying purls for commercial products.

[171] There are CPEs for some open source products, but certainly not all. Moreover, since CPEs are based on the concept of "product", which is intrinsic to proprietary

Vulnerability identifier

The purpose of a VEX document is to describe the exploitability status of one or more vulnerabilities in a particular software product or intelligent device. Of course, this means that properly identifying vulnerabilities is essential for a VEX.

By far the most widely-used type of vulnerability identifier is CVE (which used to stand for something but is now considered NBI – nothing but initials). New CVEs are reported to CVE.org, an organization that used to be referred to as MITRE. While it is still operated by MITRE staff members, CVE.org is now run as a non-profit organization, with board members from the public and private sectors.

New CVEs are described in CVE reports, which identify one or more products to which the CVE applies. Products are currently identified only with CPE names in the CPE reports, although the OWASP SBOM Forum's proposal, referred to earlier, recommends that CVE reports include purls, where applicable – although they will also include CPEs for a long time to come. When that is implemented (which will unfortunately be at least 3-4 years from now), users of the NVD will be able to search for open source products using CPE or purl.

There are other types of vulnerabilities besides CVEs. One important type is GitHub Security Advisories[172], all of which begin with "GHSA"; GHSA is just one of the vulnerability types supported by the OSV[173] vulnerability database. Both CycloneDX and CSAF support any vulnerability type, not just CVEs.

Since all vulnerability databases provide other information besides just the name and description of the vulnerability, both major VEX formats have fields available to record that information. For example, CycloneDX can record the following types of vulnerability information (and has additional free text space to add other information): Source name (e.g. "NVD"), Source URL, References (i.e. another vulnerability database that lists the same vulnerability under a different identifier), Ratings for risk or severity (e.g. CVSS score), Common Weakness Enumerations or CWEs, Advisories (URLs for advisories on other sites), Tools (used to identify, confirm, or score the vulnerability), as well as other types of information.[174]

There are two types of vulnerability information in CycloneDX that deserve special mention (there are equivalent fields for both in CSAF):

1. "justifications", found at vulnerability/analysis/justification. These are discussed in the section titled "Status justifications" in Chapter 9. A

---

software, rather than "package", which is intrinsic to open source software, it is often difficult to determine the exact open source package that applies to a CPE name. This is why it would be impossible to have a true mapping between CPEs and purls.

[172] https://github.com/advisories

[173] https://osv.dev/

[174] Available at the "Vulnerabilities" drop-down menu found here: https://cyclonedx.org/docs/1.5/json/#vulnerabilities

"justification" is only needed when the status (or "state" in CycloneDX) of the vulnerability in the product is "not affected".

2. Actions for a user to take when the status of a vulnerability is "affected". In the CSAF format, there is an "action statement" that the supplier must fill out, describing the mitigation recommended by the supplier. Normally, the mitigation will be to apply a patch, although in some cases there may be a different mitigation. In CycloneDX, there are five machine-readable "responses" that the supplier can enter:

  a. "can_not_fix"
  b. "will_not_fix"
  c. "update"
  d. "rollback"
  e. "workaround_available"

The supplier can also enter text in the "detail" field, to describe other actions or mitigations that are not listed under "responses".

Status designations

The most important field in the VEX document is the status designation for a vulnerability listed in the document. The VEX documents recognize four status designations, although both the CycloneDX and CSAF formats offer other status options. The four common status designations are:

- "affected" in CSAF and "exploitable" in CycloneDX
- "not_affected" in CSAF and "unaffected" in CDX
- "under_investigation" in CSAF and "in_triage" in CDX
- "fixed" in CSAF and "resolved" in CDX

Both the CycloneDX and CSAF VEX formats support separate status justifications for different versions of a product.

Affected component

Even though the purpose of VEX is to describe the exploitability status of vulnerabilities that are due to components of a product, the VEX document will not normally need to mention any components; this is because the "exploitability" in question is the exploitability of the component CPE in the product itself, not in the component. When a user looks up vulnerabilities for a component in an SBOM and finds one, the question then becomes whether that vulnerability is exploitable in the product itself. Of course, there should be no question that it is exploitable in the component, since otherwise it would not have been listed in the vulnerability database.

However, it may sometimes be useful to know the component that is the source of a vulnerability listed in a VEX document.

12. Advanced: The two main VEX platforms

An essential feature of VEX documents is that they are machine-readable. While software suppliers have always been able to issue both positive and negative vulnerability notifications via email or website announcement (e.g., "None of the members of our router product family is subject to the Log4j vulnerabilities"), VEX documents only make sense in a machine-readable context.

This is because VEX has always been conceived as a companion document to SBOMs, and SBOMs have always been intended to be machine-readable (although "human-readable" SBOM formats like XLS and PDF are also supported). Because of the number of components in a typical software product (around 150) and the number of vulnerabilities that might be found in those components, the analysis described earlier would be difficult to perform using spreadsheets or any other "manual" means.

VEX documents are available on two main "platforms": CycloneDX[175] and CSAF[176]. CycloneDX, an OWASP standard, is best known as an SBOM format, but is in fact a general purpose platform that can be used to produce a wide variety of machine readable documents[177], including VEX.[178] CSAF is an OASIS standard and is used by large suppliers worldwide to provide machine-readable vulnerability notifications to their customers.

While each of the two platforms has a specification, there is, as of early 2024, no specification for VEX on either platform.[179] The OWASP SBOM Forum

---

[175] https://cyclonedx.org/

[176] https://www.oasis-open.org/committees/tc_home.php?wg_abbrev=csaf

[177] See https://cyclonedx.org/capabilities/

[178] https://cyclonedx.org/capabilities/vex/

[179] Some of the fields required for a CSAF VEX document are described in a "profile" (https://docs.oasis-open.org/csaf/csaf/v2.0/csd01/csaf-v2.0-csd01.html#45-

believes that usable VEX specifications are not available because too many use cases have been proposed for VEX. The result of this has been that it has been impossible to produce consumer tools that utilize VEX documents.[180]

This is why a working group of the OWASP SBOM Forum is now (as of early 2024) developing a "tight" VEX specification – i.e., one that focuses on a single use case (the first use case described above. The working group is developing these specifications on both the CSAF and CycloneDX platforms (note that the two platforms are so different that it would be futile to try to develop a single specification for both platforms). See Part 3 of this book for further discussion of that effort.

Software suppliers need to decide which of the two major VEX platforms they will use. The two platforms are very different, and each one offers advantages and disadvantages. If a supplier has chosen CycloneDX (CDX) as their SBOM format, they will likely find it easier to utilize the same platform for their VEX documents. In addition, software tools that produce or consume CDX SBOMs will also produce or consume CDX VEX documents.

Because the author has some familiarity with CycloneDX as an SBOM platform, and especially because he finds the 100-page CSAF specification[181] daunting, to say the least, he has decided to focus on CDX VEX in Part 2. Of course, either VEX platform is usable with either SBOM format.

What is the difference between a VEX and a "traditional" vulnerability notification?

Software vulnerabilities have been present as long as there has been software. However, it was only in the 1990s, with the rapid growth of the internet, that the serious threats posed by software vulnerabilities started to become apparent. Currently, virtually all cybersecurity attacks exploit vulnerabilities in software or (in a small number of cases) firmware.

---

profile-5-vex) included in the CSAF 2.0 specification. However, as of early 2024, there is no specification for CSAF that provides all the information required to produce a CSAF VEX document, especially information on how the mandatory "Product Tree" field should be created.

[180] In this blog post https://tomalrichblog.blogspot.com/2023/10/making-vex-work.html the author conjectured that a tool meant to consume a machine-readable format would need to be accommodate the factorial of the number of independent options in the format (e.g., 4 factorial is 4X3X2X1). If there are five independent options in the format, the consumer tool needs to accommodate 120 different use cases. If there are ten options, the number is 3.6 million. And if there are 20 options (which there may be, just in the CSAF "product tree" field), the number is 2.4 quadrillion. The author does not know any developer who could create a tool to handle 2.4 quadrillion use cases, but would appreciate if any reader can inform him of such a person.

[181] https://docs.oasis-open.org/csaf/csaf/v2.0/csd01/csaf-v2.0-csd01.html

Tom Alrich

It is vitally important that software and intelligent device suppliers notify their customers of vulnerabilities, both through reporting vulnerabilities to CVE.org and through direct notifications to their customers. However, in most cases, the supplier should never report a vulnerability until they have developed a patch for it and made it available to their customers. Reporting a vulnerability before a patch or alternate mitigation is available is simply inviting hackers to exploit it.

Suppliers have been providing vulnerability notifications – along with patch notifications – to their users for years, mostly in human-readable form; there is currently no standard for these human-readable notifications. While there have previously been machine-readable vulnerability notification formats including CVRF, the predecessor to CSAF, they have not been widely used. This is mainly due to the lack of consumer tools for utilizing them.

A typical vulnerability notification might read something like, "We have discovered that our product ABC is subject to vulnerability CVE-2022-12345 in versions 3.3, 3.4 and 3.5; no other versions are susceptible to this vulnerability. We have created patch XYZ for this vulnerability. This patch can be downloaded from url12345.com. We urge all users of the affected versions of ABC either to immediately apply the patch or upgrade their product to the current version 3.6, in which CVE-2022-12345 has been patched."

These notifications were referred to earlier as positive notifications, meaning they inform a user of the presence of a vulnerability in the software they use. What about negative notifications, such as "Version X.Y of Product ABC is not vulnerable to CVE-2024-12345"? Until SBOMs became available, the main use case for a negative notification was when a particular vulnerability or set of vulnerabilities, like Ripple20 or the log4shell vulnerabilities, was widely publicized. If a supplier wanted to reassure their customers that the vulnerability or vulnerabilities did not apply to one or more (or all) of their products, they would issue a statement (probably on their web site or by email) that some or all of their products were not affected.

However, as discussed earlier, when the NTIA Software Component Transparency Initiative members started having serious discussions about SBOMs, they realized that software suppliers needed a machine-readable format for notifying their customers of component vulnerabilities that are not exploitable in one of their products, even though those vulnerabilities are exploitable in components included in that product.

To address this problem, an NTIA working group was constituted to draft a format for a document that would notify users of a product that one or more vulnerabilities are not exploitable in the product itself, even though they appear in the NVD (or another vulnerability database) as applicable to a component that is included in the product - usually a component that was listed in a recent SBOM for the product.[182] As noted earlier, this can be called a negative vulnerability notification, in contrast to the much more common positive vulnerability notification.

Does this mean that the difference between a VEX and a "traditional" vulnerability notification is that the VEX is a negative notification, while the traditional document is a positive notification? The answer is no, for two reasons:

A VEX document can provide positive vulnerability statements (that is, vulnerabilities with "affected" status in a particular product. There are several positive vulnerability notifications shown in the Section titled "Example VEX documents" in Chapter 15.

A "traditional" vulnerability notification often includes negative notification statements. For example, if a supplier puts out a notification stating that a vulnerability is present in five versions of a product and customers need to apply a patch just released by the supplier, they might also include a statement that the other versions of the product are not affected by the vulnerability.

In fact, it is safe to say there is nothing that a VEX document can do that a "traditional" machine-readable vulnerability notification cannot do. Thus, the difference between a VEX and a "traditional" vulnerability notification has nothing to do with the capabilities of the format. Rather, VEX is focused on a particular use case that only came to attention when there started to be discussions of distributing SBOMs to end users: a vulnerability is present in Component A in Product Y, when A is tested as a standalone product, but is not present in Product Y itself. Both the CycloneDX and CSAF platforms were used for both negative and positive vulnerability notifications before they were used for VEX notifications.

---

[182] It is important to note that, even though most VEX documents are likely to address the status of vulnerabilities identified in components revealed in an SBOM, there is no requirement for the VEX to refer either to an SBOM or to a component listed in an SBOM. Moreover, if the VEX does refer to a component as the ultimate source of the vulnerability being discussed, this reference is simply an "FYI"; it is almost never a statement that has any bearing on the message of the VEX itself. The VEX simply states that a particular vulnerability is exploitable or not exploitable in the product/version, without usually referring to a component or to an SBOM.

13. Advanced: Required fields in a CycloneDX VEX document

A VEX document in the CycloneDX VEX format needs to include the following fields, specified as described below:

Product name

A CycloneDX VEX document may list one or more software products. However, the author's opinion is that, while both SBOMs and VEX documents are still in their infancy, a VEX should only address a single product. Since an SBOM always addresses only one product (in fact, a single version of a single product), this will allow individual VEX documents to be matched with individual SBOMs.

The reader will learn in Part 3 of this document that being able to tie a VEX document to a single version of a product (which will always have a single SBOM) will be required to produce a "complete" component vulnerability management tool (one that ingests both SBOMs and VEX documents and outputs lists of exploitable vulnerabilities in a product/version).

Product name: One product

When only one product is being addressed in a CycloneDX VEX document, the product is identified in the metadata/component field, as shown in the example below. The code was taken from this example VEX document: https://github.com/CycloneDX/bom-examples/blob/master/VEX/CISA-Use-Cases/Case-1/vex-not_affected.json.[183]

---

[183] All code examples in this document are written in the JSON data interchange format, which is meant to be readable by both humans and computers. CycloneDX also supports the XML and protocol buffers data interchange formats. For a full explanation of the CycloneDX platform, see "CycloneDX v1.5 JSON Reference", which is available at https://cyclonedx.org/docs/1.5/json/. Note that, while these code

```
"metadata" : {
"component"184 : {

            "name" : "ABC",
            "version": "4.2",
            "type" : "application",
            "bom-ref" : "product-ABC"
              }
   },
```

Notes:

The options for "type" are listed here:
https://cyclonedx.org/docs/1.5/json/#metadata_component_type

"bom-ref" is, according to the CycloneDX documentation, "an optional identifier which can be used to reference the product anywhere in the BOM. Every bom-ref MUST be unique within the BOM." The "bom-ref" can be any character string that is unique within the CycloneDX document.

Product name: Multiple products

When multiple products[185] are described in a single VEX document, the product names are listed under the "vulnerabilities/affects"[186] field, not under

---

samples were originally developed by the CycloneDX maintainers for the CISA "VEX Use Cases" document in 2022, the author has made some simple modifications to these examples. He has not tested the revised samples, so it is possible there might be problems if a reader were to try to utilize them as is.

Also, note that these examples are not in the "tight" CycloneDX VEX format being developed by the OWASP SBOM Forum in early 2024, as described in Part 3 of this book.

[184] Even though this word is "component", it is in fact the product itself that is being referenced. The general convention in SBOMs is that the product that is the subject of the SBOM (or the VEX document, in this case) is the "primary component". While this document is in fact a VEX document, not an SBOM, the CycloneDX VEX format is built on the same platform as the CycloneDX SBOM format and therefore follows the same conventions.

[185] As mentioned earlier (and as described in Part 3 at the end of the book), the OWASP Forum is, in early 2024, developing "tight" VEX specifications for both the CSAF and CycloneDX platforms; both of these specifications require a single product. However, in the future, there will hopefully be tight VEX specifications for other VEX use cases, which will be able to list multiple products in a single VEX document (in fact, the recently announced Cisco and Red Hat VEX specifications both require that capability).

[186] The CycloneDX format uses the word "affect" in two ways. One is as part of the "affected" and "unaffected" status designations. The other is in the "vulnerabilities/affects" field. Status designations are discussed under the heading "

"metadata/component". An example of a VEX that includes a multi-product "affects" field is here: https://github.com/CycloneDX/bom-examples/blob/master/VEX/CISA-Use-Cases/Case-7/vex.json (lines 29-56).

Note that the products referenced under "affects" are not directly named in the VEX document. Instead, the products are referred to by their "bom-ref", which points to the product shown in an external CycloneDX SBOM. The two SBOMs referred to are found here: https://github.com/CycloneDX/bom-examples/blob/master/VEX/CISA-Use-Cases/Case-7/bom-1.json (for product ABC) and here: https://github.com/CycloneDX/bom-examples/blob/master/VEX/CISA-Use-Cases/Case-7/bom-2.json (for product JKL).[187]

The two SBOMs referenced in this example do not contain any data about components. In other words, the SBOM referred to in a "bom-ref" statement does not have to be the "real" SBOM for the product referred to; in fact, it does not need to refer to any components at all. It can simply be an empty shell that names the product.[188]

Product identifier

There must be an identifier for the product that will allow the product to be looked up in a vulnerability database. Because there are currently only two product identifiers that meet that description, CPE and purl, one or the other should be used (although if the vulnerability has been reported using a different type of product identifier such as one of the OSV identifiers, that should be listed instead).

Example:
```
"component" : {

        "purl" : "pkg:maven/com.acme/tomcat-
catalina@9.0.14?packaging=jar"
        "cpe"  : "cpe:2.3:a:acme:component_framework:-
:*:*:*:*:*:*:*"
```

'analysis' section" below. The "affects" field is discussed below under the heading "'affects' section".

[187] For a description of the BOM-Link capability in CycloneDX (which includes bom-ref), go here: https://cyclonedx.org/capabilities/bomlink/.

[188] In some cases, the supplier may want to have "bom-ref" refer to an actual SBOM, perhaps to refer to the component that is the source of the vulnerability in the product. However, that is not in any way "required".

Product version string

A VEX document needs to be able to list one or more versions of a product, which may have different exploitability status designations. Version strings (also called version numbers if they only contain numerals) can be identified in the following three ways:

1. Single version string

When the VEX document refers only to a single version of a single product, the version string is listed under the "metadata/component" field, as in the example below. This code was taken from this sample VEX document: https://github.com/CycloneDX/bom-examples/blob/master/VEX/CISA-Use-Cases/Case-1/vex-not_affected.json.

```
"component" : {

            "name" : "ABC",
            "version": "4.2",
```

2. Multiple version strings

If a CycloneDX VEX document refers to more than one version of a product, the version strings must be listed under the "affects" statement. Different versions of one product can have different status designations in one VEX document.[189] The code below was taken from this sample CycloneDX VEX document: https://github.com/CycloneDX/bom-examples/blob/master/VEX/CISA-Use-Cases/Case-4/vex.json.

```
"affects": [
            {
                "ref": "product-ABC",
                "versions": [
                  {
                     "version": "2.4",
                     "status": "affected"
```

---

[189] This will be a common use case for VEX documents. For example, in announcing that a vulnerability has been patched in one product, the supplier can put out a VEX that states that the vulnerability has the status "fixed" in the new patched version of the product, whereas its status is "affected" in one or more previous versions, including the current version. However, in CDX VEX, versions with different status designations need to be addressed under different instances of a vulnerability, even if the vulnerability is the same one. For further discussion of using a VEX in the case of a patch notification, see the Section titled "An illustration of real-world VEX use: patching" in Chapter 17.

Note that, while different versions of a product can have different status designations in a single VEX document, they need to be in separate "affects" sections. See the examples below.

```
    },
    {
      "version": "2.6",
      "status": "affected"
    },
  ]
  }
]
```

3. Version range

In the CycloneDX VEX format, one or more version ranges can be specified, along with one or more itemized version numbers. The syntax follows the specifications in the open source Version Range Specifier[190]. Only versioning schemes (such as semantic versioning) supported by the Version Range Specifier are supported for version ranges in CycloneDX VEX. While other versioning schemes can be included in a VEX document, how they will be interpreted by the end user's tooling if included in a version range, cannot be guaranteed (for a full discussion of this question, see the Section titled "Version Ranges" in Chapter 16).

This code was taken from this sample CycloneDX VEX document: https://github.com/CycloneDX/bom-examples/blob/master/VEX/CISA-Use-Cases/Case-4/vex.json.

```
"range": "vers:generic/>=2.9|<=4.1",
          "status": "affected"
```

This states that the status in this example, "affected", applies to every version of the product with a version number greater than or equal to 2.9 and less than or equal to 4.1. This is a way of representing the "generic" version range type, found in the Version Range Specifier.

Applicable Vulnerabilities

Every VEX document must list one or more vulnerabilities. These are usually identified using a CVE name, found in the National Vulnerability Database (NVD) and many other vulnerability databases. They may also be designated using other identifiers, such as:

- GHSA, found in the GitHub Advisories[191] vulnerability database, and

---

[190] https://github.com/package-url/purl-spec/blob/version-range-spec/VERSION-RANGE-SPEC.rst

[191] https://github.com/advisories

- The 15-20 open source vulnerability identifiers found in the OSV[192] vulnerability database.

The exploitability status of each vulnerability in the VEX document may vary by product and version listed in the VEX.

The sample below identifies CVE-2021-44228 (aka "log4shell"). It is taken from this document: https://github.com/CycloneDX/bom-examples/blob/master/VEX/CISA-Use-Cases/Case-4/vex.json)

```
"vulnerabilities":
```

```
{
    "id": "CVE-2021-44228",
    "source": {
      "name": "NVD",
      "url":      "https://nvd.nist.gov/vuln/detail/CVE-2021-
44228"
    },
```

Vulnerability information

The CycloneDX VEX format provides multiple sub-fields to describe a vulnerability. The most important sub-fields[193] are:

- ID – the vulnerability identifier, such as "CVE-2021-39182" or "SNYK-PYTHON-ENROCRYPT-1912876".
- Source/url – The URL of the database or other document that describes the vulnerability, e.g. https://nvd.nist.gov/vuln/detail/CVE-2021-39182.
- Source/name – The name of the vulnerability database, e.g. "National Vulnerability Database" or "NVD" for short.
- References – Frequently, a single vulnerability will be referenced by different identifiers in different vulnerability databases. The ID, source/URL and source/name of an alternative reference may be entered here.
- Ratings – Vulnerabilities are often rated by the degree of severity they pose. There are several rating schemes, although the most popular of these is the Common Vulnerability Scoring System or CVSS.[194] There are sub-fields for source, score, severity, method, vector, and justification.

---

[192] https://osv.dev/

[193] The complete set of available subfields is available here: https://cyclonedx.org/docs/1.5/json/#vulnerabilities

[194] https://nvd.nist.gov/vuln-metrics/cvss

- CWEs – Common Weakness Enumeration values that describe the vulnerability. Each CWE value is an integer, e.g. 399.[195]
- Description – This is a description of the vulnerability as provided by the source database (text field).
- Detail – Further detail for the description.
- Recommendation – a recommended mitigation for the vulnerability. Note this may be different from the mitigation described in the "analysis/response" or "analysis/detail" fields, described under "status designation/affected". If so, it doesn't need to be filled in. In general, the mitigation recommended by the supplier (which should be found in "analysis/response" or "analysis/detail") should take precedence over any mitigation recommended by a third-party like the NVD.
- Advisories/title and URL – The title and URL for a published advisory about the vulnerability.

"analysis" section

Every CycloneDX VEX document must have an "analysis" section. The most important field in "analysis" is "state", for which there are four possible values. The "state" designation applies to all versions of the product that are listed in the "affects" section immediately below the "analysis" section; if no versions are listed in "affects", the "state" applies to the single version listed under "component". If no version is listed there, "state" applies to all versions of the product.

Any sub-fields required are determined by the "state". There are six possible values for "state"[196], but the four that are relevant for VEX are:

1. "not affected"

When "state" is "not_affected", this means the vulnerability is not exploitable in any versions of the product that are listed in the "affects" section immediately below the "analysis" section. If no versions are listed under "affects", the "state" applies to the single version listed under "component"; if no version is listed under "component", "state" applies to all versions of the product. There are three sub-fields of "not_affected":

---

[195] https://cwe.mitre.org/
[196] https://cyclonedx.org/docs/1.5/json/#vulnerabilities_items_analysis_state

145

The "justification" sub-field is required whenever the "state" is "not_affected". This field describes why the product is not affected by the vulnerability. It must provide one of the responses listed here: https://cyclonedx.org/docs/1.5/json/#vulnerabilities_items_analysis_justification (these justifications are also listed in the Section titled "Status justifications" in Chapter 9).

The "response" sub-field may be used when "state" is "exploitable" or "not_affected", although its use is not required. If used, it must indicate one of the items shown on this page: https://cyclonedx.org/docs/1.5/json/#vulnerabilities_items_analysis_response

- "can_not_fix"
- "will_not_fix"
- "update"
- "rollback"
- "workaround_available"

Note that, when "state" is "not_affected", the only one of these responses that makes sense to use is "will_not_fix".

The "detail" sub-field is described in the CycloneDX documentation as "Detailed description of the impact, including methods used during assessment. If a vulnerability is not exploitable, this field should include specific details on why the component or service is not impacted by this vulnerability."[197] Note that, when "state" is "not_affected", either the "justification" or the "detail" field, or both, must be filled in.

Below is an example of the "analysis" section with a "state" of "not_affected". The code is taken from this example: https://github.com/CycloneDX/bom-examples/blob/master/VEX/CISA-Use-Cases/Case-1/vex-not_affected.json

```
"analysis": {
            "state": "not_affected",
            "justification": "code_not_present",
            "response": ["will_not_fix"],
            "detail": "This version of Product ABC is not affected
by the      vulnerability. Class with vulnerable code was removed
before shipping."
            },
```

2. "exploitable"

When "state" is "exploitable", this means the vulnerability is exploitable in any versions of the product that are listed in the "affects" section immediately

[197] See
https://cyclonedx.org/docs/1.5/json/#vulnerabilities_items_analysis_detail.

below the "analysis" section. If no versions are listed under "affects", the "state" applies to the single version listed under "component"; if no version is listed under "component", "state" applies to all versions of the product.

The code below is taken from this example: https://github.com/CycloneDX/bom-examples/blob/master/VEX/CISA-Use-Cases/Case-1/vex-affected.json.

```
"analysis": {
        "state": "exploitable",
        "response": ["will_not_fix", "update"],
        "detail": "Versions of Product ABC are affected by the
vulnerability. Customers are advised to upgrade to the latest
release."
    },
```

c. "resolved"

When "state" is "resolved", this indicates that the version of the product listed under "component", or the multiple versions listed in the "affects" section, have been patched for the vulnerability (or the vulnerability has been mitigated by the supplier in another way, other than by patching). This is equivalent to the "fixed" status designation in CSAF.

Note that, since only one version of the product may be listed under "component", this means that "resolved" can apply to only one version of the product (however, if multiple versions of the product have been patched, the other versions could be listed with "not_affected" status).

The code below was taken from this example: bom-examples/vex-fixed.json at master · CycloneDX/bom-examples · GitHub.

```
"analysis": {
        "state": "resolved",
        "detail": "This version of Product DEF has been
fixed."
        },
```

d. "in triage"

When "state" is "in triage", this means it is not yet known whether the version of the product listed under "component", or the multiple versions listed in the "affects" section, are or are not affected by the vulnerability. This is still being investigated and the result will be provided in a later VEX. This is equivalent to the "under investigation" status designation in CSAF.

Note that, since only one version of the product may be listed under "component", this means that "in triage" can apply to only one version of the product, with respect to one vulnerability. This code is from the example found here: https://github.com/CycloneDX/bom-examples/blob/master/VEX/CISA-Use-Cases/Case-1/vex-under_investigation.json

```
"analysis": {
            "state": "in_triage",
            "detail": "This version of Product GHI is under
investigation to determine if product is affected."
          },
```

"affects" section

The "affects" section of the CycloneDX VEX document describes the "status" of the vulnerability referred to above, as it applies to each version of each product listed in the section. The product is referred to by its bom-ref, which is simply a character string that is unique within the VEX document. In the examples, the bom-ref always includes the name of the product, for clarity's sake (this is a good practice in general, when creating CycloneDX SBOMs or VEX documents). Note that the "status" of each version of the product does not need to be the same within the VEX document as a whole, although the versions listed under one instance of a vulnerability need to have the same status[198].

The code below was taken from this example: bom-examples/vex.json at master · CycloneDX/bom-examples · GitHub

```
"affects": [
  {
      "ref":                    "urn:cdx:cbb2cd68-2857-43b8-a10b-
e8c03d277d18/1#product-ABC",
      "versions": [
        {
          "version": "2.4",
          "status": "affected"
        },
        {
          "version": "2.6",
          "status": "affected"
        },
        {
          "range": "vers:generic/>=2.9|<=4.1",
          "status": "affected"
        }
      ]
```

---

[198] In other words, if a VEX document needs to specify different versions of a product that have different status designations for CVE-2023-12345, they will need to be listed under separate instances of CVE-2023-12345. See the example in the Section titled "C. Single Product, Multiple versions, Single Vulnerability, Multiple Statuses" below.

This example indicates that versions 2.4, 2.6, and the version range between and including 2.9 and 4.1, are all affected by the same vulnerability.

14. Advanced: Optional fields in CycloneDX VEX documents

Following are optional fields in CycloneDX VEX documents:

Affected Component

Because the purpose of VEX is to describe the exploitability status of a component vulnerability in a product/version, there is usually no need to refer to the component that is the source of the vulnerability, since that should almost always be known beforehand. For example:

A user receives an SBOM for Product A Version 2.3. One of the components listed in the SBOM is XYZ Version 4.5.

The user looks up XYZ Version 4.5 in the NVD (or a tool does this on their behalf) and discovers that it is vulnerable to CVE-2023-12345. The user wants to know whether Product A Version 2.3 is also vulnerable to this vulnerability, since one of its components is vulnerable.

Meanwhile, the supplier makes a VEX document available that states that the exploitability status of CVE-2023-12345 in Product A Version 2.3 is "not affected", so the user (and the supplier's help desk) will not waste their time pursuing this vulnerability. Note that this statement does not mention Component XYZ, even though it is the source of the vulnerability. That information is not relevant at this point.

Of course, it will not cause any harm to list the vulnerable component in the document using the "Components" field (this is different from "Metadata/component", which specifies the product that is the subject of the VEX). However, the only reason to do that would be for informational purposes, in case downstream users may consider it important to know which component is the source of the vulnerability.

Timestamp for VEX document

It is important for a VEX document to have a timestamp, even though this is an optional field. The reason a timestamp is needed for a VEX is the same reason it is needed for an SBOM: the order in which VEXes for a product are released is important. For example, one VEX may assert that a vulnerability is "exploitable" in a product/version, while a subsequent VEX may assert that the product is "not_affected" by the vulnerability, perhaps because the supplier realized that their original "verdict" on the vulnerability was mistaken. A timestamp will eliminate any question about which VEX document is the more recent.

Example:
```
"metadata" : {
        "timestamp" : "2022-03-03T00:00:00Z",199
    },
```

Product supplier

This should be treated as an optional field. The supplier of the product or component does not need to be known for the VEX document to be useful, if there is a unique identifier for the product (e.g., CPE or purl). However, if two products from different suppliers have similar names, including the supplier's name in the VEX will eliminate any confusion. Here is an example:
```
"metadata" : {
        "supplier" : "Example, Inc.",
    },
```

One reason not to include the product supplier in the VEX document is that supplier names are notoriously unreliable. Ten people who work for the same company may very well give ten different names for the company: XYZ, XYZ Inc., XYZ Corp., XYZ EMEA division, XYZ Minerals, etc. Trying to determine the "real" company name is a fool's errand. It will never yield a useful result unless a very specific question is asked, e.g. "Under what name is XYZ Corp. registered in the state in which it is incorporated?"

In this case, the question is how the supplier will be listed in the NVD. Since the decision on the supplier name is up to the individual NIST person that assigned the CPE name, and since there is no "official" directory of supplier names and never will be, there is simply no good answer to this question. This is a good example of the "naming problem", described in the Chapter with that title earlier in this book.

---

[199] This is in the ISO 8601 timestamp format, described here: https://en.wikipedia.org/wiki/ISO_8601#:~:text=As%20of%20ISO%208601%2D1, hour%20between%2000%20and%2023.

Author(s)

This field is also recommended, although not required. Usually, the name of the organization that created the VEX document will be entered here. If the person or persons who authored the VEX are not employed by any organization, or if they were not acting on their employer's behalf when they authored it, their name(s) should be entered here. For example, a security researcher might create a VEX as an individual, even though they are employed by a larger organization, if this was not done as part of their job. They should enter their name as the author of the VEX document.

The author of a VEX will normally be the supplier of the software product that is the subject of the VEX. The supplier is the organization best able to answer the question whether a particular vulnerability is exploitable in the product. However, it is possible that some suppliers will for various reasons not produce or distribute SBOMs and VEXes. Thus, third parties may produce these on their own, using whatever information is available to them[200].

It is also possible that a third-party researcher will discover that a vulnerability is exploitable in a product and wish to inform users of the product of this discovery. Following the rules for coordinated vulnerability disclosure, the researcher should first try to discuss this with the supplier, and only issue their own notification (whether it is called a VEX or just a vulnerability notification) if the supplier refuses to do that.

The CycloneDX VEX format provides fields for the Author's name, email address and phone number, as shown here: https://cyclonedx.org/docs/1.5/json/#metadata_authors.

---

[200] While this is still a topic of active discussion, the author's opinion is that, in most cases, exploitability in the VEX sense can only be determined by the organization or person that developed the code. See the discussion in the Section titled "The concept of exploitability" in Chapter 9.

15. Advanced: Example VEX documents

B elow are examples of CycloneDX VEX documents, developed to illustrate the important "building blocks" of a VEX. These are taken from the CISA document "Vulnerability Exploitability eXchange (VEX) – Use Cases".[201] All page numbers refer to that document. Line numbers refer to the online version of each example. Other than the line numbers, the examples are the same, both online and below.[202]

The examples below are all preceded by a table that describes the JSON VEX example shown below the table. Each subject starts with the beginning field and ends with the ending field. Note that the beginning and ending fields are sometimes at different levels of indentation in the CDX document.

A. Single Product, Single Version, Single Vulnerability, Single Status – "not affected"

This example makes a statement about the exploitability status of a single vulnerability in a single version of a single product. The "state" is "not_affected". This example is discussed in the section headed "Not Affected" on page 4 of the CISA document. The example code is found here: bom-examples/VEX/CISA-Use-Cases/Case-1/vex-not_affected.json at master · CycloneDX/bom-examples · GitHub

---

[201] Available at
https://cisa.gov/sites/default/files/publications/VEX_Use_Cases_Apr22.pdf.

[202] These CycloneDX VEX examples all use the version 1.4 specification, since that was current when the CISA document was created. As of early 2024, version 1.5 is current, and version 1.6 will soon be available.

Subject	Beginning field	Ending field	Comment
Document metadata	"Bom format"	"Timestamp"	
Product (i.e., subject of VEX document)	"component"	"BOM-ref"	Only one product is addressed in this VEX document. The author believes that should be the norm for the time being, at least for the first and second use VEX use cases described earlier.
Info on CVE-2021-44228	"vulnerabilities"	"url"	
State of CVE in product	"analysis"	"detail"	The fact that the state is "not affected" means that the product or version(s) referred to below have a status of "unaffected" (in this case, the status of the entire product is "unaffected"). The justification (status justification) is "code_not_present ". The detail field explains the justification by saying "Class with vulnerable code was removed before shipping."
Product or versions with "unaffected" status	"affects"	"ref"	The entire product has "unaffected" status.

```
{
    "bomFormat": "CycloneDX",
    "specVersion": "1.4",
    "version": 1,
    "metadata" : {
      "timestamp" : "2022-03-03T00:00:00Z",
      "component" : {
        "name" : "ABC",
        "version": "4.2",
        "type" : "application",
        "bom-ref" : "product-ABC"
      }
    },
    "vulnerabilities": [
```

```
{
    "id": "CVE-2021-44228",
    "source": {
      "name": "NVD",
      "url":     "https://nvd.nist.gov/vuln/detail/CVE-2021-
44228"
    },
    "analysis": {
      "state": "not_affected",
      "justification": "code_not_present",
      "response": ["will_not_fix"],
      "detail": "This version of Product ABC is not affected
by the vulnerability. Class with vulnerable code was removed before
shipping."
    },
    "affects": [
      {
        "ref": "product-ABC"
      }
    ]
  }
 ]
}
```

Notes

"Type" can be any of the items listed here:
https://cyclonedx.org/docs/1.5/json/#components_items_type.

The "bom-ref" is any character string that is unique within the VEX document. The "bom-ref" will be used elsewhere in the document to refer to the product that is addressed in this VEX. The "bom-ref" may, but does not have to, include the name of the product, which in this example is ABC.

Since the "state" is "not affected", one of the nine "justifications" needs to be listed:
https://cyclonedx.org/docs/1.5/json/#vulnerabilities_items_analysis_justification
. In this case, the "justification" is "code_not_present".

The "response" subfield needs to include at least one of the five responses found   here:
https://cyclonedx.org/docs/1.5/json/#vulnerabilities_items_analysis_response. In this case, the "response" is "will_not_fix". The supplier will not fix the vulnerability because it does not affect the product/version in question.

The "detail" subfield is a text field, intended to clarify the "justification". It is not mandatory to include data in this field, but it is recommended.

B. Single Product, Multiple versions, Single Vulnerability, Single Status

In this example, there is a single product and a single vulnerability. The VEX reports the "status" of the vulnerability in multiple versions of the product. In this example, the status of the vulnerability is the same in all versions. This example is discussed in section 3.2.4 on pages 6 and 7 of the CISA document. The example code is found here: https://github.com/CycloneDX/bom-examples/blob/master/VEX/CISA-Use-Cases/Case-4/vex.json

Subject	Beginning field	Ending field	Comment
Document metadata	"Bom format"	"Timestamp"	
Product (i.e., subject of VEX document)	"component"	"BOM-ref"	One product, ABC, is addressed in this VEX document, although multiple versions are addressed.
Info on CVE-2021-44228	"vulnerabilities"	"vector"	
State of CVE in product	"analysis"	"detail"	The fact that the state is "exploitable" means that the version(s) referred to below have a status of "affected". The "response" field includes two of the five machine-readable responses: "will_not_fix" and "update". The detail field clarifies that the customer needs to upgrade to the latest release.[203]
Versions with "affected" status	"affects"	"status"	The versions with "affected" status are 2.4, 2.6 and the range between and including 2.9 to 4.1.

```
{
     "bomFormat": "CycloneDX",
```

---

[203] See Chapter 13 for a discussion of the "response" field, in the section titled "not affected".

```
    "specVersion": "1.4",
    "version": 1,
    "metadata" : {
     "timestamp" : "2022-03-03T00:00:00Z",
     "component" : {
      "name" : "ABC",
      "type" : "application",
      "bom-ref" : "product-ABC"
     }
    },
    "vulnerabilities": [
     {
      "id": "CVE-2021-44228",
      "source": {
       "name": "NVD",
       "url": "https://nvd.nist.gov/vuln/detail/CVE-2021-44228"
      },
      "ratings": [
        {
         "source": {
          "name": "NVD",
          "url":            "https://nvd.nist.gov/vuln-metrics/cvss/v3-
calculator?vector=AV:N/AC:L/PR:N/UI:N/S:C/C:H/I:H/A:H&version=3.1"
         },
         "score": 10.0,
         "severity": "critical",
         "method": "CVSSv31",
         "vector": "AV:N/AC:L/PR:N/UI:N/S:C/C:H/I:H/A:H"
        }
      ],
      "analysis": {
       "state": "exploitable",
       "response": ["will_not_fix", "update"],
       "detail": "Versions of Product ABC are affected by the vulnerability.
Customers are advised to upgrade to the latest release."
      },
      "affects": [
        {
         "ref": "product-ABC",
         "versions": [
           {
            "version": "2.4",
            "status": "affected"
```

```
        },
        {
          "version": "2.6",
          "status": "affected"
        },
        {
          "range": "vers:generic/>=2.9|<=4.1",
          "status": "affected"
        }
      ]
    }
  ]
}
]
}
```

Notes

The last field in the VEX document is "affects". Notice that it refers to the "ref", which is the same as the "bom-ref".

The version range notation indicates that the status of the vulnerability is "affected" in every version of product ABC, that falls in the range starting with version 2.9 and ending with version 4.1. See the section titled "Version Ranges" in the next Chapter.

C. Single Product, Multiple versions, Single Vulnerability, Multiple Statuses

In this example, there is a single product and a single vulnerability. The VEX reports the exploitability status of the vulnerability in multiple versions of the single product. The status of the vulnerability is different in different versions of the product.

This example is discussed in section 3.2.6 on pages 7 and 8 of the CISA document. The example code is found here: https://github.com/CycloneDX/bom-examples/blob/master/VEX/CISA-Use-Cases/Case-6/vex.json

Subject	Beginning field	Ending field	Comment
Document metadata	"Bom format"	"Timestamp"	
Product (i.e., subject of VEX document)	"component"	"BOM-ref"	
Info on first instance of	"vulnerabilities"	"vector"	This is the first instance of this CVE

CVE-2021-44228			in the VEX. Because all the versions listed in the "affects" section under one vulnerability instance need to have the same status, there needs to be one instance of the vulnerability for each status type used in the document.
State of CVE in product	"analysis"	"detail"	The fact that state is "exploitable" means the versions referenced below have a status of "affected".
Versions with "affected" status	"affects"	"status"	Includes two versions and one version range.
Second instance of CVE-2021-44228	"id"	"vector"	The CVE has not changed, but has been cited again. This time, the versions listed below it have a different status. It is not possible to list versions with differing status under a single instance of a CVE.
State of CVE in product	"analysis"	"detail"	The fact that state is "not_affected" means the versions referenced below have a status of "unaffected". Note that, since the state is "not_affected", a "justification" ("status justification") has

			been provided, as required; it is "code_not_present". A "response" of "will not fix" has also been included, although this is not required.
Versions with "unaffected" status	"affects"	"status"	Two individual versions have "unaffected" status, as well as two version ranges.

```
{
        "bomFormat": "CycloneDX",
        "specVersion": "1.4",
        "version": 1,
        "metadata" : {
         "timestamp" : "2022-03-03T00:00:00Z",
         "component" : {
          "name" : "ABC",
          "type" : "application",
          "bom-ref" : "product-ABC"
         }
        },
        "vulnerabilities": [
          {
          "id": "CVE-2021-44228",
          "source": {
           "name": "NVD",
           "url": "https://nvd.nist.gov/vuln/detail/CVE-2021-44228"
          },
          "ratings": [
            {
             "source": {
              "name": "NVD",
              "url":          "https://nvd.nist.gov/vuln-metrics/cvss/v3-
calculator?vector=AV:N/AC:L/PR:N/UI:N/S:C/C:H/I:H/A:H&version=3.1"
             },
             "score": 10.0,
             "severity": "critical",
             "method": "CVSSv31",
             "vector": "AV:N/AC:L/PR:N/UI:N/S:C/C:H/I:H/A:H"
            }
          ],
          "analysis": {
```

```
        "state": "exploitable",
        "response": ["will_not_fix", "update"],
        "detail": "Versions of Product ABC are affected by the vulnerability.
Customers are advised to upgrade to the latest release."
        },
        "affects": [
          {
            "ref": "product-ABC",
            "versions": [
              {
                "version": "2.4",
                "status": "affected"
              },
              {
                "version": "2.6",
                "status": "affected"
              },
              {
                "range": "vers:generic/>=2.9|<=4.1",
                "status": "affected"
              }
            ]
          }
        ]
      },
      {
        "id": "CVE-2021-44228",
        "source": {
          "name": "NVD",
          "url": "https://nvd.nist.gov/vuln/detail/CVE-2021-44228"
        },
        "ratings": [
          {
            "source": {
              "name": "NVD",
              "url":                    "https://nvd.nist.gov/vuln-metrics/cvss/v3-
calculator?vector=AV:N/AC:L/PR:N/UI:N/S:C/C:H/I:H/A:H/CR:X/IR:X/AR:X
/MAV:X/MAC:X/MPR:X/MUI:X/MS:X/MC:N/MI:N/MA:N&version=3.1"
            },
            "score": 0.0,
            "severity": "none",
            "method": "CVSSv31",
```

```
            "vector":
"AV:N/AC:L/PR:N/UI:N/S:C/C:H/I:H/A:H/CR:X/IR:X/AR:X/MAV:X/MAC:X/
MPR:X/MUI:X/MS:X/MC:N/MI:N/MA:N"
            }
          ],
          "analysis": {
            "state": "not_affected",
            "justification": "code_not_present",
            "response": ["will_not_fix"],
            "detail": "These versions of Product ABC are not affected by the
vulnerability. Class with vulnerable code was removed before shipping."
          },
          "affects": [
            {
              "ref": "product-ABC",
              "versions": [
                {
                  "range": "vers:generic/>=1.0|<=2.3",
                  "status": "unaffected"
                },
                {
                  "version": "2.5",
                  "status": "unaffected"
                },
                {
                  "range": "vers:generic/>=2.7|<=2.8",
                  "status": "unaffected"
                },
                {
                  "version": "4.2",
                  "status": "unaffected"
                }
              ]
            }
          ]
        }
      ]
    }
```

Note (refer to table below this section)

In the first "affects" section, customers running one of the affected versions are advised to upgrade to the latest version. Which version is that? The answer: The most recent of the "unaffected" versions listed at the end of the document is version 4.2. This is obviously the version to which affected users should upgrade.

The table below will make it easier to follow what is going on in the different sections of this VEX example.

Instance	Vulnerability	State	Product	Status	Versions
1	CVE-2021-44228	exploitable	ABC	"affected"	2.4, 2.6, 2.9-4.1
2	Same	not affected	ABC	unaffected	1.0-2.3, 2.5, 2.7-2.8, 4.2

D. A CSAF example

Below is an example of a CSAF VEX document. It comes from the same CISA "VEX Use Cases" document from which the above CycloneDX VEX examples were taken: https://github.com/oasis-tcs/csaf/tree/master/csaf_2.0/examples/csaf.

In fact, this CSAF VEX example addresses the same use case as the first of the CycloneDX VEX examples, found in the earlier Section "A: Single Product, Single Version, Single Vulnerability, Single Status – "not affected".

The document states the following:

As in the CycloneDX VEX example shown in Item A above, this CSAF VEX refers to Product ABC, version 4.2. The vulnerability listed in the VEX document, CVE-2021-44228, is the infamous log4shell vulnerability.

Also as in the CDX example, the status of the vulnerability in Product ABC version 4.2 is "not affected". The reason for this, described in the CSAF "impact statement" which is described in the "details" field (and the CDX "analysis/detail" field), is "Class with vulnerable code was removed before shipping."

Product ABC is not directly referred to in the CSAF document. Instead, the document refers to "CSAFPID-001", which has been defined with the statement " "product_id": "CSAFPID-0001" ". This is similar to how CycloneDX refers to ABC, although it does this in the "bom-ref" statement: "bom-ref": "product-ABC".[204]

---

[204] One difference between the "product_id" in CSAF VEX and the "bom-ref" in CycloneDX VEX is that the former refers to the combination of the product name and the version number, i.e. "ABC 4.2", while the latter just refers to the product name; the version number is identified separately in the document. The reason for this difference is that CSAF does not support identification of versions separately from identification of a product, while CycloneDX does. In other words, CSAF does not deal with either products or versions separately, but with an object that combines the two.

As discussed earlier, a VEX document should always contain a machine-readable status justification when the status of a vulnerability is "not affected"; yet this document does not contain one. This is because the concept of status justification was introduced by the CISA VEX working group in the CISA "Status Justifications" document, which was published in June 2022. Since the CISA "VEX Use Cases" document, from which these examples were taken, was published in April 2022, and since status justifications were added to CSAF after that document was published, the CSAF document does not contain one.

Because CycloneDX has included "justifications" since around 2020, a justification is included in the CDX example.

```
{
  "document": {
    "category": "csaf_vex",
    "csaf_version": "2.0",
    "notes": [
      {
        "category": "summary",
        "text": "Example Company VEX document. Unofficial content for demonstration purposes only.",
        "title": "Author comment"
      }
    ],
    "publisher": {
      "category": "vendor",
      "name": "Example Company ProductCERT",
      "namespace": "https://psirt.example.com"
    },
    "title": "Example VEX Document Use Case 1 - Not Affected",
    "tracking": {
      "current_release_date": "2022-03-03T11:00:00.000Z",
      "generator": {
        "date": "2022-03-03T11:00:00.000Z",
        "engine": {
          "name": "Secvisogram",
          "version": "1.11.0"
```

The disadvantage of the CSAF approach is that a range of versions must consist of a series of separate product/version pairs; that is, if there are six versions between v2.0 and v2.7 (i.e. v2.1, v2.2, v2.3, v2.4, v2.5, v2.6), they must be listed in separate objects: "ABC v2.1", "ABC v2.2", etc. However, this means that CSAF is currently incapable of representing version ranges in a way that will always be interpreted correctly by consumer tools (see the discussion of "Version ranges" later in this Part). The author has heard that changes will soon be made to the CSAF specification that are intended to fix this problem.

```
      }
    },
    "id": "2022-EVD-UC-01-NA-001",
    "initial_release_date": "2022-03-03T11:00:00.000Z",
    "revision_history": [
      {
        "date": "2022-03-03T11:00:00.000Z",
        "number": "1",
        "summary": "Initial version."
      }
    ],
    "status": "final",
    "version": "1"
  }
},
"product_tree": {
  "branches": [
    {
      "branches": [
        {
          "branches": [
            {
              "category": "product_version",
              "name": "4.2",
              "product": {
                "name": "Example Company ABC 4.2",
                "product_id": "CSAFPID-0001"
              }
            }
          ],
          "category": "product_name",
          "name": "ABC"
        }
      ],
      "category": "vendor",
      "name": "Example Company"
    }
  ]
},
"vulnerabilities": [
  {
    "cve": "CVE-2021-44228",
    "notes": [
```

```
        {
          "category": "description",
          "text": "Apache Log4j2 2.0-beta9 through 2.15.0 (excluding security releases 2.12.2, 2.12.3, and 2.3.1) JNDI features used in configuration, log messages, and parameters do not protect against attacker controlled LDAP and other JNDI related endpoints. An attacker who can control log messages or log message parameters can execute arbitrary code loaded from LDAP servers when message lookup substitution is enabled. From log4j 2.15.0, this behavior has been disabled by default. From version 2.16.0 (along with 2.12.2, 2.12.3, and 2.3.1), this functionality has been completely removed. Note that this vulnerability is specific to log4j-core and does not affect log4net, log4cxx, or other Apache Logging Services projects.",
          "title": "CVE description"
        }
      ],
      "product_status": {
        "known_not_affected": [
          "CSAFPID-0001"
        ]
      },
      "threats": [
        {
          "category": "impact",
          "details": "Class with vulnerable code was removed before shipping.",
          "product_ids": [
            "CSAFPID-0001"
          ]
        }
      ]
    }
  ]
}
```

16. Advanced: Other versioning options

Version ranges

Version ranges are a powerful tool for making statements about the status of vulnerabilities. "Traditional" vulnerability notifications often refer to a range of versions, as in the statements:

- "CVE-2021-12345 is exploitable in versions 4.3 to 4.9."
- "CVE-2020-12345 is not exploitable in all versions before 3.5."
- "CVE-2022-56789 is not exploitable in versions after 5.2, up to and including 6.0."

However, using version ranges in a machine-readable document like VEX, as opposed to simply enumerating the versions in that range, can cause problems in interpretation. It might seem at first glance that there is no difference between specifying a version range and simply enumerating all the version numbers within that range. For example, the range "v5.0 to v5.6" might seem quite simple. That's just versions 5.0, 5.1, 5.2, 5.3, 5.4, 5.5 and 5.6, right? Could there be confusion about how this range would be interpreted by a computer?

In fact, there could be a lot of confusion. For example, there could be many more version numbers in between 5.0 and 5.6, such as 5.24, 5.4e, 5.1.2, etc. The version of a software product should change whenever there has been any change in the code at all – meaning that a patch, a new build, etc. should each have their own version string. All these versions need to be included in a version range.[205]

The big advantage of specifying a version range rather than enumerating the individual versions, is that the person doing the specifying does not have to know each version within the range. For example, suppose the supplier in question follows the versioning scheme known as "semantic versioning".[206] In this scheme, versions are represented as "X.Y.Z", where X is the major version, Y the minor version, and Z the patch level. X, Y and Z are all positive integers.

---

[205] CycloneDX VEX allows the author to make exceptions for particular versions in a range; i.e. "CVE 123 is exploitable in all versions between 2.4.0 and 2.6.0, excluding 2.5.2."

[206] See https://semver.org/

Now, suppose a supplier that follows semantic versioning wants to state in a VEX document that a particular vulnerability is exploitable in every version of a product, starting with v5.0.0 and ending with v5.6.0. If they just enumerate versions 5.0.0, 5.1.0, 5.2.0, 5.3.0, 5.4.0, 5.5.0 and 5.6.0 (i.e., all the minor versions between 5.0.0 and 5.6.0), they may miss patched versions like 5.0.1, 5.2.3, etc. This is why specifying a version range will often be both easier and more accurate than trying to enumerate all the versions within the range.

However, there is another important consideration regarding the accuracy of machine-readable version ranges: Will the interpretation of a machine-readable range specification always lead to identification of the same set of versions by the consumption tool?

For example, if a range is specified as v6.1 to v7.3, will all interpretation algorithms identify "v7.1" as falling within that range? That is likely. How about "v6.9.2"? It's also likely that most algorithms would identify that as being within the range, although that shouldn't be assumed. But how about "v7.3a" or "v6.1 patch 3"? Neither of these is certain to be evaluated as falling within that range, although they both might be considered to do so in at least some cases.

Moreover, there are some complex versioning schemes in which it is impossible to tell which of two versions is the more recent, without having a level of knowledge of the scheme that is unlikely to be found in an automated tool that hasn't been specifically programmed to do that. For example, a Cisco™ IOS version might be numbered "12.2(33)SXI9". Is IOS version "12.2(35) SX17" more recent than that? One algorithm might answer yes, because 35 is greater than 33. However, another algorithm might answer no, because 19 is greater than 17.

For that reason, many versioning schemes are simply not amenable to machine interpretation; the only way to unequivocally indicate every version within such a range is to enumerate each of them. But, if a customer wonders whether their version of a product was accidentally left out of an enumeration, they will most likely have to contact tech support to ask this question, which somewhat defeats the purpose of enumerating the versions in the first place. To eliminate problems like this, suppliers should consider migrating to a standardized versioning scheme like semantic versioning.

The CycloneDX VEX specification provides full support for version ranges that conform to one of a specified set of standardized versioning schemes: those included in the "Version Range Specifier".[207] For example, if a supplier follows "generic" versioning (one of the supported schemes), they can enter a statement "vers:generic/>=2.9|<=4.1". This indicates the range between and including versions 2.9 and 4.1, which is to be interpreted using the generic versioning scheme.

---

[207] Available at https://github.com/package-url/purl-spec/blob/version-range-spec/VERSION-RANGE-SPEC.rst.

Any supplier that does not follow one of the versioning schemes supported by the Version Range Specifier can never be certain that a version range they want to communicate in a machine-readable format will be interpreted as they intend it to be by the end user's tool.

Patch and build levels

Many suppliers track "patch levels" and/or "build levels" separately from version numbers, meaning that a user seeking support for a problem might need to know all three numbers, not just their version number. While in general there is nothing wrong with this practice, these suppliers will have to change it when they start creating VEXes. This is because the VEX format does not provide a field for either patch or build level; there is only one field for version string. The patch and build levels will somehow have to be encoded in the version string.

If a supplier finds itself at the point where it needs to consolidate version numbers with patch and/or build levels, they should seriously consider moving to semantic versioning or another version supported by the Version Range Specifier (known as "VERS"). That will allow them to safely specify version ranges in CycloneDX VEX documents, as well as documents created in other formats that support VERS.

17. Advanced VEX applications

The examples listed earlier in this document are based on simple applications of the VEX concept, which state the exploitability status of a particular vulnerability or vulnerabilities in one or more versions of one or more products. These are the "bread and butter" applications for VEX.

However, there are also advanced applications that address more complex scenarios. Today, these are handled through detailed human-readable vulnerability notifications, which suffer from problems like:

The end user's vulnerability and asset management systems will need to be manually updated to reflect the contents of the advisory. If the advisory covers a complex scenario, there is no assurance that the systems will be properly updated, or even that they will be updated at all. This means that important actions that should be taken (such as a mitigation that should be applied because a patch will not be available soon) could be missed.

There is no assurance that the notification will reach all the people who should know about it, or that they will understand what actions they need to take based on the notification. This is especially true if some of the actions in the notification are contingent on others, or if there are "if...then...else" statements.

Before VEX, applications like the following would usually have to be handled through direct interaction with help desk personnel. However, VEX documents, combined with tooling on the user end to ingest and interpret SBOMs and VEX documents, will allow the required actionable information to be made available to the user and automatically integrated into their existing asset or vulnerability management systems.

Utilizing VEX, the supplier can inform their customers about the varying status of a vulnerability (or vulnerabilities) in multiple versions of their product. At the same time, they can advise them of different remediation options they have, depending on their version – all without requiring the user to contact the help desk. Below, we discuss two advanced applications which can only be accomplished efficiently using VEX documents (or other automated machine-readable vulnerability notifications).

Advanced application 1: Patching multiple versions of a product

When a supplier patches an important vulnerability, they often do a lot more than develop a patch for a single version of their product. For example, a supplier might do the following:

1. Develop a patch for the most recent version of the product. The patched version needs to have its own version number and will have a "fixed" status. The original version will have "affected" status.

2. If a user applies a patch to the version they are operating, the version number on their system needs to be incremented to the number of the patched version (this should happen automatically when the patch is applied).

3. If there are recent affected versions that are still in widespread use, the supplier may patch those as well; the version number will similarly be incremented in those patched versions.

4. For some older versions, even though they are still supported, the supplier will require users to upgrade to the current version.

5. Some versions of the product are not vulnerable. Of course, nothing needs to be done with them.

6. A new SBOM needs to be developed for every patched version of the product, not just the current version.

Below is a hypothetical scenario like what was just described. In this scenario, the supplier needs to make the following statements to their users in one or more VEX documents:

1. The current version is 6.0.0 and the patched version of that is 6.0.1. The supplier announces that v6.0.0's status is "affected" and v6.0.1's status is "fixed".

2. Versions greater than and including 4.0.0, and less than 5.3.0, are "unaffected" by the vulnerability. No action needs to be taken regarding these versions, and no patch will be made available.

3. Versions in the range of 5.3.0 up to (but not including) 5.6.0 are "affected" by the vulnerability. No patch will be developed. Users should upgrade to the current version 6.0.1.

4. Versions greater than 5.6.0, up to and including 6.0.0, are also "affected". A patch is available for these versions. The patched versions are numbered with the third digit incremented by 1 – e.g., the patched version of v5.7.0 is v5.7.1. There are four affected versions in this range: 5.7.0, 5.8.0, 5.9.0 and 6.0.0. They are itemized in the example below. They were not included in a version range, because the range would have to include the patched versions 5.7.1, 5.8.1 and 5.9.1, which have a different status ("fixed") than the affected versions.

As noted earlier, the supplier needs to develop a new SBOM for every patched version of the product. This includes all patched versions in the range of v5.6.0 to v6.0.1. After they have developed the patch and made it available to customers, the supplier will release a VEX document that includes the CDX equivalents of the English statements listed above.

This table describes the JSON VEX example shown below the table. Each subject starts with the beginning field and ends with the ending field. Note that the beginning and ending fields are sometimes at different levels of indentation.

Subject	Beginning field	Ending field	Comment
Document metadata	"Bom format"	"Timestamp"	
Product (i.e., subject of VEX document)	"component"	"BOM-ref"	Only one product is addressed in this VEX document. The author believes that should be the norm for the time being, for the first and second VEX use cases.
Info on first instance of CVE-2022-12345	vulnerabilities	"vector"	This is the first instance of this CVE in the VEX.
State of CVE in product	"analysis"	"detail"	The fact that state is "exploitable" means the versions referenced below have a status of "affected".

Versions with "affected" status	"affects"	"status"	Includes four versions and one version range.
Second instance of CVE-2022-12345	"id"	"vector"	The CVE has not changed but has been cited again. This time, the versions listed after it have a different status. It is not possible to list versions with differing status under a single instance of a CVE.
State of CVE in product	"analysis"	"detail"	The fact that state is "not_affected" means the versions referenced below it have a status of "unaffected". Note that, since the state is "not_affected", a "justification" ("status justification") has been provided, as required. A "response" of "will not fix" has also been included, although this is not required.
Versions with "unaffected" status	"affects"	"status"	Includes one version range.
Third instance of CVE-2022-12345	"id"	"vector"	The CVE has not changed but has been cited for the third time. As with the second instance, the versions listed below the third instance of the CVE have a different status.
State of CVE in product	"analysis"	"detail"	The fact that state is "resolved" (the CycloneDX word for "fixed") means the versions referenced below have a status of "unaffected". Note that, since the state is "resolved", a

			"justification" is not required, even though the status is "unaffected". This is because "resolved" indicates the vulnerability has been patched in the versions listed.
Versions with "unaffected" status	"affects"	"status"	Includes one version range.

The following JSON code is based on the example listed in the earlier Section titled "C. Single Product, Multiple Versions, Single Vulnerability, Multiple Statuses":

```
{
        "bomFormat": "CycloneDX",
        "specVersion": "1.4",
        "version": 1,
        "metadata" : {
          "timestamp" : "2022-03-03T00:00:00Z",
          "component" : {
            "name" : "ABC",
            "type" : "application",
            "bom-ref" : "product-ABC"
          }
        },
        "vulnerabilities": [
          {
            "id": "CVE-2022-12345",
            "source": {
              "name": "NVD",
              "url":      "https://nvd.nist.gov/vuln/detail/CVE-2022-
12345"
            },
            "ratings": [
              {
                "source": {
                  "name": "NVD",
                  "url":                      "https://nvd.nist.gov/vuln-
metrics/cvss/v3-
calculator?vector=AV:N/AC:L/PR:N/UI:N/S:C/C:H/I:H/A:H&version=3.1"
                },
                "score": 10.0,
                "severity": "critical",
                "method": "CVSSv31",
                "vector": "AV:N/AC:L/PR:N/UI:N/S:C/C:H/I:H/A:H"
              }
            ],
            "analysis": {
              "state": "exploitable",
```

```
        "response": ["will_not_fix", "update"],
        "detail": "Versions of Product ABC are affected by the
vulnerability. Customers using one of these versions are advised to
upgrade to one of versions 5.6.1, 5.7.1, 5.8.1, 5.9.1, or 6.0.1."
        },
        "affects": [
          {
            "ref": "product-ABC",
            "versions": [
          {
            "version": "5.6.0",
            "status": "affected"
          },
          {
            "version": "5.7.0",
            "status": "affected"
          },
          {
            "version": "5.8.0",
            "status": "affected"
          },
          {
            "version": "5.9.0",
            "status": "affected"
          },

              {
              "range": "vers:semver/>=5.3.0|<5.6.0",
               "status": "affected"
              }
            ]
          }
        ]
      },
      {
        "id": "CVE-2022-12345",
        "source": {
        "name": "NVD",
        "url":     "https://nvd.nist.gov/vuln/detail/CVE-2022-
12345"
        },
        "ratings": [
          {
            "source": {
              "name": "NVD",
              "url":                "https://nvd.nist.gov/vuln-
metrics/cvss/v3-
calculator?vector=AV:N/AC:L/PR:N/UI:N/S:C/C:H/I:H/A:H/CR:X/IR:X/AR:X
/MAV:X/MAC:X/MPR:X/MUI:X/MS:X/MC:N/MI:N/MA:N&version=3.1"
          },
```

```
            "score": 0.0,
            "severity": "none",
            "method": "CVSSv31",
            "vector":
"AV:N/AC:L/PR:N/UI:N/S:C/C:H/I:H/A:H/CR:X/IR:X/AR:X/MAV:X/MAC:X/MPR:
X/MUI:X/MS:X/MC:N/MI:N/MA:N"
          }
        ],
        "analysis": {
          "state": "not_affected",
          "justification": "code_not_present",
          "response": ["will_not_fix"],
          "detail": "These versions of Product ABC are not
affected by CVE-2022-12345. Class with vulnerable code was removed
before shipping."
        },
        "affects": [
          {
            "ref": "product-ABC",
            "versions": [
              {
                "range": "vers:semver/>=4.0.0|<5.3.0",
                "status": "unaffected"
              },
            ]
          }
        ]
      }
    ]
  }
  {
    "id": "CVE-2022-12345",
    "source": {
      "name": "NVD",
      "url": "https://nvd.nist.gov/vuln/detail/CVE-2022-12345"
    },
    "ratings": [
      {
        "source": {
          "name": "NVD",
          "url":      "https://nvd.nist.gov/vuln-metrics/cvss/v3-
calculator?vector=AV:N/AC:L/PR:N/UI:N/S:C/C:H/I:H/A:H/CR:X/IR:X/AR:X
/MAV:X/MAC:X/MPR:X/MUI:X/MS:X/MC:N/MI:N/MA:N&version=3.1"
        },
        "score": 0.0,
        "severity": "none",
        "method": "CVSSv31",
        "vector":
"AV:N/AC:L/PR:N/UI:N/S:C/C:H/I:H/A:H/CR:X/IR:X/AR:X/MAV:X/MAC:X/MPR:
X/MUI:X/MS:X/MC:N/MI:N/MA:N"
      }
    ],
      "state": "resolved",
```

```
    "detail": "This version of Product ABC has been fixed."
  },
"affects": [
  {
    "ref": "product-ABC",
    "versions": [
      {
        "version": "5.6.1",
        "status": "unaffected"
      },
      {
        "version": "5.7.1",
        "status": "unaffected"
      },
      {
        "version": "5.8.1",
        "status": "unaffected"
      },
      {
        "version": "5.9.1",
        "status": "unaffected"
      },
      {
        "version": "6.0.1",
        "status": "unaffected"
      }
    ]
  }
]
  }
]
}
```

Notes

The "severity" of CVE-2022-12345 is "critical" in the first instance, but "none" in the second and third instances. This is not because the official CVSS score (the one shown on the CVE report) changed between the first and second instances; it is still 10.0. However, since the "state" is "not_affected" in the second instance and "resolved" in the third instance, in effect the severity is 0 in both instances.[208]

---

[208] The author is not sure he agrees with the idea of changing the CVSS score based on the exploitability status of the vulnerability in one or more product/versions; the author believes the score should not be changed from the way it is listed in the NVD. The CVSS score is meant to apply to the vulnerability in all environments, absent other mitigating factors. In the author's opinion, the presence of mitigating

The supplier should develop a new SBOM for each "resolved" version.

Advanced VEX application 2: A new product version with a previously patched vulnerability

VEX documents, of course, make assertions about the status of vulnerabilities in current or previous versions of a software product; they do not make assertions about future versions. This is because there is no way to assert with certainty that, even if a particular vulnerability has been patched in the current version, it will never become exploitable in a future version because of some other change in code in the product (for example, if the code of the patch for the vulnerability is inadvertently altered as part of a separate change, so that it no longer mitigates the vulnerability).

Because of this fact, suppliers who issue VEX documents for their products will need to be careful when they release a new product version that includes patches for previous vulnerabilities. With the new version, they should issue one or more new VEX documents that state explicitly that the vulnerabilities previously patched are still not exploitable. Here is an example of why this is a good practice:

The supplier of product XYZ releases an SBOM for their current version 4.5.0, which lists component YYY version 3.0 as included in the product.

After version 4.5.0 is released, customers discover in the NVD that YYY v3.0 is subject to CVE-2022-34567, which has a CVSS score of 10.0. They immediately notify the supplier, who first verifies that the vulnerability is exploitable in version 4.5.0, then develops a patch for the vulnerability. When the patch is applied, it increments the version number to 4.5.1 (the supplier follows semantic versioning for their products).

The supplier releases a VEX document that lists the status of CVE-2022-34567 as "affected" in v4.5.0, but "unaffected" (or "fixed" in CSAF) in v4.5.1.

The supplier subsequently releases a new major version of the product, v5.0.0, along with a new SBOM for that version. The version still contains component YYY, so the SBOM still lists YYY v3.0. However, v5.0.0 also contains the code for the patch, so CVE-2022-34567 is still not exploitable in v5.0.0.

But since YYY v3.0, taken by itself, is still vulnerable to CVE-2022-34567, customers who look up the components of ABC v5.0.0 in the NVD will still notice that vulnerability, and assume it is exploitable in v5.0.0 (this should be the default assumption whenever a new component vulnerability is identified for a product).

Customers will start calling the supplier about CVE-2022-34567 and asking when it will be fixed in v5.0.0. The supplier's help desk will experience a high

---

factors (as in this case) does not change the severity of the vulnerability considered by itself.

volume of calls about this problem, even though the answer is always the same: the vulnerability was fixed in the previous version, and the vulnerability is still fixed in v5.0.0.

To quiet the help desk calls, the supplier releases a VEX document stating that the status of CVE-2022-34567 is "unaffected" in v5.0.0.

Later, the supplier releases a minor update to product ABC, version 5.1.0, which still contains component YYY v3.0, as well as the code that fixes CVE-2022-34567. They release a new SBOM with the update, which shows that YYY v3.0 is still a component. Because the NVD still shows that YYY v3.0 is vulnerable, the supplier once again receives a lot of calls about this vulnerability – and once again, they must tell every caller that CVE-2022-34567 isn't exploitable in v5.1.0.

Of course, by this point the supplier has learned their lesson: Whenever a serious component vulnerability was fixed in a previous version of a product, but the version of the component that was the source of that vulnerability in the previous version of the product is still present in a new version, the supplier needs to check in the NVD to determine whether the component version is still shown to be affected by the vulnerability. If the component is still affected, the supplier needs to issue a VEX document that indicates the status of the vulnerability in the new version is "unaffected".

When the supplier releases version 5.2.0 of XYZ, they issue the VEX document shown below.

The supplier needs to do this for every vulnerability that was patched in the previous version, if a) the component version that was the source of the vulnerability remains in the product, and b) the component version is still affected by that vulnerability (i.e., it is affected when considered by itself, not when it is a component of Product ABC). Moreover, the need to issue a VEX regarding this vulnerability will continue in all future versions as well, until the component is removed from the product or upgraded to a non-vulnerable version.

The bottom line of this discussion is that a supplier needs to track every component vulnerability they have patched in any previous version of their product, along with the component and version with which the vulnerability is associated in the NVD (or another vulnerability database like OSS Index). Whenever the supplier releases a new version which includes the same component version, and that component version is still listed as vulnerable in the NVD, the product supplier should also release a VEX document that indicates the status of the vulnerability is "not affected" in the new version.

As in the previous Section, here is an example JSON VEX document, preceded by a summary table:

Introduction to SBOM and VEX

Subject	Beginning field	Ending field	Comment
Document metadata	"Bom format"	Timestamp	
Product (i.e., subject of VEX document)	"component"	"BOM-ref"	Only one product is addressed in this VEX document. The author believes that should be the norm for the time being, for the first and second VEX use cases.
Info on CVE-2022-34567	vulnerabilities	"vector"	
State of CVE in product	"analysis"	"detail"	The fact that state is "not affected" means the version referenced below has a status of "unaffected". The justification is "protected_by_mitigating_control", meaning the vulnerability was patched. Note that the detail field points out that the CVE was patched in a previous version.
Versions with "affected" status	"affects"	"status"	Includes one version: the new version of the software.

```
{
  "bomFormat": "CycloneDX",
  "specVersion": "1.4",
  "version": 1,
  "metadata" : {
    "timestamp" : "2022-03-03T00:00:00Z",
    "component" : {
      "name" : "XYZ",
      "type" : "application",
      "bom-ref" : "product-XYZ"
    }
  },

    {
      "id": "CVE-2022-34567",
      "source": {
        "name": "NVD",
        "url": "https://nvd.nist.gov/vuln/detail/CVE-2023-12345"
      },
      "ratings": [
        {
          "source": {
            "name": "NVD",
```

```
        "url":       "https://nvd.nist.gov/vuln-metrics/cvss/v3-
calculator?vector=AV:N/AC:L/PR:N/UI:N/S:C/C:H/I:H/A:H/CR:X/IR:X/AR:X
/MAV:X/MAC:X/MPR:X/MUI:X/MS:X/MC:N/MI:N/MA:N&version=3.1"
        },
        "score": 0.0,
        "severity": "none",
        "method": "CVSSv31",
        "vector":
"AV:N/AC:L/PR:N/UI:N/S:C/C:H/I:H/A:H/CR:X/IR:X/AR:X/MAV:X/MAC:X/MPR:
X/MUI:X/MS:X/MC:N/MI:N/MA:N"
        }
      ],
      "analysis": {
        "state": "not_affected",
        "justification": "protected_by_mitigating_control",
        "response": ["will_not_fix"],
        "detail": "This version of Product XYZ is not affected by
the vulnerability, because it was fixed in a previous version. The
fixed code remains in this version."
      },
      "affects": [
        {
          "versions": [

            {
              "version": "5.2.0",
              "status": "unaffected"
            },
```

Only when the vulnerable version of the component is no longer in the product (either because the product supplier upgraded the component to a new version or they replaced it with another component) should the product supplier stop doing this.

18. Advanced: VEX Playbook

T he following are examples of use of VEX documents to meet specific situations. As with the examples discussed earlier, all of these are part of the general use case of component vulnerability management.

Coordinating VEX documents and SBOMs

It is important to note that, while VEX announcements may be triggered by information found in an SBOM (e.g., "Component Y, which is found in Product A, is vulnerable to the serious vulnerability CVE-2021-98765"), there is no necessary connection between a VEX document and an SBOM. A VEX document simply states the exploitability status of one or more vulnerabilities in a particular version of a product (e.g., "CVE-2021-98765 is not exploitable in Product A Version 2.1").

In some cases, the message that a particular vulnerability is not exploitable in the product may be needed because of the presence of a vulnerable component. However, in other cases the message may be needed to reassure customers that the "celebrity vulnerability" *du jour* isn't present in the product, with no reference to any component.

Despite this fact, it is a good idea for a supplier to release a VEX document for a version of one of their products soon after they have produced an SBOM for that product/version. The VEX document will inform the users (through the tool they use for component vulnerability management) which of the vulnerabilities listed for components in that product/version – in the NVD or another major vulnerability database – are exploitable and which are not exploitable. It will also inform the user which vulnerabilities remain "under investigation". The VEX document should be revised and re-issued whenever the exploitability status of a vulnerability has changed, usually from "under investigation" to "affected" or "not affected".[209]

---

[209] Currently, asking a supplier to release a new VEX document whenever there has been a change in status of any component might sound like a huge task that could require multiple people producing and distributing VEX documents full time (since a new VEX document could well be needed every day for every supported version of any of a supplier's products). If a supplier were to attempt to do that today, it certainly *would* be a huge ask.

However, there are two developments in progress which should substantially change this calculus. Both of these are likely to come to fruition in 2024:

1. The CycloneDX project is going to release their "Transparency Exchange API", which will allow an application to automatically download a new

However, there are also some special cases in which it is important to coordinate the release of VEX documents and SBOMs. Here are some example scenarios:

Emergency patch

The product security team for the supplier of product A receives an SBOM for a new version of A. They discover in the NVD that there is a serious vulnerability CVE-2021-12345 that applies to component XX, which is included in A. Moreover, the product security team realizes – to their dismay – that CVE-2021-12345 is in fact exploitable in product A.

Fortunately, the team building the software is confident they will have a patch for the vulnerability ready for distribution in two days. Should the product security team go ahead and issue a VEX now, which indicates that the status of CVE-2021-12345 in their product is *affected* and that the mitigation (included in the "detail" field) is to apply the patch when it is available? Certainly not! Two days is an eternity in the hacker world, and if this VEX is issued, it's possible there will be exploit code for an attack based on CVE-2021-12345 available on the dark web within hours – meaning that some customers might be successfully attacked during the two days before the patch is available.

In this situation, the supplier should a) not disclose the vulnerability outside of their security team and developers who need to know about it; b) expedite development of the patch as much as possible; and c) cross their fingers and hope word of the exploitable vulnerability doesn't leak out in the next two days.

Let's assume the supplier does release the patch before any of their customers are compromised. Of course, they will then release a new version of the product with the patch applied (and perhaps other changes as well). Is there anything more they need to do? Yes, they need to do three things:

SBOM (in SPDX or CycloneDX SBOM format) or a new VEX document (in CSAF or CycloneDX VEX format) from the supplier of a product whenever the document is made available; the supplier will simply need to post each SBOM or VEX to a server that makes it available to the API (third parties may develop and maintain these servers).

2. The OWASP SBOM Forum is developing "tight" specifications for VEX documents developed on both the CSAF and CycloneDX platforms and will also develop sample code for producing and consuming (parsing) those documents. When those specifications and code are developed, it will be possible to develop "complete" component vulnerability management tools, as described in Part 3 of this book. Using the Transparency Exchange API, those tools will automatically download and analyze the SBOM and VEX documents as they become available.

1. Issue an SBOM for the new version (i.e., the previous version with the patch applied);
2. Issue a VEX statement that says the status of CVE-2021-12345 in the current version is "affected". The statement should also include the URL for the patch in the mitigation field;
3. Include in the same VEX document the statement that the status of CVE-2021-12345 in the patched version is "not affected" (or "fixed"); and

If CVE-2021-12345 is exploitable in any previous versions of the product, issue a new VEX statement (possibly in the same VEX document as the above statements) for all supported previous versions in which the vulnerability is exploitable, listing the status of CVE-2021-12345 as "affected". The mitigation statement will notify users of those versions (in the "detail" field in CycloneDX VEX or the "action statement" field in CSAF VEX) that, to fix this vulnerability, they need either to apply the patch (if available for their version), or else upgrade to the patched version.

Delayed patch

In some cases, a supplier is unable to quickly produce a patch for a serious vulnerability. The supplier needs to provide multiple messages to their customers, although with a lot of care. These messages can be delivered with the help of SBOMs and VEX documents. The scenario might include:

1. The serious vulnerability CVE-2021-44555 has recently been discovered in many software products. It was first discovered by hackers, who posted exploit code and are now actively probing for vulnerable systems.
2. A software supplier discovers that Component XX in their product ABC is affected by CVE-2021-44555. To their dismay, the developers also discover that the CVE is exploitable in the current version of ABC itself.
3. In addition, CVE-2021-44555 affects the six most recent versions of ABC, which also contain XX.
4. However, technical reasons prevent the supplier from developing a patch for CVE-2021-44555 within the next month.

Unlike in the previous example, it isn't possible – or ethical – to withhold an announcement of this vulnerability, even though a patch is not available. The vulnerability itself is well known and is beginning to be exploited. Customers will need to apply a temporary mitigation measure until the patch is available, perhaps including removing the product from their networks altogether.

Fortunately, the supplier has identified a mitigation measure that doesn't require a lot of work to implement; the mitigation is to close two firewall ports. Since these ports are not commonly used, this should be achievable in most cases.

The supplier issues a VEX document (using the upcoming Transparency Exchange API, which pushes SBOM and VEX documents to tools like Dependency Track) that lists the status of CVE-2021-44555 as "affected" in the seven vulnerable versions (including the current one). It also describes the mitigation in the "detail" field. They accompany this with an urgent email to all users of the product, since not all of them will be able to utilize a machine-readable notification.

After about a month has elapsed, the supplier is able to develop a patch for this vulnerability. It fixes all seven of the vulnerable versions.

The supplier issues an SBOM for each of the seven patched versions, each of which has a new version number. Since the supplier follows semantic versioning, the number of each patched version is a simple increment of the previous version number; for example, v5.3.3 is the patched version of v5.3.2.

If the user applies the patch to any of the affected versions, the version number automatically increments to the new version number.

The same vulnerable version of component XX remains in the product through the next four versions of the product. The NVD continues to list CVE-2021-44555 as exploitable in XX.

To prevent customers from panicking about the presence of the serious vulnerability in component XX, the supplier issues a VEX with every new major or minor version. This VEX lists the status of the vulnerability as "not affected" in the patched versions. The VEX includes similar statements for other vulnerabilities that were previously patched, if the NVD still indicates that a component of the product is affected by any one of those vulnerabilities.

Several product versions later, the supplier replaces the vulnerable version of component XX with the current version, which is no longer affected by CVE-2021-44555; the SBOM for the next version of the product lists the fixed version of XX, not the version that is affected by the vulnerability.

The supplier stops issuing an "unaffected"[210] VEX statement about this vulnerability with every new version of ABC, since customers that look up components in the NVD will no longer find that Component XX is vulnerable to CVE-2021-44555.

---

[210] The VEX will need either to itemize every version of the product that is not affected by the vulnerability or include them all in one or more version ranges. The version range might well be from version 1.0 through the current version. However, trying to translate the statement, "No version of this product is affected by CVE-2020-12345" into either CSAF or CycloneDX code, without itemizing the versions or using a version range, is likely to produce more problems than it is worth. See the Section titled "None of our products is affected by..." in Chapter 18.

Erroneous vulnerability attribution

A software supplier experiences an unfortunate incident in which some unknown party spreads a rumor on social media that the current version of their product is vulnerable to a serious new vulnerability that affects a particular component YY.

Not only is the product not affected at all; it doesn't even contain YY. The supplier issues a VEX (as well as a press release and email to all customers) stating that the status of the vulnerability in all versions of the product is "unaffected". The supplier also re-publishes (to customers) their most recent SBOM, which shows that YY is not in the product.

Because the rumor refuses to die on social media, the supplier releases a new VEX with each new version of the product, stating that the status of the vulnerability in the new version is "unaffected", until the rumor finally dies down.

"Will not fix"

Software suppliers do not have infinite resources for software vulnerability management at their disposal. Therefore, a supplier may decide not to invest a lot of time patching vulnerabilities of low severity, perhaps indicated by a CVSS or EPSS score below a certain threshold. The supplier should make this policy, including the current threshold, known to all customers.

For example, suppose a supplier discovers that the current version of their product is affected by a new vulnerability with a CVSS score of 3.8; this falls below their threshold for patching, which is a CVSS score of 4.0. Therefore, they issue a VEX that states the following:

1. The status of the vulnerability in the current version is "affected".[211]

2. The status in all previous versions is "unaffected".

3. Under "analysis", the "state" is listed as "exploitable". The "response" is "will not fix". The "detail" field reads, "The CVSS score falls below our pre-announced threshold for patching. Any concerned customer should close the following port on their firewall…"

The vulnerability remains in the next four versions of the product, so the supplier issues a similar VEX with each of those versions. Since by assumption the supplier had previously announced their "threshold" for patching a

---

[211] Some people have suggested that, when a supplier is deliberately not fixing a vulnerability in one of their product/versions, they should list its status as "not affected". They say this because they think the supplier's decision not to fix the vulnerability is effectively a statement that the vulnerability is so insignificant that it can be ignored. However, this overlooks the fact that many high-assurance users think any vulnerability at all should be patched; they will want to know about any vulnerability, whether or not the supplier agrees to patch it.

vulnerability (and they maintain the announcement on their customer portal), most customers should not have any problem with this.

Can VEX handle vulnerabilities in "first-party" components?

The discussion in this chapter has deliberately not made a clear distinction between two types of components: third-party (developed by an entity other than the product supplier) and first-party (developed by the product supplier). Most statements made so far could be applied to both types of components. However, it is important to remember the difference between the use cases for third-party and first-party components; this difference applies to both SBOMs and VEX documents.

As stated at the beginning of this book, the main use case discussed in the book is that of a software supplier issuing SBOMs and VEX documents, so that its customers will be able to identify and track exploitable vulnerabilities in third-party components included in the product. Of course, suppliers also create components for use by their own developers in their products. Should these be included in SBOMs that are distributed to customers, and should the exploitability status of vulnerabilities in those components be tracked in VEX documents?

To answer these questions (which come up very often in SBOM discussions), it is important to remember that the suppliers are not expected to disclose vulnerabilities in third-party components. Instead, they're expected to disclose the components themselves in an SBOM, including an identifier – purl or CPE – that can be used to look up vulnerabilities in those components in a vulnerability database. The recipient of the SBOM (which will often be a third-party service provider acting on behalf of end users or software suppliers) will use a tool like Dependency Track to identify component vulnerabilities.

Of course, if a component cannot be found in a vulnerability database, the end user will never be able to learn about vulnerabilities in that component (which is why listing a purl or CPE for every component in the SBOM is so important). But first-party components will almost never be listed in a vulnerability database, since the only individuals that should be concerned about vulnerabilities in first-party components are the developers that use those components; these will usually only include employees or contractors of the supplier.

Does this mean that vulnerabilities in first-party components should not be disclosed to customers of the products that utilize those components? Absolutely not! It means that, if a supplier's product includes one or more first-party components and these components have vulnerabilities, the supplier should report these vulnerabilities to their customers and to CVE.org, just as they report vulnerabilities in the first-party code included in their product. In other words, the fact that a vulnerability is found in a first-party component and not in what the supplier refers to as their own code is irrelevant. It should all be considered first-party code.

Another important difference between first- and third-party components is there should not normally be any question about the exploitability of vulnerabilities in the former: If the supplier reports a vulnerability in a component they wrote (under the name of the product, of course), that is the same thing as saying the vulnerability is exploitable. It is not at all likely that a supplier would report a non-exploitable vulnerability to either their customers or to CVE.org, since neither the supplier nor their customers would benefit from their doing so.

Distributing VEX documents

Because VEX documents are meant to be utilized with SBOMs (at least in the SBOM and VEX use cases discussed in this book), they need to be distributed through the same channel as SBOMs. Currently, the small number of SBOMs and VEX documents that are being distributed to users of proprietary software are usually being provided via an authenticated customer portal.

There are three problems with this approach. The first is that, as both SBOMs and VEX documents start to be distributed more frequently and in larger quantities, requiring customers to download them from a portal will prove not to be a scalable solution. The second problem is that, once there are "complete"[212] end user component vulnerability management tools available, users will find it tiresome to have to manually download each document and make it available to the tool.

The third problem is that users need to be notified as soon as a new SBOM or VEX document is available for a product/version they use; this is currently being done by email. As the volume and frequency of documents being released grow, software customers will find it increasingly difficult to keep up with them, let alone download them all and load them into their tool. This is especially true for VEX, since – as we learned earlier in Part 2 - it is not at all inconceivable that a software supplier will need to issue a new VEX document once a day, for each of their supported products and versions.

The author believes that the upcoming Transparency Exchange API (described in the Section bearing that name in Chapter 4 of this book) will address all three of these problems, because 1) being an API, it will be able to operate independently of the user; 2) since it will be embedded in a tool, the downloaded document will automatically be made available for ingestion into the tool; and 3) the tool can utilize the API at whatever frequency the user has set. That is, the tool should be able to check for new SBOMs and VEX documents for a particular product/version every month, every week, every day, or every hour – whatever is appropriate for that product/version.

---

[212] For a description of a complete tool, see Part 3 of this book.

As of early 2024, the author has not seen the Transparency Exchange API in action, since it is still under development. Therefore, the above statements are not based on direct knowledge of the API. However, the author has been told that the API is under development.

Product families

The CSAF format allows a supplier to make a statement about the status of a vulnerability in a "family" of their products, not just in a single product. A family might be "routers", "office productivity software", "infusion pumps", etc. It may be tempting for a supplier simply to state in a VEX that an entire family of infusion pumps is "unaffected" by the log4shell vulnerability, rather than include in one VEX a statement regarding the vulnerability status of each member of the family.

However, it is better for suppliers to resist this temptation. It is only useful for a supplier to make a statement about a product family in a VEX if they are sure that every consumption tool that ingests the VEX will "understand" the family name in the same way as the supplier does. In other words, if the supplier understands a product family to include a set of 96 specific products and a specific version or versions of each product, the consumption tool will have to understand the family name in the same way. Moreover, any "guidebook" to the product families of a particular supplier will need to be updated constantly as members of the family are updated, added or removed.

This means there will need to be the same client software on every device that receives a VEX with a product family reference; it will need to be developed and maintained by the supplier. Unless all of this happens, a supplier will never be sure that, if they designate a product family in a VEX document, all end user tools will "understand" the family to correspond to the same set of products and versions as the supplier understands.

"None of our products is affected by…"

It is often said that an important use case for VEX is to make machine-readable statements like, "None of our products is affected by (*vulnerability name, e.g. log4shell*)." As in the case of product families (discussed earlier), the problem with assertions like this is that they are not usually based on much, if any, consideration of how statements like this will be interpreted by consumption tooling – or whether they even can be interpreted.

Of course, it is always possible to put any statement in a text field of a machine readable document; it will very likely be faithfully reproduced by almost any consumption tool. However, if the only goal of creating a VEX document is to be able to convey statements in English from a supplier to its customers, a much easier way to do this would be to send a PDF attachment by email. Only if the statement can be read by a consumer tool and utilized as part of an automated vulnerability management process will it be useful to make a statement like this in a machine readable VEX document.

Consider this scenario:

1. Because a serious new vulnerability CVE-2023-12345 has been the subject of a lot of scary articles lately, Supplier A, which develops and distributes over 1,000 software products, wishes to notify every one of their customers that none of their products are subject to this vulnerability. Specifically, Supplier A wishes to put out a PDF statement saying, "None of our users need to worry about the CVE-2023-12345 vulnerability, since none of our products are affected by it."

2. The supplier, of course, has a relationship with every one of their customers and knows the email addresses of multiple people in each of those organizations. They can easily send out an email to every one of those people, and in fact they do that.

3. However, the Director of Product Security (DPS) for the supplier thinks it will impress their customers if they also send out a machine-readable VEX notification that makes the same statement.

4. The DPS understands that, for a machine-readable statement like the one in question to be useful to an end user, something like the following must occur:

   a. The end user (an organization whose main business is not software development) needs to operate a tool like Dependency Track or Daggerboard, that ingests SBOMs and looks for vulnerabilities in the components. That tool will be attached to a database that tracks the set of component vulnerabilities found in product/versions that are in use by that organization. Fortunately, almost all of Supplier A's customers utilize Dependency Track (DT), which is by far the most widely used tool for this purpose.

   b. The supplier puts out a new SBOM to all customers of a product whenever a new major version of the product is published. Their customers know they should feed each new SBOM into DT to learn about component vulnerabilities. Because three of the supplier's products are erroneously flagged in the NVD as affected by CVE-2023-12345, the DPS is sure that customers are already seeing that vulnerability show up in DT searches.

5. The DPS wishes to provide some type of pre-notification to all their customers that they can safely ignore any such findings. The DPS considers the options for doing this. First, she wonders if there's an easy way to do it, for example by developing code to run under DT, which will interpret the phrase "All of our products" to mean "Any product/version for which Supplier = Supplier A." But then she remembers that their products list different supplier names, including "Supplier A, Inc.", "Supplier A, Europe", etc. Not to mention names of companies they acquired, which are identified in the NVD under those supplier names.

6. Then she wonders if they can bypass that problem by making DT interpret "All of our products" to mean, "Any product which is included in the Supplier A product list". This list is maintained internally and could be made available on Supplier A's web site. However, she quickly realizes this won't work. Because A sells thousands of products, the list of current products will need to be updated daily to take account of new products, discontinued products, product name changes, etc. Supplier A will have to update the list daily on their website and develop an API to allow DT to download the list daily.

7. In fact, the product list will need to include not only product names, but the name of every supported version of every product. Thus, it will really need to be updated hourly, not just daily. And DT will need to download the list whenever it encounters a VEX statement regarding "all of our products", since that phrase only has meaning if it's backed up by a list maintained locally.

8. Of course, before creating the VEX document, the Product Security team will need to thoroughly scan every currently supported version of every product on the list to make sure it isn't vulnerable to CVE-2023-12345. If even one version of one product is vulnerable, Supplier A can't make the statement they want to make. This alone will be a huge undertaking.

9. Before any new product or version is added to this list, the DPS will need to make sure it has also been thoroughly scanned for the presence of CVE-2023-12345. The company might be in serious legal trouble if a customer or independent researcher found that the vulnerability was in fact present in it.

10. Assuming that problem is overcome, the supplier will need to:

a. Develop code to run in Dependency Track. Whenever it encounters a VEX statement from Supplier A that mentions "All of our products" or "None of our products", it will utilize an API to retrieve the product list from the website and download it into DT. Of course, doing this will require forking Dependency Track. It will also require Supplier A to develop and support the API.

b. When the code encounters a VEX statement like "None of our current products is affected by CVE-2023-12345", it will interpret this as an instruction to go through the database attached to DT and change the status of any instance of CVE-2023-12345 in the list of component vulnerabilities for any product/version on Supplier A's list to "not affected". There will also need to be a status justification, probably "vulnerable code not present".

c. Since it is likely that a subsequent lookup to the NVD will unintentionally change the status of one or more instances of CVE-2023-12345 to "affected" or at least "under investigation" (which a high assurance user will probably interpret to mean "affected"), the code in DT will probably need to repeat step b at least weekly for the foreseeable future.

11. Moreover, all the above steps will need to be repeated continually in the future, until the DPS believes that the likelihood that a vulnerability due to CVE-2023-12345 will be reported for one of their products is close to zero.

12. Of course, the above steps will need to be repeated whenever Supplier A wants to make this statement about another vulnerability. This includes scanning every supported version of every product for the vulnerability before putting it on the list.

13. Finally, this list of steps is likely to be incomplete. There are probably many more steps that need to be taken.

Of course, having understood what is involved with trying to put out the seemingly simple statement that none of their products is affected by the vulnerability, it is highly unlikely that the Director of Product Security will go ahead with the idea of putting it out. Just emailing a PDF to all customers will look more attractive all the time! After all, a human being can understand what "None of our products" means, even though it is very hard for a computer to do so.

Accommodating high assurance users

For VEX to become widely accepted, it will need to overcome the doubts of "high assurance" users: i.e., those in critical fields like hospitals, military contractors and large electric utilities. Security professionals at these organizations are in general skeptical when they hear a software supplier make a bland statement that their product will not be affected by a certain component vulnerability because the supplier has, for example, blocked all paths by which an attacker could reach the vulnerable code.

Moreover, these people have every reason to be skeptical of such statements, for a simple reason: Proving a statement like this one requires proving a negative. If a supplier asserts that they have blocked all paths that an attacker might take to reach the vulnerable code in their product, the question becomes, "How could you possibly prove that, unless you can itemize all possible paths and prove that each one is blocked? Even worse, how could you possibly prove that no future change in the product would ever unblock one of those paths, so there would now be a path for an attacker?"

Of course, most end user organizations that are not in the high assurance category will be inclined to trust their supplier. When the supplier's VEX document states there is no path available for an attacker to compromise their product using the vulnerability in question, they will believe that statement.

But where does that leave the high assurance users? Will they just ignore all VEX statements and demand that their suppliers patch every component vulnerability, whether exploitable or not exploitable? There are undoubtedly some who will do that. However, that is probably an overreaction. This is because there are at least two types of cases in which the supplier can "prove" that a vulnerability is not exploitable in their product.

To understand these two cases, the reader should review the excellent CISA "VEX Status Justifications"[213] document, which was discussed earlier. This document describes five machine-readable statements that a supplier can include in a VEX document when a vulnerability is given a "not affected" status. The point of including a status justification in a VEX document is that it allows the user of a product to make fine-grained distinctions between status designations they feel are acceptable and those that are not. The five status justifications discussed in the document are:

- Component_not_present
- Vulnerable_code_not_present

---

[213]

https://www.cisa.gov/sites/default/files/publications/VEX_Status_Justification_Jun2 2.pdf

- Vulnerable_code_cannot_be_controlled_by_adversary
- Vulnerable_code_not_in_execute_path
- Inline_mitigations_already_exist

Some software security professionals believe that the first two justifications are of a different quality from the other three. "Component not present" indicates that the vulnerable component, which appeared in the SBOM for the product, was not in fact included in the product. There are multiple reasons why this might occur: For example, the component may have been removed from the product after the SBOM was generated but before the product was shipped to customers. Or the tool that created the SBOM may have erroneously identified a different component as the vulnerable one. If the vulnerable component is not present in the product at all, this obviously means the vulnerability is not present and the supplier can prove it.

"Vulnerable code not present" means that, even though the vulnerable component is present in the product, the vulnerable code is not in it. This might also be because the developer of the product edited an open source component to remove the vulnerability, before they installed the component in the product. It also might be because the compiler stripped out the vulnerable code from an open source component before installing it. Again, this is something the supplier can prove.

For the remaining three status justifications, there can be no real proof, since even if they are true today, there is no way for the supplier to prove that a future change in the product will not inadvertently make the vulnerability exploitable. Therefore, high assurance users may be inclined not to accept the "not affected" status designation when the accompanying status justification is one of these three.

Let's return to the question that started this discussion: whether high assurance users will have any use for VEX at all. We can now answer that question in the affirmative. The status justifications (called "justifications" in CycloneDX, where there are nine, not five) are machine readable. As long as the consumer tool allows the user to decide which status justifications they are willing to believe and which they are not, both high assurance and "normal" users can be accommodated.

If given the choice, high assurance users will usually believe just the first two status justifications, meaning that, whenever the status of a vulnerability is "not affected" and one of the first two status justifications is present, they will agree that the status of the vulnerability should remain "not affected".

However, if the status of a vulnerability is shown as "not affected" and one of the other three status justifications is present (or one of the seven other "justifications" in CycloneDX), high assurance users will want the status to change to "affected" from "not affected". Again, most non-high assurance users will probably be pleased to leave the status of each vulnerability as it appears in the VEX document, since they trust the supplier's statements. Both types of users will be able to get what they want from a VEX document, if the option to do this is present in the software tool they use.

Tom Alrich

The author hopes that this proposed change will result in end users, especially high assurance ones, having an appropriate level of trust in VEX information. They will then be less reluctant to utilize vulnerability information derived from SBOMs and VEX documents.

19. Other VEX use cases

The author has focused on the two VEX use cases described earlier (which he together calls the "main use cases") because in his opinion, the fact that there is no end user tooling available to make use of VEX documents based on these use cases is one of the two major impediments to widespread distribution of SBOMs.

However, in 2023, two new use cases called "VEX" were introduced. These are different from the first and second use cases, meaning that different tooling will be required to implement them. However, they are both valid use cases. As long as discussions of VEX distinguish among the different VEX use cases, the organizations promoting them are welcome to continue to utilize the VEX name.

The first of these two new use cases is using VEX information to remove "false positive" vulnerability identifications by scanning tools. In this case, the supplier of a product issues VEX documents that can be ingested by a scanning tool. The documents include statements about multiple vulnerabilities which have "not affected" status designations in a certain product and version; these are presumably based on reports to the supplier, from scanning tool vendors, of false positive scan results their users have encountered in different software products. The main group promoting this use case is the OpenVEX[214] project.

The second use case is one that is the basis for the document types called "VEX", which are now being produced by Cisco[215] and Red Hat[216]. While these documents probably do not follow exactly the same format, they both appear to have the same purpose: to advise customers which product/versions in the supplier's product line are affected by a particular vulnerability.

---

[214] https://github.com/openvex

[215] https://tomalrichblog.blogspot.com/2023/09/ciscos-important-vex-announcement.html

[216] https://www.redhat.com/en/blog/vulnerability-exploitability-exchange-vex-beta-files-now-available

Of course, this is very different from the first and second VEX use cases described earlier, which deal with the exploitability of one or more vulnerabilities in a single product, although in either one or multiple versions. So, the main use cases deal with exploitability of many vulnerabilities in one product/version, while the Red Hat and Cisco use cases deal with exploitability of a single vulnerability across a broad product line.

The author wishes these organizations well. However, given that the OWASP SBOM Forum wishes to focus on removing the current impediments to widespread use of SBOMs, and given that the group has identified the lack of implementation of the two main VEX use cases as one of the two main inhibitors of widespread distribution of SBOMs, the group wants to focus on implementing the tooling and procedures for those two use cases.

Part Three: The Way Forward

Tom Alrich

20. Summing up

In the first two parts of this book, the author has made the following points:

1. While there are multiple cybersecurity use cases for software bills of materials and VEX documents, there is one that is usually assumed to be the main use for them: identifying and tracking exploitable vulnerabilities in a version of a software product (or an intelligent device) that are due to the components (dependencies) used by the product. This book uses the term "component vulnerability management" to describe this process.

2. Both software developers (usually called "suppliers" in this book) and organizations whose main business is not software development (usually called "end users") can benefit from this use case[217]. Suppliers benefit because SBOMs produced for a product in development can be utilized (with a tool like Dependency Track) to identify vulnerabilities due to components in the product. Learning about these vulnerabilities enables the supplier to manage risks by patching component vulnerabilities before the product is made available to end users.

---

[217] There is a third use case, which is system integrators. These entities both procure software from open source and commercial suppliers and sell it (as part of integrated systems) to end users. Therefore, integrators need to be treated both as end users and suppliers (fortunately, the functions are distinct enough that it is unlikely the two roles will be confused).

In fact, almost every software developer today can be considered to be an integrator. This is because almost all developers procure components from upstream suppliers (including open source projects) and integrate them into a software product. They then provide that product to one or more downstream users (who might themselves be software suppliers that integrate the software they procure into another product for users further downstream). In fact, large software suppliers purchase (or download, in the case of open source components) large numbers of software components, making them integrators of software.

199

3. End user organizations can benefit from SBOMs and VEX documents, because they allow the organization to learn about vulnerabilities found in the software products that they use to run their operations, which are due to the third-party components found in those products. Components make up the greatest part of the code found in almost any software product today. Therefore, learning about component vulnerabilities is essential for any organization that wants to understand the risks it faces from the software it uses.

4. Suppliers are successfully using SBOMs to manage component risks in the products they are developing. While it is certain that the number of suppliers doing this today is relatively small compared to the total number of suppliers, it is nevertheless a significant number; moreover, it is growing very rapidly. For that reason, this book does not focus on the supplier use case.

5. However, the end user use case is a very different story. Almost no end user organizations today (including the IT departments of large software developers) regularly receive[218] SBOMs from any of their third-party software suppliers. The main reason for this is not that most suppliers do not want to provide SBOMs to their customers (although there are certainly some suppliers for which this is true), but that there is almost no demand for SBOMs from the users[219].

---

[218] By "regularly", the author means the end user organization receives an updated SBOM whenever they upgrade to a new version of the product. An SBOM is no longer valid once the user has upgraded to a newer version, or even applied a patch.

[219] Executive Order 14028 from May 2021 required federal agencies to ask for an SBOM from each of their suppliers of "critical software", although there is no penalty if the supplier does not provide one (an Executive Order only applies to federal government agencies, not private organizations like software suppliers). In practice, it seems the main result of this provision in the EO has been that a lot of single SBOMs have been provided to federal agencies, where they were promptly stored and forgotten. Since an SBOM cannot be trusted if the software has been updated since the SBOM was developed, and since most software is regularly updated, with new versions, patches, etc., it is likely that almost none of these SBOMs will ever be put to practical use.

However, the EO was not a failure when it comes to SBOMs. It sent a signal to many thousands of public and private organizations about the importance of managing risks due to third-party components in software products. This step alone has made a huge contribution to software security.

6. Why are software users not requesting SBOMs from their software suppliers? The author has talked to many software end users who would be pleased to have regularly updated SBOMs for the software they use. However, the required software tools are not available in the form that end user organizations require: "complete", easy to use, low-cost and commercially supported.

What would a "complete" component vulnerability management tool do? It would automate the following workstream:

1. The tool ingests a newly released SBOM for a software product/version being used by the end user organization.

2. The tool parses the list of components in the SBOM and looks up vulnerabilities applicable to each component in the NVD or another vulnerability database.[220]

3. The tool stores all the component vulnerabilities identified for the product/version in a "VEX database". Besides the vulnerability identifier, other fields in the database will include exploitability status (the four VEX status designations), status justification (when the status is "not affected"), and mitigation (when the status is "affected").

4. Information about the vulnerability will also be stored. Optionally, the identifier for the component affected by the vulnerability can be stored.

5. Initially, the status of every vulnerability stored in the VEX database for the product/version will be set to "under investigation". However, as the supplier determines whether each vulnerability is exploitable in this product/version, they will update the status of the vulnerability accordingly.

6. Every time the status of a vulnerability changes, the supplier will issue a new VEX document containing the updated contents of all the VEX fields for every component listed in the database instance for the

---

[220] This assumes that the software supplier addresses the naming problem themselves and identifies a purl or a CPE name for most components in the product/version. Even though it is certain that many suppliers will not be able to do this themselves, the author believes that "name resolution" should be the supplier's responsibility, even if they have to pay a service provider to do this for them. See Chapter 8, "The naming problem".

product/version. The document will be made available to the user tool via the Transparency Exchange API.

7. The VEX document will be ingested by the user tool; the data will be stored in the database in the user tool, in the instance for the product/version.[221]

8. The tool repeats steps B through G every day (or more often, if needed).

9. As a result of the above, the VEX database in the user's tool will always include the most recent exploitability status of every component vulnerability for each product/version utilized by the user organization.

10. The user organization will always be able to retrieve from their tool a list of component vulnerabilities and their status designations (as well as status justifications and mitigations, where applicable) for a product/version that they utilize. They will be able to retrieve this data in "raw" form, or in a format required for ingestion by their vulnerability, configuration, or asset management tool.

11. The above process will continue as long as the product/version is supported.[222]

The end user tool described above will not be difficult to build, since all the steps in this workstream are quite basic. However, the presence of the naming problem means the workstream cannot be completely automated. Given that end user organizations cannot be expected to mitigate the naming problem on their own, this means the tool cannot today be produced in the form that end users need: fully automated, low cost and commercially supported. In fact, it will probably be at least 3-4 years before it is possible to do that.

Until complete tools become available, very few end user organizations will be interested in receiving SBOMs directly from their suppliers, except perhaps to satisfy their curiosity. However, just because an end user organization does not

---

[221] Because of these updates, the contents of each product/version instance in the user's VEX database will essentially be a "mirror" of the contents of the instance for the same product/version in the supplier's VEX database. However, the user's database will include instances for products/versions from many suppliers, while the supplier's VEX database will only include the supplier's own products/versions.

[222] The author does not expect the SBOM (i.e., the list of components) for a product/version to change over the version's lifetime. If for example a component were to be replaced, that would require a new version to be declared, as well as a new SBOM to be generated. In other words, the above process would start over from A, for the new product/version. However, the database instance for the previous product/version would be maintained, along with daily lookups to the NVD and ingestion of VEX documents whenever delivered, as long as the product/version was still under support.

want to receive SBOMs directly from a supplier does not mean they are not interested in learning about exploitable component vulnerabilities found in the software they use; it just means they don't want to spend a significant amount of money purchasing a software tool and invest the time required to learn how to use it, as well as need to address the naming problem on their own.

This is where third-party service providers come in. They will be able to develop their own tools or chain together open source tools (or both), to perform the above set of steps on behalf of end users. They will be able to ingest SBOMs and VEX documents and provide end user organizations the information they need to manage component vulnerabilities in their environment; moreover, they will be able to update this information continually, making it available on demand to their customers.

Given the ultimately huge potential demand for this service, it is likely that the cost of providing it will decline rapidly, as the service providers gain both experience and customers. This will be especially true for the naming problem. Even though that problem creates a big barrier to end users who wish to utilize data from SBOMs, it will not do that for service providers. This is because there are many *ad hoc* ways to deal with the naming problem; these are being utilized today by software developers and their consultants. Since the service providers will be dealing with the naming problem every day, they will quickly develop the expertise to mitigate it (but not defeat it, unfortunately. Others will have to do that).

An end user organization needs to know what *exploitable* component vulnerabilities are present in each of the software products (and intelligent devices) their organization uses. Moreover, they need to have that information updated regularly (preferably daily), as software suppliers come to understand the exploitability status of the component vulnerabilities found in their products and issue new VEX documents to communicate changes in that status information.

The service providers will need to make this information available not simply in standalone reports, but in a continuously updated data stream that the user can access and utilize at any time. The data in the stream will need to be made available in a format or formats that are compatible with tools the organization utilizes for vulnerability management, asset management or configuration management.

The VEX specification problem

Besides naming, there is another serious problem that needs to be addressed (although not "solved" in any absolute sense) before even semi-automated third-party service provider solutions are possible. This is the problem that there is no agreed upon specification for VEX on either the CycloneDX or the CSAF platform (there is also no VEX specification applicable to both platforms – which of course would be impossible, given how different the two platforms are).

The lack of VEX specifications is probably because there are now at least five or six different use cases that all claim to be VEX. Of course, there is nothing wrong with having many meanings for the word "VEX", but trying to accommodate this many use cases makes it almost impossible to create a single specification that encompasses all of them. And the lack of a specification means there will not be commercially supported, low cost end user tools that can parse VEX documents and utilize the information as part of a component vulnerability management workstream. After all, what commercial vendor is going to invest in developing a tool to ingest documents whose format will never be consistent?

In the fall of 2023, the OWASP SBOM Forum formed a workgroup called VEX Playbooks. The purpose of the group is to standardize VEX formats and practices to the point that it will be possible for commercial vendors to safely develop tools that utilize VEX documents as part of a fully automated component vulnerability management workstream[223].

From the start, the group realized that we would not be successful at our task if we did not specify which VEX use case(s) we would address and which we would not. Because the whole purpose of the SBOM Forum is to identify and try to mitigate the problems that are preventing widespread distribution and use of SBOMs, we immediately focused on the VEX use case that is most needed to achieve that purpose. Not coincidentally, this is the use case addressed by the NTIA Software Component Transparency Initiative, which is described at the beginning of Chapter 9, "Why do we need VEX?".

The first task of the workgroup was to develop "tight" specifications for both CSAF and CycloneDX VEX documents (CSAF is being addressed first). These specifications are both focused on a single use case; other use cases will require separate specifications (which will not be hard to develop).

Once these two specifications have been developed, the group will work with one or more developers to create open source proof of concept VEX production tools. The tools will produce documents that follow the specification and do not introduce options that are not part of the spec. as well as consumption tools that ingest and parse documents that follow the specification, so the data from the document can be utilized by tools for component vulnerability management. The group is describing its progress in this Google Docs document.

As of early 2024, the group is developing "tight" VEX specifications for both the CycloneDX and CSAF VEX platforms (CSAF will be first). These focus entirely on the first VEX use case, described early in Chapter 10, "The two principal VEX use cases". The purpose of these tight specifications is to include just the minimum fields required to describe the first use case.

---

[223] As of early 2024, the VEX Playbooks workgroup is tracking its progress in this Google Docs document:
https://docs.google.com/document/d/1i8p5LtYj3cXWlp1R4CLpRtl7b_5SYKQMIN6m4Xjt2bU/edit.

One developer[224] who is a member of the workgroup is now developing demonstration code (which will be made publicly available) for the following:

- Code for a producer's tool that creates a "tight" CSAF VEX document. To use the tool, the producer will only need to answer questions on what should be in the VEX; they will not be required to understand the CSAF format itself.

- Code for a "consumer's" tool that can parse the CSAF code produced by the producer's tool, and pass that data onto another tool (e.g., an end user organization's asset or vulnerability management tool).

- Code for a similar producer's tool for the CycloneDX format.

- Code for a similar consumer's tool for the CycloneDX format.

Once these four projects are completed, they will be tested to make sure that VEX documents produced by the producer's tools are correctly parsed by the corresponding consumer's tools. Once that is confirmed, the code will be made available to any organization that wishes to create tools that utilize VEX documents in a tool, hopefully like the "complete" tool described above.

The author believes that the "tight" VEX specification is the last important piece of the puzzle that needs to be in place before there can be complete tools for component vulnerability management. There are already lots of tools for producing and consuming SBOMs, although a set of agreed practices regarding SBOM production and distribution needs to be developed and followed. These practices will include tight specifications for both SPDX and CycloneDX SBOMs. Creating these specs should just require choosing which fields from each format need to be included and limiting the spec to those fields.

A big proof of concept

While the activities described above are essential to realizing the goal of widespread use of SBOM information by end users of software, they are not sufficient. There are many questions regarding associated practices and policies that are still up in the air – for example, the question of how to standardize the SBOM Types[225]. For example, if an end user organization wishes to receive a particular Type of SBOM from their software suppliers, such as "Build", they need to be able to formulate their request so that it will be understood in the same way by all suppliers, regardless of development tools or languages used.

---

[224] Anthony Harrison of Manchester, UK.

[225] See the Section titled "SBOM Types" in Chapter 4.

Some of these questions can be resolved just by discussion among suppliers and end users, but a lot of them can only be answered through experience. And "experience" can only be attained through…well, *experience*. How can suppliers and end users get the experience they need to answer questions of best practice for SBOMs, when exchange of SBOMs and VEX documents between suppliers and users will normally require that some sort of contract be in place between the parties – and having such a contract will require already being in agreement on questions like the one above?

The solution to this conundrum is fairly simple: a "proof of concept" exercise in which both suppliers and end users agree that everything that goes on is "just for fun". In other words, no end user organization will hold a supplier responsible for any particular deliverables regarding SBOMs or VEX documents, including accuracy, suitability to purpose, etc.

The OWASP SBOM Forum wants to use a proof of concept exercise (probably running for months) to demonstrate the software component vulnerability management process end-to-end, using SBOMs and VEX documents produced by suppliers. The PoC will also demonstrate to end user organizations how the information derived from SBOM and VEX documents can be used to manage component vulnerabilities in the software they use to run their organizations. In other words, we want to prove the concept of using SBOMs and VEX documents to enable end users of software to manage the risks due to component vulnerabilities in the software they use.

The two SBOM proofs of concept, that the author knows of, that are currently exchanging SBOMs are based on the model of software suppliers exchanging SBOMs and VEX documents directly with their customers (these are the Healthcare SBOM Proof of Concept previously operated by the NTIA Initiative and now operated by the Healthcare-ISAC, and the Autos SBOM Proof of Concept, operated by the Autos-ISAC. Note that only the Healthcare PoC is releasing information on their activities to the public). However, the problem with that model today is that the end user organizations do not have tools to utilize those documents in an automated component vulnerability management workstream.

The SBOM Forum's Proof of Concept (PoC) will include one or more third-party service providers to mediate the exchange of SBOMs and VEX documents between suppliers and end users. The suppliers will provide SBOMs and VEX documents to the service provider(s). The service providers will operate "complete" tools that a) ingest SBOMs and VEX documents for individual product/versions, and b) output, for each product and version tracked, continually updated lists of exploitable component vulnerabilities in each product/version[226].

---

[226] End users may also be able to receive the complete set of VEX information from the product supplier, not just the list of exploitable component vulnerabilities. That is, they may be able to receive the complete list of component vulnerabilities in the product/version, and the exploitability status of each one. They may also be able to receive the status justifications and mitigations associated with those vulnerabilities.

These lists will be made available online to end user organizations that have been specifically authorized to receive them by the suppliers of the products (of course, these will usually be current customers of those products, although the supplier is free to set whatever criteria they want for an organization to receive the component vulnerability information).

Here are very preliminary ideas for how this will work:

1. All participants (suppliers, end users, and service providers) will sign an NDA saying they understand that:

   a. No information from SBOMs and VEX documents will be shared with end user organizations that have not been authorized by the suppliers of those documents to receive it.

   b. No information the end user receives may be shared outside of their organization. If the supplier requires more protection than this (e.g., only certain named individuals may see the information), they will need to discuss this directly with the end users.

   c. All information is provided strictly for learning purposes; no supplier will be held responsible for deficiencies or errors in the SBOMs or VEX documents.

   d. End users promise they will not make business decisions based on the information they receive as part of the PoC.

   e. If a supplier requires it, information in SBOMs and VEX documents will be encrypted during transmission between the supplier and the service provider, and between the service provider and the end user.

2. Since there are currently no complete, commercially supported component vulnerability management tools available to end users and there probably will not be for years, the service providers will develop (or integrate) and operate the tooling required to accomplish the tasks for the complete tool which were listed earlier. Their tooling will ingest SBOMs and VEX documents provided by suppliers and make available continually updated lists of exploitable component vulnerabilities and their mitigations to end user organizations[227]. If the supplier desires,

---

[227] It is possible that the complete set of VEX information could be provided to end users as part of the PoC, not just the list of exploitable component vulnerabilities.

they may restrict access to the information in their SBOMs and VEX documents to customers who have signed an NDA directly with them, in addition to the overall NDA described earlier. The lists will be for one or more product/versions operated by the end user organization.

3. The service providers will charge for their services, but they will be required upfront to charge a rate agreed to by all the PoC participants as "reasonable". If multiple service providers participate in the PoC, they will all need to charge the same rate, perhaps based on the number of product/version pairs tracked for an end user. Rates may be changed at any point by mutual agreement among PoC participants, based on lessons learned. The incentive for the service providers to agree to reasonable rates is that they will gain valuable experience that they will not be able to gain in any other way.

4. Both end users and suppliers will be responsible for paying service provider charges, although how the responsibility will be split among the two groups needs to be agreed on before the PoC begins.

5. Because there will be direct expenditures required to establish and operate the PoC, all participants will be encouraged to donate to OWASP, a non-profit 501(c)(3) organization. Donations will be directed to the SBOM Forum and will be applied to the PoC project.[228] Of course, the SBOM Forum will welcome contributions from non-PoC participants as well – that is, from organizations that recognize the importance of proving that SBOM is not just an academic talking point, but a tool that can produce significant benefits in practice.

This includes, for a particular product and version, a current list of all component vulnerabilities and their exploitability status, status justifications for "not affected" status designations, and mitigations for "affected" status designations.

[228] Any organization wishing to donate to the OWASP SBOM Forum is encouraged to contact the author at tom@tomalrich.com, although donations can be made online at any time by going to https://owasp.org/www-project-sbom-forum/ and clicking on the "Supporters" button. Please read item 3 on that page (regarding "restricted" donations, which go directly to one OWASP project) and then donate by clicking on the "Donate" button at the top right of the screen.

To make a restricted donation, you then need to click on "Other" and enter an amount greater than $1,000 (this is the minimum for restricted donations. Any lower amount goes to support the general work of OWASP). Of course, please enter your name and email address where indicated and check the box requesting "Please restrict this gift for OWASP SBOM Forum." Thanks for your support!

6. The main goal of the PoC will be learning. The participants in the PoC will discuss their experiences regularly. These experiences and lessons learned will be shared with the public, perhaps as an e-book.

7. Most importantly, the participants will learn important lessons regarding their own operations. The software suppliers will learn what their customers require in SBOMs and VEX documents, as well as how they can provide it. The service providers will learn about the tooling and training required to deliver their services, as well as what they might reasonably charge for the services. Most importantly, the end users will learn how they can utilize the component vulnerability information provided to them by the service providers, to secure the software they use.

While there are obviously a lot of questions that still need to be answered about how the PoC will work, the author believes that something like this is needed to finally break the logjam that is preventing end user organizations from utilizing information derived from software bills of materials and VEX documents, to manage third-party component vulnerabilities in software.

21. Conclusion

It should be obvious that this book is just the first chapter in an ongoing story. While the SBOM and VEX concepts have made huge progress in both articulation and acceptance by the software development community in recent years, they also have a long way to go before they can be said to have truly had a big impact on the security of the software used by just about every organization in the world today (as well as software used by individuals, of course).

Fortunately, as the previous chapters have shown, a lot of progress has been made toward widespread use of SBOMs by software suppliers, and much more will be made soon toward widespread use by software end users.

The author hopes to be able to provide regularly updated versions of this book, which will describe both further progress that has been made and tasks that still need to be accomplished. Of course, a huge amount remains to be done, so there will be much to discuss for years to come.

If you are looking for more frequent updates on developments regarding SBOMs, you should follow the author's blog;[229] you are always welcome to email him at tom@tomalrich.com. You can also follow CISA's SBOM efforts.[230] And you should consider joining in or supporting the OWASP SBOM Forum's activities to promote broad use of SBOMs for software component vulnerability management. Please email the author if you wish to join the SBOM Forum.

---

[229] https://tomalrichblog.blogspot.com/
[230] https://www.cisa.gov/sbom

About Tom Alrich

Tom Alrich has consulted in cybersecurity since 2001, working previously for Honeywell and Deloitte; he is now independent. He writes Tom Alrich's Blog (https://tomalrichblog.blogspot.com/), which has a worldwide following and addresses topics including SBOM and VEX, security of IoT devices, software naming, and cybersecurity regulation.

Tom has actively participated in the SBOM efforts of the US National Technology and Information Administration (NTIA) and the Cybersecurity and Infrastructure Security Agency (CISA). In 2022, Tom founded what is now the OWASP SBOM Forum. Tom lives in Evanston, Illinois and has a BA in Economics from the University of Chicago.

www.ingramcontent.com/pod-product-compliance
Lightning Source LLC
LaVergne TN
LVHW051228050326
832903LV00028B/2297